Jewish Continuous
Presence in the Land of Israel

and

The Israeli-Palestinian Conflict

By

Harold J. Margolis, Ph.D.
Silogram

For information, write to SILOGRAM Corporation
3168 Benedict Canyon Drive, Beverly Hills, Ca. 90210
halmargolis@aol.com

First Edition

Margolis, Harold J.

Jewish Continuous Presence in the Land of Israel

1. Jewish History   2. Middle East History

3. The Israeli-Palestinian Conflict

Includes Index

Library of Congress Control Number: 2003094360
ISBN 1-879646-01-3 (pbk.) $18.95
Printed in the United States of America

SILOGRAM CORPORATION
SAN: 254-5403

FORWARD

It was in Tiberias when verification of a continuous Jewish presence came together for me -- the day, September 11, 2001. Early that day while walking through the centre of the city I had remarked that the flags in front of the large hotel by the waterfront of the lake were not of all the nations of the world, but were of the few nations which were friendly to Israel. When we returned to the tourist information office for an interview with the local historian, I remarked that the American flag in front of the hotel was upside down, an international sign of distress. Hal did not make much of it and thought that someone just made a mistake; but I felt then as I do now that it was an omen. The time was twelve noon in Tiberias, two in the morning in Los Angeles, and five in the morning in New York and Washington, DC.

The historian concurred with our impression of the continuous presence of Jews in Israel. He suggested visiting Piki'in, a village with a record of Jewish people residing there for over two thousand years. Outside of the office of tourist information is an archeological park in which are the remnants of a planned Jewish community which moved from higher on the hillside to this walled and protected city about the year 1000. It was a time when few people lived in the geographic area; and marauding hordes were causing anarchy. The site had residences, immersion pools, and a synagogue with a beautiful mosaic floor.

On our way home, I learned that our government changed the campaign from "Infinite Justice" to "Enduring Freedom" which I believe is a mistake. The Moslems, who insisted that 'Infinite Justice' can only come from Allah, have a good point. Freedom has one meaning for people who think in terms of the vocabulary of a democracy; and another meaning for people living under autocratic rule. It is my understanding that with civil rights come responsibilities. For example, there is free speech; but one does not have the right to yell "Fire!"when there is no fire, as the panic may endanger other lives. If one lives in a society where one behaves solely out of fear of punishment, anarchy and chaos will ensue when restraints are removed. Where oppressive regimes have been removed, there is often looting, murder, and generalized anarchy, as occurring now in Iraq and Afghanistan. In a society in which individuals accept responsibility for valued rights, the expectation is that one inhibits impulses; then the conduct follows a mutually expected pattern. Even if one is frustrated, angry, aroused, it is not an excuse to act out in a socially unacceptable manner.

If it is okay to make people dead just because of who they are or what they believe; then no one is safe. World War II had a religious zeal "to make the world safe for democracy." Our world in the United States changed on December 7, 1941 with total mobilization; the allied powers insisted on unconditional surrender. Something else was going on with our spirit: popular songs were "Praise the Lord and Pass the Ammunition", "Coming in on a Wing and a Prayer". After September 11, 2001, a "War on Terror" was declared; but it seems that most people did not understand that we were challenged to a "religious war". Americans have trouble now conceiving of a religious struggle; after all, individuals have the right to practice religion according to the individual's conscience; so what is the problem? But for a person who follows the Koran, the world is of two spheres; there is the "World of Islam" and the "World of War". It is not only okay to make people dead to advance the faith; but doing so is honourable and such will be rewarded in the Afterlife. As part of unconditional surrender of World War II, the Japanese made a modification in their religion; the emperor spoke over the radio and allowed people to realize that he was a man and not a god. And the war crimes trials established that one is accountable for individual behaviour regardless of the order from a superior.

The meaning of the word, Islam, is submit. The social structures created under the rule of Islam are authoritative and autocratic. The governmental organizations are either monarchies or dictatorships; the families are dominated by a strong father figure. These same social structures occur under other faiths, too. But much of the rest of the world does not function under exclusionist theocracies and do have social and philosophical altitudes based on the respect of the dignity and human rights of individuals. Americans share the deeply ingrained value that all people are entitled to specific rights. The Declaration of Independence in which the United States declared its independence from England states, "all men are endowed by their Creator with certain unalienable rights."

We must understand that the way people think is based on language. Our safety depends upon it. For a person living and thinking in the words of a democratic system as ours, it is in conceivable to think that one has to 'submit' to anything. Words such as 'freedom' 'terror' and 'religion' hold different meaning in different cultures.

There are nations who do not want to recognize the reality of Israel. There are now such distortions of reality that maps in classrooms in Syria, Palestinian areas, and other Arab countries have no Israel. Children are being taught that it is of more value in what takes place after death than to deal with the reality of living. The world is not safe as long as terror is tolerated in any form; for it is not safe for any of us so long as people act on the judgement that it is all right to eliminate Jews, Christians, Shiites, or any other group. Respect of human rights and reality has to come before the world is again safe for democracy.

The terror attacks in the United States occurred at a time that we were experiencing terrorist action in Israel; then having to travel through New York ignited us to act together and fulfill what we considered a responsibility to write up what we saw, experienced and of our thoughts on the matter.

Hannah Margolis

PREFACE

Our first trip to Israel was to be a pleasure trip, to be together, to visit Jerusalem and leisurely see the country and visit some interesting sites. There was to be no tour. No people to visit. We wanted to travel by whim, to be free of the influence of guides, to experience Jewish life in Israel and visit interesting sites. It was to be our thing! We traveled in March of 2001, the month of the visit of the Pope to the Middle East. The outlook for Israel, the Palestinians, and nearby Arab states seemed the most peaceful and the most promising of any year that we could recall.

We had followed the development of Israel, a land quite far away but from a distance of nine thousand miles across the U.S., the Atlantic and Europe. Israel is quite small as she appear on a map, much the size of New Jersey, with a population of only seven million. Yet, because of interest over the years by parents, relatives, Jewish and Christian friends, colleagues, acquaintances, rabbis, priests and ministers, political and governmental leaders and media -- I became aware that the interest seems way elevated beyond the proportion of its size and population. I tell of the how and of the why this is indeed the case.

The land was full of surprises. The pages reveal our impressions and how expectations measured against the realities. The first three chapters tell of our first impressions as a tourist, of our first brief visit to Jerusalem, Ashkelon, of our drive past Beersheva through the Negev, a stop at Mitze Ramon to view the world's largest crater, then to Eilat and the Dead Sea. The style of writing changes upon our visit to Masada and En Gedi, reflective of our change in historical outlook as we learned of events reflecting Jewish history that differed widely from what we were taught. We began to rethink our own conception of Jewish presence over the years and how it was that we had developed attitudes towards history that were incompatible with what we were seeing in archaeological sites.

Another change in our outlook occurred shortly when we attempting to visit the Tomb of the Patriarch in Hebron. There we got caught up in the unrest between two Palestinian youths and the Israeli Army and two different perceptions of reality. Were it not for some quick thinking on a soldier's part, we might have all been part of an unfortunate international event.

During our first visit to the Old City of Jerusalem, we developed a greater discomfort with our own precepts of Jewish history as we viewed centuries of history pass before us while walking block after block through areas that were rebuilt and restored. Later, upon surveying the ruins and restorations of the ancient city of Katzr'in in the Golan and areas of Tiberias and Safed, we generally began to reach the conclusion that our conceptions of the Jewish past in *Eretz Ysrael* was indeed significantly different than that of what we now believe. By the time we had to leave Israel, we knew we had to come back. But this next time I would do some concerted study on the matter of Jewish presence.

After some study, we returned to Israel. We arrived in mid August, 2001. This time I was prepared to see for myself the evidence, or lack of it, for continued and unbroken Jewish presence in Israel from the days of the First and Second Temples, an unbroken period of over three thousand, two hundred years. It seemed quite important to me to ascertain the evidence for continual Jewish presence, especially at this juncture of time when Arabs, Moslems and most notably, Palestinians claim an unpaired entitlement to the land. The project by this time had taken on a major part of its present form -- the nature of the Jewish and Arab/Moslem claim of entitlement to the Land of Israel.

As we traveled throughout the country to outlying sites, we heard explosions, rifle fire, the rat-a-tat-tat of machine gunfire, cannons and tank firing every day. Low flying aircraft appeared daily. The skies over Jerusalem, Safed, the Golan and Tiberias were marked by flashes of light. Because of bombings or bomb threats, we were cardoned off the sidewalk at various times in Jerusalem and the Old City, in Safed and Tiberias. Barricades prohibiting traffic flow because of shootings as we drove through Jericho, Tiberias and Tel Aviv. Armed solders were seen individually patrolling the streets in Jerusalem. Small infantry units were on mobile patrol throughout the north. The front pages of local newspapers carried text and images of destruction, killings and terror attacks, claimed by Hamas, PFLP and Al Aqsa Brigade.

We were really taken aback following the attack on the Twin Towers in New York City and the Pentagon in Washington. Though I had already decided to write up the project, I became further embroiled as we realized that more people were killed in the New York attack than killed in the last few years here in Israel. I tell of our experiences and the reactions of the people about us and of the changes we saw in the outlook of Israeli Jews and Arabs.

We were quite close to many acts of violence. I discovered that local opinion surveys of the Arab populace revealed considerable support for the violence going on at the time. As a psychologist, I felt impelled to understand what is motivating the perpetrators to cause such macabre acts, not only at the risk of their lives, but often in spite of their lives. I wanted to know, to my own satisfaction, what is the content and source of the precepts that guide such people to commit such violent acts. The second part of the book describes the violence about us, Moslem precepts derived from the Qur'an, links with imperialism and colonization, Arab/Moslem sentiments for objectives of the Central and Axis Powers, the impact of the British Mandate of Palestine, precepts regarding the "illegitimacy of Israel", precepts of entitlement to the land, refugee matters, the development of Palestinian nationalism, and justification offered for terror attacks. These matters are explored in their historical and religious context.

x

CONTENTS

PART I
VISITS TO ISRAEL

PROLOGUE

March - April 2000
A Year of Peace and Hope

The outlook for Israelis, the Palestinians and nearby Arab states seemed as peaceful and promising of any year that Hannah and I could recall.[1] It was a time to be together and experience Jewish life in Israel. There was to be no tour. We wanted to travel by whim, free of the influence of guides. Our first trip to Israel, was to be a leisurely visit to Jerusalem and a drive through the countryside to visit interesting sites.

The land was full of surprises. The journal reveals how our expectations measured against the realities in Israel. The text, in journal style, reflects our change in outlook over time as we became aware of the actualities of cultural clash, the significance of historical events, the importance of how they are perceived and the extent that history, religion and culture affects everyday life.

The first change occurs following our visits to Masada and En Gedi. What we learned there differed widely from what we were taught and had learned. We soon began to rethink our conception of history, particularly the nature of the Jewish past in this area. A significant change in our attitude also occurred when we attempted to visit the Tomb of the Patriarch in Hebron whereupon we got caught up in the unrest between two Palestinian youths and the Israeli Army. Were it not for some quick thinking on a soldier's part, the soldier, the teenagers, Hannah and I might have all been part of an unfortunate international event. The next day, during our first visit to the Old City of Jerusalem, centuries of history appeared before us while strolling through areas that were rebuilt and restored. A few days later in the Golan, upon surveying the ruins and restorations of the ancient city of

---

1. Palestinians, in this book, refers to (1) Arabs and their families claiming residence in what is now Israel, Syria, Lebanon and Jordan after 1946 and (2) Arabs residing in these areas today that associate themselves with the development of Palestinian nationalism starting in 1964, the Palestinian Liberation Organization (PLO) and the Palestinian Authority (PA), the current governing power in the West Bank and Gaza areas.

Katzr'in, then subsequent visits in Tiberias and Safed in the Galilee, our conception of the Jewish past in *Eretz Yisrael,* the Land of Israel,[2] had changed significantly. We gradually came to believe that Jews have been in this land continuously for over three thousand years, and more often than not, flourishing. I began to wonder how it came to pass that I had believed otherwise.

---

2. In this book, *Eretz Yisrael* refers to the land within the greater perimeters of ancient Israel during the First and Second Temple periods (1000 BCE - 137 C.E.). This area includes what is today central and northern Israel, and adjacent parts of Lebanon, Syria, and Jordan.

Chapter 1.
Our First Few Days in Israel

We arrive at Ben Gurion Airport, March 12, late at night. In the quietness of the airport, a man is seen in the baggage area holding up a sign with our name. He leads us to his waiting car. In about twenty minutes we approach Jerusalem and find the city quiet this time of night.

We find ourselves at the historic King David Hotel. The bellhop greets us and shows us to our room. He hesitates as we step into the room, steps around in front of us, catches our eye, and states in a matter of fact manner, "We are in the suite where Anwar Sadat stayed when he, as president of Egypt, came on his peace mission twenty years ago." He takes a few steps forward to the drapes covering the far wall. He reaches for the drawstring, hesitates again then withdraws the drapes with a swoosh exposing a large glass door. We look out over the balcony into the dark night. We see, five hundred yards away, a huge wall perpendicular to us at eye level, surrealistically visible in the darkness of the night.

The imposing wall appears unreal. The image is like a specter materializing after a long lapse of time. Awakened now, we excitedly step outside onto the balcony to get a clear view. The wall, built by the Turks in 1587, sits atop a forested ridge a quarter mile to our east. The base of the wall lies at an elevation somewhat above our third floor elevation. At the base of the wall are a series of floodlights, perhaps fifty yards apart, illuminating the entire length of the wall in a brilliant contrast to the darkness of the night. The lights reveal the light golden texture of the large stones forming the ramparts. As we look over the scattered rooftops on the downward slopes below us we find ourselves holding hands transfixed as history suddenly comes alive.

March 13, Monday AM: King David Hotel, Jerusalem

In the morning we feel a need to be anchored a bit in Israel before visiting Jerusalem. We agree to see some of the country before digesting the Old City. We will return to Jerusalem after we get a glimpse of the nation. We rent a car.

Now, in the bright light of midday, we are impressed with what we see. We drive out of downtown through the western portion of Jerusalem. We see structures and landmarks we've seen only in photographs. Our drive takes us past the Knesset area, through a short commercial section before striking Highway 1, the Tel Aviv to Ammon freeway. From the freeway we see the hills are carpeted with sparse chaparral growth similar to that of drier sections of southern California. There are occasional abandoned small military vehicles along the nearby hillsides. Small trucks were deliberately left following the war for independence in 1948. Their presence reminds us that for nineteen years Jerusalem lay at the eastern terminus of a narrow canyon-like corridor flanked on both sides by Jordanian forces.

We continue eastward for about half an hour. We decide to head for Ashkelon National Park. We turn southward short of the coast to avoid the congested seaside cities. As we approach Ashkelon we opt to cruise by residential areas. We randomly go up and down streets, some wide and some narrow. Each block we pass appears unique and different. There are small storefronts. The kind of store and merchandise are identified by modest advertisements in many styles and languages. Almost all signs contain at least some Hebrew, the common denominator in this part of Ashkelon. There is much residential housing, some of several stories high. People here are dressed informally as if they might be close to home. People seem preparing for some activity or another. They appear busy with routine domestic tasks. Conversation is going on everywhere, and in various languages and gestures.

There is barely enough English signs to navigate safely, but not enough to keep us from getting lost. We find the national park containing ancient historical sites a couple of miles to the south. As the hour is getting late, we decide to look for overnight accommodations. We opt to recuperate at a nearby hotel, a Holiday Inn on the banks of the Mediterranean. Though quiet today, the staff is busy preparing for a convention tomorrow. We find we are limited to one night's booking. Because we are still experiencing jet lag, we decide to make reservations for our next night at a hotel in Eilat, a leisurely day's drive southeast through the Negev. In our room, we look to the south along the beach. We see small ancient-looking structures in various states of ruin dotting the coast line leading south to Gaza.

March 14, Tuesday AM: Holiday Inn Motel, Ashkelon

After a morning of experiencing our first Israeli hotel breakfast, we opt to leave and drive further around the nearby neighborhoods. We meander through different communities in and about Ashkelon. We pass through congested areas mixed with populations of Ethiopian and Russian Jews. The way the people are dressed, the outdoor signs and storefront advertisements are all consistent with this mix of a subculture in the area. We stop at a couple of small grocery stores. Many of the products have labels in Russian as well as in Hebrew. Other than the labels on the foods, these stores are not unlike the small grocery-delicatessen stores

I've seen in western parts of Los Angeles or in the San Fernando Valley that reflect a Russian influence. We are impressed with this mix of eastern European, Israeli-Middle-East and African culture. Though diverse in geographical and national background, all the people are quite Jewish. This diversity of culture takes place from one block to the next, mile after mile. We are indeed impressed with Israel! We cannot help now but see parts of our own cultural roots, til now perceived as merely historical, told by parents about life in "the old country," read in books or seen through images in illustrations and motion picture.

We reluctantly leave the coast for Eilat. We find ourselves soon on Highway 40, driving through some more active suburbs, then through rich agricultural areas. We are gradually leaving the coastal plain. To the west, the Mediterranean coast gradually turns toward the southwest as we head southerly. As we travel along this major thoroughfare, we find farming sectors slowly becoming intermixed with areas of native chaparral-covered growth.

The land becomes partly hilly and drier as we leave the coastal plain. We are in the beginning of the desert. There is some agriculture, but there is low lying sparse chaparral growth on the hills as we approach Beersheva. Though we are aware of attractions in the area, we continue to drive south on Highway 40 towards Eilat. The seasonal agriculture now becomes limited to the lowlands. Once passed Beersheva, we find we are in the desert. The chaparral is short and sparse. Soon after departing Beersheva we enter and pass through the more barren Negev landscape.

After about an hour of driving through the Negev Desert the road climbs somewhat to eventually reach a summit of about 3,000 feet. Nearby is a rest stop and visitor site, *Mitzpah Ramon*, an overlook, or view site, of Ramon. A visitor center sits on a knoll overlooking a huge crater. A mile to the east we view the largest known natural crater in the world. We stroll through the center, have a snack, but find no explanation as to how the crater was created. The available literature on site and our Guidebook recognizes that little is known as to how it was formed. We see the entire perimeter of this crater. The width is 4.34 miles and its length is 24.8 miles, far larger, more extensive , deeper and older looking than that of the noted crater in central Arizona. The depth is measured as 1,637 feet. The road winds down following the contours of the crater wall to finally cross the bottom. Once in the crater, it appears quite barren and not altogether much different in appearance than the area about, perhaps more barren and darker in color.

Our Route 40 now leads south by southeast through the barren Negev Desert. The major thoroughfare parallels the Egyptian border, about 15 miles to the southwest. After leaving the great crater, the road goes up and down a bit but generally maintaining a thousand feet before a short climb and descent to near sea level where it strikes Highway 90. This major highway follows the length of Israel from Lebanon to the Gulf of Aqaba, about 350 miles. This major north-south thoroughfare follows the sink from the northern Hula Valley near Lebanon, cuts along the west side along *Yom Kinneret*, the Sea of Galilee, then south along the west bank of the Jordan River to the Dead Sea, then on to the Gulf of Eilat to connect with highways through Jordan and Egypt.

We turn right and take this historical route southward thirty miles to the northeast extremity of the Gulf of Aqaba at Eilat, our more immediate destination. A transition takes place from barren desert to widely scattered agricultural areas as we approach Eilat.

Eilat is a bustling commercial and resort area where lies a tiny corner of Israel with borders to Jordan to the immediate east and Egypt to the immediate south. We look for our hotel. In so doing we meander around the resort area hoping to find our home for a couple of days. We drive through the sprawling resort area passing one hotel after another, each one larger and more grand than the next, reminiscent of the strip in Las Vegas and that of the curving shore line and inlets of Honolulu. Some of the large structures appear to be in the latter stages of construction. Some are receiving guests while construction is continuing. Only about half of the large hotels seem to be completed. The street signs, advertisements and posted directions are new and constantly being modified to account for new streets and connections. We eventually find our hotel, the Holiday Inn, a large, but more mature looking hotel than the more recently constructed hotels in the area on the shores of the Gulf.

We walk down the hall from our room. The aisle turns into a balcony that overlooks the large dining room and adjacent lounge a couple stories below. We can see from our vantage point a large group of teenagers seated in the large dining room. They are escorted by two or three young men standing about with watchful eyes holding machine guns pointed downward. Here, we have our fist sign of unease experienced by citizens throughout their fifty years of statehood. We walk down the flight or two of stairs and find these youngsters are celebrating the finishing of their senior year at high school. These teenagers are dressed and behaving like groups of students anywhere throughout the U.S. As others before them, they soon will be entering a required tour of active duty with the Israel

Defense Forces.   The casualness, chatting and humor displayed among the students and young armed guards reveal their unique style growing up in an environment that can be quite hostile.

March 15, Wednesday: Holiday Inn, Eilat

In the morning we drive south along the west bank of the Gulf of Aqaba. We pass a number of bathing beaches, tourist attractions and more hotels. Out to the broadening Gulf of Aqaba are a number of large cargo ships. Here, the waterway serves Israel, Jordan and Egypt. The ships are too far away to see in much detail, but have flags from all over the world. There are several Israeli patrol type craft on our Israeli side. A number of housing tracts can be seen on the hills overlooking the gulf. We see the product of peaceful coexistence. After the fun self tour and a walk along the beach, we return to our hotel to make reservations for tomorrow night, *Shabbot* (Jewish sabbath, dusk Friday to dusk, Saturday) at a hotel at Ein Boqeq on the banks of the Dead Sea.

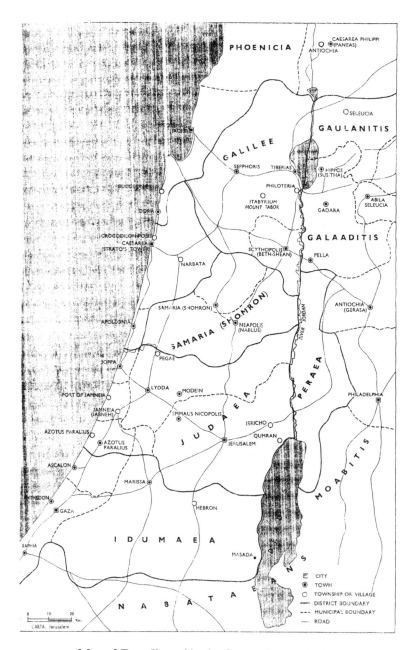

Map of *Eretz Yisrael* in the Graeco-Roman Period
The Second Temple (332 B.C.E. - 70 C.E.)
Jewish, Roman and Byzantines (70 - 633)
Modifed from Avi-Yonah (2001), p 114

Chapter 2
Masada

March 16, Thursday AM: Leaving Eilat

Traffic is heavy this late morning as we leave the busy Eilat-Aqaba area. Trucks are in line. There is much importing and exporting of goods among the states of Israel, Jordan and Egypt and a lot of transporting within Israel. The Eilat airport is busy. Large planes are taking off and landing. The border crossings are busy. But traffic goes by well. A sense of peace and purpose permeates the whole area. There are little indications that twenty years earlier Israel was existing without a peace treaty with these neighbors. Now, the border crossings are busy with cargo passing in all directions.

Our four lane highway reduces to the standard Israeli two lane rural highway. We are pleased to find the Israeli highways uniformly wide, well paved and graded with adequate shoulders. Traffic becomes lighter. The roadside business and activity soon thins out. A number of date palms and tropical fruit groves are seen in the flat and lower areas to the east where they are accessible to irrigation. Beyond the groves to the east, in Jordan, all appears arid, as do all areas to the west.

We drive north along the first stretch of Highway 90, now somewhat familiar and approach the junction with Highway 40 to Beersheva. A review of our maps suggests that in a couple of hours we will reach the great sunken salt lake. If we were so inclined, it would take us additional forty-five minutes to reach the west-east Jerusalem-Ammon highway. From this junction it is but a half an hour traveling west to Jerusalem. If we were to head eastward, we would reach Jordan in about three miles and could be in Ammon also in a half hour. To continue north would bring us to the Sea of Galilee in just over an hour, and in another hour or so to reach Metulla and step across the Lebanese border. We are impressed with the proximity of one city and one country to another. Now, we come to understand how small Israel is.

After a few more miles of the junction to Highway 40, we become aware of widely distributed deserted concrete shelters with old military signs posted nearby. We become mindful of being on a frontier between two countries. There are extensive networks of barbed wires. More often than not, they are deteriorating and in poor condition, a hopeful sign that perhaps they are not needed anymore. The soil looks eroded, sandy, rocky and whitish in color. The chaparral-like growth becomes even more sparse and low to the ground as we put on milage. There are occasional agricultural activities on the west side, characterized by plastic green-house-like structures over young plants. Other than vehicles on this highway, nothing is moving. We pass several small Israeli military bases that are quiet.

We find the horizon to the north and east becoming obscured by a growing haze over the sunken terrain. We imperceptibly drop in altitude. The air becomes dense, very thick. We let go of our pleasant thoughts of Ashkelon and Eilat. We are approaching the Dead Sea. The haze reduces visibility to a few miles.

Sooner than expected we reach the southwest banks of the Dead Sea. It is mid afternoon. It is quiet. The air is still. The long and narrow lake is now seen obliquely from just a few feet above its level. The sun is playing on the surface at this hour. The sea looks like a piece of wet glass. There is no activity on or near the water as we pass abeam the Dead Sea. An occasional rise to the road over a knoll reveals an overview of the Dead Sea. Beyond the lake, to the east, lies the rise of the east bank, barely visible through the pervasive murky haze. To our immediate west the barren and rounded Judean Hills appear to rise more sharply. As we approach the large lake we see fingers of large sharp escarpments and gullies coming down from the western ridge, about 2,000 feet or more above us. Some of these gullies reveal signs of intermittent streams or washes, hints of possible springs or surface moisture in this vast dry area..

We arrive at Ein Boqeq and readily find the Crown Plaza Hotel. We are assigned a room adjacent to a group of Israeli military officers that had just been relinquished, and now available. We unload our baggage. I wash some socks and hang them out to dry. We decide we may have sufficient time this afternoon to visit Masada if we forego the afternoon stay at the hotel.

3:30 PM: Masada

We arrive at the base of Masada, uphill, just off to the west about a mile from the highway. On approaching the area the steep escarpment appears golden in color reflecting the hazy afternoon sun. Beside the imposing mountain are two distinct gullies forming a small but dry streambed with sparse low plants.

Our attention is soon directed to a large parking lot with various rest areas and small businesses. It is now late afternoon. We head for the main structure at the base of the tramway. We luck out in finding the tramway to the summit still operating. It is relatively quiet this afternoon; many of the tourists had already left. Stepping into the gondola we sit forward to catch the drama enfolding before us as we sharply climb up 700 feet in altitude to the top of the Masada plateau, almost 1,300 feet above the valley and Dead Sea below.

We develop an unexpected insight which is to change the nature and purpose of our trip in Israel. Going up the gondola is a small group of American tourists and a couple of guides. We quietly listen to their overview of history. An inquiry from the group occurs as to the nature of the Roman attack and the legendary suicidal response of the Jews. The two guides point out that they had come to the conclusion that the mass suicide described by Josephus Flavius (37-100 C.E.) in his book, *The Jewish Wars*, was an invention on his part. Both of us having read translations of his work,[3] were taken aback by the guide's denial of the mass suicide. It wasn't so much the case that we would like to agree with the guides, as it was that it suddenly occurred to us that there may be a perceived reality of another account of the dreadful event, the Jewish response to being overpowered by the Roman legions. Before the issue is finished, the ride is over and we are at the top. We step out of the gondola wishing to hear more, but we realize the guides are staying with their group, have a job to do. We continue on our way letting the subject rest.

4:30 PM: On Top of Masada

We are impressed with the extensiveness of the area. It is huge on top. Here is a large plateau, isolated from its surroundings by deep gorges on all sides, roughly a half mile long and a quarter of a mile wide. According to the brochure (2000), the plateau is 2,132 feet long and 984 feet wide. The flat top is 1,443 feet above the Dead Sea (164 feet above mean sea level). The area on

---

3. Josephus Flavius was a Jewish general active during the Jewish-Roman Wars of the first century. Josephus is the sole source of the legendary suicide account. He defected to the Romans at the end of the war. While in Rome he was commissioned to write up an account of the battles. Not only has Josephus became recognized as providing the only known historical account of the war, his work contains a wealth of first hand description of terrain, climate, flora and depiction of Roman and Jewish life.

top reveals signs of ancient improvements including terracing and construction. On top is a gentle slope rising perhaps fifty feet from one end to the other with occasional dips and rises and small knolls. Here are remains of agricultural plots, terraces, cisterns and pools. Some of the pools are *mikvot*, unique bathing pools for the Jewish ritual of immersion. Jewish communities are required by *Halacha*, Jewish Law, to have a *mikveh*. This requirement prevailed throughout all periods of Jewish history up to the present day. It is a rule of thumb that whenever a *mikveh* is uncovered, the host community is viewed as Jewish.

Israel still maintain much of *Halacha*, Jewish Law, and this one is still in effect as it was throughout the last 3,000 years. Whereas *mikvot* are of a similar size, cisterns and pools here are of varying sizes and dimensions. Some appear practical, most likely were used as wells, whereas other pools appeared ornamental. A synagogue on top is partially restored as are many structures of various sizes and dimensions. Such structures extend along the length and breadth of the hilltop plateau.

All quadrants provide dramatic panoramic views except when one is very near the center of the plateau. All quadrants of outlook appear barren. We wonder how this barren area below might have appeared 2,000 years ago.

We are impressed with the ancient engineering feat and signs of comfortable and affluent living of the inhabitants at the time of the Roman occupation and Second Temple. A great deal of care was taken by the work crews to excavate the area. The success of the Israelis in uncovering details of the dwellings existing two thousand years ago is understated like many things the Israelis have done. Many of the structures are amazingly well restored. More is being excavated. But most of the ancient improvements remain underground. What we see by way of structure and landscape is but the very tip of an iceberg.

The brochure lists the periods of occupancy. According to the brochure, the area had been populated during the time of the First Temple from the 10th to 7th centuries BCE, the Hasmonean period during the time of the Second Temple, 103-40 BCE, the relatively shorter Herodian period, 40-4 BCE, during the time of Herod's successors and Roman procurators, 4 BCE-66 CE, through the great Revolt and beyond, 73-111 CE and by a few Christian monks adapting a number of caves as dwellings during the Byzantine period of the 5th -6thcentury, staying for more than a hundred years. When they left, Masada became desolate again.

7:30 PM: The Crown Plaza Hotel at Ein Boqeq

We head back to Ein Boqeq. We are tired but stimulated after trekking along the top of Masada. We find the hotel area is more congested than earlier in the day. There are no parking places close to the front of the hotel. While I look for a parking place, Hannah goes up to the room. As soon as she opens the room's door, the telephone rings.

A man's voice speaking in good English says, "There is a problem with the electricity in the room. The lighting is not working properly. I'd like to come over and fix it."

Since she is alone in the room, she does not want to give permission for this man to enter the room. Her response is, "I do not observe any problems with the lighting. We will notify the desk if any problems develop."

The person on the phone then went on to state some observations of a person that had been in our room, "There is make-up left out on the counter in the bathroom and socks are drying on the balcony." He continued on with some more questions as if attempting to size us up or get a profile on us. As Hannah hangs up the phone, she noticed a lovely gift basket of wine, cheese, crackers, cakes, and candies. It is not unusual to find food baskets in rooms of the Israeli hotels. We've already had baskets in our rooms in Jerusalem and Askelon. This one is a bit more elegant. Entering the room, I see Hannah on the bed, her feet are up as she is leisurely sampling bits of chocolates from the basket. We talk about the unusual phone call and conclude that it may be part of a security measure. We recall that as we were bringing our luggage up to the room hotel staff were carrying roll away beds and extra bedding to a large suite next to our room. We had recalled the bell hop explaining that a "big ranking military officer and staff" will be spending the weekend next door to us.

We begin to sample more of our delights in the basket. As Hannah gets into more of the chocolate we hear a knock on the door. A uniformed bell hop , the same one that brought in our luggage earlier, struggles to explain something in English. The more he speaks, the more incoherent it becomes. He is becoming more and more flustered and embarrassed especially as he sees us sampling the goodies in the basket. He says in a half questioning, half accusing way, "You have a basket of wine and cakes!"

"Yeah, that was very thoughtful. We got into it."

He says, "Inside you got?"

"We though it was for us."

"There's a big general next door."

"Oops, sorry about that. We didn't know it was for someone else."

He now explains in better English, "There was an extensive search for a missing wine basket. It was supposed to be for the officers next door."

"At least the wine is all there. I'll be glad to give it to them."

He takes the basket with him. As he leaves, I say, "Well, good for them, too bad for us."

The bellhop completes his mission; he heroically retrieves the wine; he does not commit himself to a smile.

We try to settle down for the afternoon and cannot help but begin addressing the significance of what we learned at Masada. We are both impressed with what we heard from the guides going up on the gondola. We again began to question what had really occurred during the Roman siege. Our understanding was based on our reading of Joshephus's account in his book, *The Jewish Wars*. We were led to believe the event at Masada and the failed Bar Kochba revolt occurring sixty years later in 137, as sealing the fate of Jews in *Eretz Yisrael*. We were taught that the two events foretold the end of Jewish life in what is now Israel until immigration 1,300 years later, but will soon learn otherwise.

Chapter 3
En Gedi

March 17, Friday: AM: Crown Plaza Hotel, Ein Boker:

During breakfast, in the ambience of the dining room set up as a buffet, we unhurriedly discuss our experience yesterday at Masada. We are impressed with the quality of the structures and the affluent life that seemed to exist on top of the mountain. A number of questions on Jewish life arise. Would it make a difference if the Jews did not commit suicide? Where might they have escaped to? What became of the Jewish presence in the area at the time? Plenty of questions, but at the moment, no answers. We begin to wonder about the nature of our precepts and of our presumptions of history. These complexities are put aside as we prepare for the short drive to En Gedi.

We drive north about twenty miles to reach Ein Gedi National Park. Here in a canyon, according to scripture, the not-yet King David hid from King Saul, 3,000 years ago. We enjoy the day hike through the extensive deep canyon. Sheer walls and waterfalls abound in shaded areas offering rest areas from the heat of the day. There are streams with a number of pools, some shaded with riparian growth and semi-tropical forests. Children fill the more attractive pools. On both sides are steep escarpments rising upward to a thousand feet. Animal trails and narrow foot trails are seen contouring up the high and steep slopes on all sides of this curving and gorge-like canyon. The foot trails lead to a number of historical landmarks. After dunking our heads in one of the waterfalls and our feet in the stream, we head back down the easy trail looking forward to experiencing our first Shabbot in Israel and wonder how it will be managed in a large resort hotel with international and multi-cultural guests.

3:30 PM: En Gedi, the Ancient historical community

On the drive back, an interesting sign catches our eye. The sign indicates an ancient archaeological site nearby. Though shabbot is on our minds, we head for the site wondering what it might lie ahead. The road leads through a glade of date trees to the remains of the ancient community of En Gedi. Here, we find an extensive but close network of restored structures surrounding a synagogue. The mosaic floor to the synagogue remains perfectly intact. Here, dug out, we see indications of much Jewish presence. We see more *Mikvot*, cisterns, storage facilities and residential quarters for a large number of people. The area is but partially excavated.   We can see from the plots that it served a large geographical area. How wide an area the structures may have covered and where might have laid the perimeters of the city is not clear. We note there are no signs of walls nor fortifications to be seen. Looking about today we see non-irrigated groves of date palms and other large trees throughout the area. Jericho is but twenty five miles to the north, a two days walk. Over the barren Judean Hills in a northwesterly direction lies Hebron, about seventeen miles northwest. We learn from pamphlets available that the site had been active with a Jewish population from a time well before the destruction of the Second Temple to somewhere around the 500s.

. . . . . .

The archaeological site was discovered accidentally in 1965. Excavation occurred between 1970-1972 and again between 1995-1999. According to Avivat Gera, of the Israel Antiquities Authority (2000), this extensive settlement existed from the time of the 2nd Temple at least through the sixth century C.E. Below the revealed strata was found remains of an earlier Second Temple period. The settlement and its synagogue were destroyed by fire; signs of a fire were evident during excavations. A hoard of linen-wrapped coins was found in an adjacent building courtyard. The latest coin was dated to the reign of Emperor Justinian the First (527-565). It is known there was a wave of persecution throughout the area in 530.

. . . .

We attempt to deduce what might have happened at the time of the Masada siege. Here lies En Gedi, 10 miles away, as the bird flies, within a day's walk from Masada. We conclude that most likely the two community centers were co-active before and following the destruction of the 2nd Temple. At the time that Masada fell, En Gedi apparently was quite active. This community not only endured Roman occupation, but remained active as part of a commercial center for at least 500 years after the incident at Masada, well into the Byzantine era

As a result of visiting En Gedi, we seemed to gather a new light as to the matter of Jewish existence during and following the Roman occupation. It takes little imagination to visualize that the view from here and also from the top of

Masada 2,000 years ago might have revealed a more hospitable agricultural land than seen today.

March 17, Friday Afternoon

We return to Ein Boqeq in a state of cognitive dissonance on the matter of Jewish presence in this part of Eretz Yisrael. It was at this point in time, after visiting the historical sites at Masada, reflecting on the words of the guides on tramway to Masada, and unexpectedly seeing the site at Ein Gedi the next day, and reviewing the historical material that the germ was set to pursue matters of Jewish presence in this area of *Eretz Yisrael*. Though we had not yet set out to study the presence of Jews throughout all of *Eretz Yisrael*, we began to sort out what we had learned and picked out what we considered significant.

We learn later upon returning home that according to Ben-Sasson (1977) after Alexander's death in 323 BCE, the entire region was swept by a wave of wars of 'successors' who fought over the inheritance. Palestine changed hands several times, often with disastrous results for its land, towns and population.[4] In 301 BCE, the area including En-Gedi finally fell to Ptolemy I of Egypt, to remain so until the year 200 BCE, at which time its history remained linked for many years to that of Ptolemaic Egypt. Such areas in *Eretz Yisrael* shared in the general economic prosperity of the Ptolemaic Kingdom during the time of its greatness. There was much trade shared in *Eretz Yisrael*. Important commodities at the time were a quality olive oil, asphalt from the Dead Sea (for embalming), and balsam which grew in groves near En-Gedi and Jericho.

At the end of the Second Temple era, the majority of *Eretz Yisrael's* population was Jewish. Most of the Jews were concentrated in Judea, Galilee and the Peraea, but many lived in other parts of the country (Ben Sasson, 1977, Ben Gurion, 1974, Abba Eben, 1974, 1984). Many Jews lived on the Hellenized coastal cities, such as Caesarea, Ashkelon and Acco, and further inland in such places as Scythopolis and Gerasa in Trans-Jordan. At the end of the 2nd Temple period, the village system was still the pattern of settlement and social cohesion for most Jews.

Ben-Sasson (1977) reviews estimates of Jewish population during the end of

---

4. Palestine, as used in this book, refers to the land contained in the British Mandate of 1917-1948, what is today Israel, Jordan and parts of Syria and Lebanon.

the 2nd Temple. Ancient sources usually gave exaggerated figures. Josephus gave the number of dead in Jerusalem following the destruction of the Temple as 1,100,000; prisoners taken as more than 97,000. He also claimed there were 3,000,000 participants in the Passover celebrations in Jerusalem. According to McEvedy (1978), and other specialists in world population growth, population estimates offered by writers including Josephus, military officers, historians of the past as well as population estimates offered in The Old Testament were consistently highly exaggerated. It is nevertheless clear that *Eretz Yisrael* was quite densely settled. In this respect the land did not differ from its neighbors, Syria and Egypt, which also had large populations during the days of the Roman Empire.

Table 1 provides our estimate of time line for the Masada and En Gedi areas. Unless otherwise indicated, all tables in the books are original.

Estimates of population, including demographic breakdown, were attempted following our site visits. Very little information on numbers of people were available by way of plaques or published material at the sites. Numbers were based on a number of factors, including related data posted at the sites, consideration of the existing infrastructure at the time, caches of coins in the area, review of tax records, burial sites, visits to museums, and contemporary writings from a wide variety of sources. Appendix B, page 223-225, provides a compilation of our sources of information on the presence of Jews throughout the annals of history.

Table 1
Time Line for Masada and En Gedi Areas
Estimated Highest Population

Year	Administration Occupier	Population
B.C.E.		
300	Jewish	4,000+
200	Jewish	4,000+
100	Jewish/Roman	4,000+
C.E.		
	Jewish/Roman	4,000+
100	Roman	4,000+
200	Roman	4,000+
300	Roman	4,000+
400	Not Clear	4,000+
500	Not Clear	4,000+
600	Persian/Umayad	Trace
2000	Israel	10,000+

At the time of the Massada incident and for years following, En-Gedi and Jericho were major centers of an agricultural area that flourished throughout the Jordan valley and to the east to the areas of Gerasa and Philadelphia and in the north to Machaerus, and to the Dead Sea in the south. According to Ben-Sasson (1999), Jews of the Peraea followed the fortunes of Judea and fought side to side with the Judeans in the Great Revolt 132-135 C.E.

During the first years of the revolt, Bar Kochba had re-occupied all of Judea. A "duumvirate" was appointed over En Gedi. In caves in the Judean Desert, during the time of the revolt, letters have been discovered belonging to refugees from En-Gedi and other places in the vicinity where shelter had been sought. We assume that after the failure of the revolt against Rome, the center of Jewish activity soon shifted from Judea and the south to the north centering in the Galilee.

During these times, a considerable part of the country was defined by its ethnic character. The status of a region was determined according to the nation or ethnos to which its population belonged (e.g. Judea, Samaria, Edom). In areas with such a clear ethnic character, the Ptolemaic authorities were forced to consider local traditions and leadership.

We assume, unless we learn otherwise that the population center at En Gedi, at its height served an area comprising of greater than 4,000 people, probably all Jews. Also, the fall of Masada did not signal the end of Jewish life in the area, but that Jewish life continued in the immediate area, and went on for more than five hundred years. Quite likely a high proportion of the descendants of these people settled northward over time to more hospitable areas in and about the Galilee.

There is much to reconsider in our understanding of history of the area. Much of the trouble I have in trying to absorb the history of the area is unlearning what I had taken for granted as "facts"and struggling with the mental gymnastics to replace them with meaningful new concepts. For us to better understand the present political and military conflicts in this part of the world, we first have to go through a process differentiating that which we had believed to have occurred from that which had actually happened or more likely had really occurred. In Israel, differences among people in their perception of the reality of historical events from that which had really occurred is responsible for much angst. The differing precepts of past events among people here are often the source of much of the current strife and conflict.[5]

We have come to accept that the defeat of the Jews at Masada did not mark the end of Jewish presence in Judea. It may have more likely have been the case that there were no mass suicides occurring during the withdrawal from Masada. The number of bodies found during the excavations are consistent with the rate of natural deaths of a population of the size that was estimated to reside on top of the mountain. Jewish life in En-Gedi co-existed with that of Masada. Jewish life persisted in the area in and around En-Gedi, including areas about Masada, on both sides of the current Jordanian and Israeli border, from at least 300 B.C.E. on through to at least 550 C.E., and for how many centuries beyond, it is for us now not clear, but Jews prevailed throughout the area for more than 800 years -- with En-Gedi as an example of such a community.

For the time being, we put such matters of history and Jewish presence behind us as we prepare for our first Shabbot in Israel, interestingly enough, in one of the larger hotels, The Crown Plaza here on the banks of the Dead Sea.

Business goes on, but in a different manner than during the rest of the week. We find "Shabbot Elevators" automatically stop at each floor. The lights in the rooms have dimmer controls that also turn the lights on and off automatically if not set. From Friday evening on, and throughout Saturday, all restaurant food is kept warm from the day before. There is no necessity to exchange funds for meals, nor anything to sign. All happens with smooth execution and Israeli know how. And, all service needs of all guests are met, Jews, Christians, Moslems and a number of people with other interesting backgrounds.

In this way, all people can easily observe Shabbot if they so choose. It may be fair to say that all people are participating in some form of recognition of Shabbot. The guests are seen to go along with the conventions of Shabbot.

---

5. It is indeed normal and expected for people to react with distress when faced with unlearning something in order to adapt to a new way of behaving. I have written of the nuances of this phenomenon (Margolis, 1962, 1964, 1971, 1991). All of us, regardless of culture, are susceptible to this kind of distress. When we are not aware of the connections between what is to be learned and what is to be unlearned (suppressed) the resultant distress experienced can be called, anxiety (Margolis, 1991). As I am a clinical psychologist and Hannah, a psychiatric social worker, we are familiar with how defense mechanisms and styles of living can be erected to offset arousal of such distress and anxiety.

Most choose to ride the Shabbot elevator, choose not to write in public places, avoid signing for meals, avoid driving, avoid use of the cellular phone, and a host of other such patterns associated with conduct during Shabbot. Because we usually cannot tell by looking at someone to whether they are Jewish, Christian, Moslem, or something else, we have the feeling that the wide majority, regardless of their ethnicity, seem to go along with the restrictions, and are not experiencing any inconvenience by the hotel's adherence to customs of Shabbot. We do not feel in any way special because we do or do not observe any of the traditions of Shabbot. The staff attempts to meet the needs of all their guests without any indication of discrimination. As millions of others before us had concluded, here in Israel, an observant Jew can feel comfortable in a public and private accommodation without hassle.

March 19, Sunday Morning: The Judean Hills to Hebron

After a dunk in the now cooled Dead Sea, a swim in the heated salt water indoor pool and another luxurious breakfast, Hannah and I leave the hotel at Ein Boqeq on Sunday, the day before Purim (a Jewish and Israeli holiday of the saving of Jews from a planned massacre in Persia). We drive back on Highway 90, fourteen miles south along the west bank of the Dead Sea to Highway 31. We then head westward and immediately upward through the southern Judean Hills. The air thins out a bit as sea level is reached, a few miles into the climb as the road winds up through the barren rolling hills. After about ten miles of hilly desert driving we approach the higher desert city of Arad lying in the midst of the Judean Hills, only about seven air miles from the Dead Sea. Here we find the hills are less barren, and in fact have new grass growing among the sparse and low forms of chaparral. As we enter the city, we see our first hint of Purim. We see young girls dressed in costume on one of the street corners. Later, on the highway out of town, perhaps distracted by avoiding a herd of sheep on the road, we believe we see a sign indicating a right turn to Hebron. We turn north and head for Hebron where we hope to visit the structures associated with the Tomb of the Patriarchs.

We soon find ourselves on dirt roads that wind through the Judean Hills. The entire area is rather desolate with low growth of scattered chaparral and signs of ancient ruins everywhere. Along the unmarked road that cuts northward toward Hebron and Jerusalem the ruins are so extensive that there seems little area left other than a garden plot size area that can be plowed without interference of rocks and stones. Remnants of very old ancient looking decayed walls appear to criss-cross the entire landscape forming terraces that have an ancient look to them.

It dawns upon Hannah and me that we are now on the hills to the west of the banks of the Jordan River, The West Bank. We are on the grounds of the ancient Jewish state of Judea. Here is the area where Jews had settled before constructing the First Temple. Here, Jews had a presence over 3,000 years ago. We'll find out how long it lasted. This is also an area of land which Palestinians now claim an entitlement, as do Jews, Christians and Moslems. We begin to feel compelled to explore the matter.

We soon pass through residential sections that are obviously Arab. There is no English, no Russian, no Hebrew; all is in arabic script. The road takes us through the middle of the town, a "main drag" lined with active businesses, shoppers and strollers on both sides of the street for about half a mile. The traffic slows down sufficiently permitting a close glimpse of the life style in this community. The area is a mixture of the old and new. The structures are all small and poorly cared for, as is the general property adjacent to the businesses. Nearby, people can be seen cleaning clothes in the slowly moving streamlets in nearby gullies. The hillsides are heavily terraced with piled rocks giving an ancient look to the perimeters. Driving slowly, we can see the modern advertisements, contemporary goods and hardware on display in the front of the stores which are typical of that for sale anywhere throughout the United States. Here, to us, the modernity of goods seems out of context with the immediate and distant environmental conditions. We seem to be getting non-reactive, quick looks, perhaps cold stares from people we pass along the way. Many seem to "be hanging around" the sidewalks watching one another on this nice sunny day.

We leave the traffic behind as we leave the town. We reach an intersection of dirt roads. No cars, no signs, no structures. We don't know where we are, nor do we know where to go. I say to Hannah, "If being lost means not knowing where you are, and also not knowing how to get where you want to go, then we're lost!"

"This is not a good place to get lost, Hal."

"I know. I can't read the signs. What's more, there aren't any!"

We pull over to the side shoulder at the intersection, stop and look over our road map. Suddenly, from out of nowhere, behind us, comes an armed military patrol vehicle, a jeep with an in-placed machine gun in its midst. Fortunately, they are Israeli! There are two soldiers, both personally armed. One comes to the car, the other stands some distance, on guard. The one closest asks something in Hebrew.

I say, "Manishma? Do you speak English?"

The soldier says something unintelligible.

The second soldier says something like, "Anglit."

"We can speak English."

"Hello, why are you here?"

"We are looking for Hebron."

"I don't understand."

I try to pronounce the word in Hebrew, "Chev'ron."

I bring out the map and point to Hebron. Hesitant to get closer, they remain too far away to read it. They ask us a few more questions. But we cannot understand their Hebrew nor broken English. They continue to gesture indicating they need to know our intent. With gestures, the communications runs like this:

"What are you doing in this area?"

"We are looking for Chevron."

"Why Chev'ron?"

"To see the Tomb of the Patriarchs."

"What's that?"

Out of desperation I spit out "Bei't abba' v'eema" which means literally, house of dad and mom.

Now, they look at one another. They laugh and speak rapidly to one another in colloquial Hebrew. I now can tell they understand our intent.

The soldier now communicates by word and gesture. They pull up beside us, give us directions in English, then wave high in the air for us to follow them. They lead us uphill on a dirt road. After a couple of turns we find ourselves on a paved highway. They slow down. He calls out and sticks his hand up in the air pointing to upcoming signs along the road. The armed jeep disappears from view as we continue driving keeping our eye on the signs. The tri-lingual road signs, Hebrew, Arabic and English, now offer assurance this is a main thoroughfare. We are approaching Hebron!

Chapter 4
Hebron

March 19, Sunday, noon

We drive through some hilly, arid area with scattered light chaparral before reaching Hebron. At a sign indicating *Chev'ron,* I turn left off the road on a paved spur around a curve to a barricade and check point. Before us is a protective barbed wire fence and gate with checkpoint, the periphery of a Jewish community completely surrounded by a high protective barbed wire fence. We explain we wish to visit the Tomb of the Patriarchs. He lets us in. The guard politely offers directions on how to drive through the enclosure to reach the gate on the opposite, western side of the community where we can get directions. On the way through, we sense this community is self-contained. There is a governmental look to the area. The contemporary modern warehouses, public buildings and residential facilities have a standard, non-commercial look to them. Children are seen freely meandering home from school. Many of the children are in costume; today is Purim. While exiting the community from the west, we engage the security guards. Their English is limited. We have a bit of a problem explaining our intent. Fortunately, nearby is an Israeli resident in his car. He overhears Hannah. He recognizes we are American, introduces himself with a fluent English. He explains how to get to the Tomb of the Patriarchs, but makes a point of for us to take care while traveling in that area, to take care not to get lost as some of the local Arabs are dangerous. The Tomb of the Patriarchs is said to be a mile or so away, reached by driving through a winding hillside road through Arab residential property. He tells us again that the Arabs around the immediate area can be quite hostile and tells us to take care. We thank him, follow his instructions, and drive a little more carefully.

We drive through some narrow streets as we follow the contours of a rather steep hill through residential neighborhoods that overlook parts of the city below. The streets and homes do not appear unusual as does the people milling about of the people. We find the people, as the man indicated, appearing hostile. It's not so much what they do when we pass, but it's largely what they don't do. Perhaps it is their glance, a recognition that we must be tourists, probably Jewish. Their body movement and glance, if they were to speak would say, "stay away...I don't want to be seen communicating with the likes of you."

12:30 PM: Before the Tomb of the Patriarchs

We are now in Hebron, *Chev'ron,* "friend, or loved one," near the Tomb of the Patriarchs, the four patriarchs and matriarchs recorded in the Old Testament. We are in the oldest of existing Jewish centers, active during the time of Abraham and Sarah. According to the bible (Genesis 23:9), it was here that Abraham is said to have purchased and had built the tomb for his first wife, Sarah, the mother of Isaac. Also said to be buried here is Isaac's wife, Rebecca, as is their son, Jacob and his second wife, Leah. The Hebrew word and the Israeli name, *Chev'ron* serve as reminders that the Tomb of the Patriarchs, *Me'orat ha'machpela* (family or ancestral burial site), is a place for friends and "loved ones." We conclude that the Israeli soldiers who interrogated us as we were approaching Hebron knew of the terminology so that when I referred to Abraham and Sarah as *abba* and *eema*, mom and dad, they caught on and understood of the place we wished to visit.

The Arabic word for the site is *Al-Haram Al-Abrahimi.* We presume Moslems residing in the area grasp the fact that this site is central to Jewish history and has some importance beyond that of being used as a mosque and the burial site of Abraham. It is noteworthy that Jews and Christians are taught from Genesis that Sarah gave birth to their son, Isaac, who later was saved "from the sword" by the word of God on the Temple Mount.

The distinctive looking building is across the street from a small business section and city park. The immediate surroundings are monitored and heavily secured by local police, Israel Defense Forces, Palestinian police and uniformed personnel of the United Nations contingency. The area is relatively quiet. We readily park close by, almost in front of the building. There are some children playing about in a park and playground across the street. There are no tourists about. There are "guard houses" and tall structures that tower obtrusively around the old building. We park nearby and head for the stairway leading to the large, almost massively large, structure. Before us on the wide stairs stands a tall and young Israeli armed guard in the uniform of the Israeli Defense Force (IDF).

As we step towards him, two older teenagers confront the guard as we approach him. We stand off, give ground, as they inch their way towards the solo soldier. Their left shoulders are up as they approach the guard. They begin to taunt the Israeli to take them on in a fight. Their body language is saying, We're not afraid of you. I look at the soldier, offer a slight smile and back off giving them room. He shrugs his rifle butt at them. They laugh and circle him. He remains in control. As we leave his presence, they also leave sauntering in the characteristic gang style I've seen in the streets of Los Angeles.

We come across another young man in uniform. We are told the disappointing news that we are not permitted free access to the area. Another guard tells us that Christians can go in at this time, but not Jews. Jews can enter an area set aside as a study center outside the building. We climb the steps leading to the entrance. The military presence seems tense. The air is thick with hostility, so thick you can cut it with a knife! Men in different uniforms appear grim-faced, giving the impression they do not enjoy this kind of duty. They are alert for trouble.

We start up the stairway. We approach another armed Israeli soldier guarding this part of the structure. He asks us, "Are you travelers? "

We tell him, "We are Americans and have passports."

He politely says, "If you tell me you're Christian, I can let you in."

"We're Jewish."

He points in another direction. He says "You can go up there." He points to a walkway leading up to a courtyard. We head in that direction and venture up the walkway. We find a courtyard with a study area nearby. A few elderly Jews are sitting about studying silently. We find no plaques, memorabilia or the like. The study area has a few books on a shelf with a lit memorial candle. A few men are *dovening,* reading and chanting routine prayers, while facing north to Jerusalem.[6] The area inside and adjacent to this Jewish section was without special mention nor identification. The courtyard seemed to us not unlike a very small and barely maintained small neighborhood center. The small "Jewish" area seems to have no special connection to the importance of the building nor

---

[6]Jews recite prayers facing Jerusalem. This was the first time in my experience that one does not face east.

to any of the significant events that took place here over a period of three thousand years.

We are deeply hurt and puzzled by what we are experiencing -- the hostile attitude among the Arab populace towards us, the confrontation between the teenagers and the Israeli guard, not being able to visit an area that Moslems and Christians indeed can, but not us.   Such discrimination is outside our experiences of the last fifty years. We try to make sense of how it is that we are discriminated in this manner. We are also puzzled as to how it is that this structure, so central to Judaism and important to Christianity, now a mosque is available to Moslems is off limits to all Jews.

The structure houses a memorial series of concrete coffins, cenotaphs. They are empty. These memorials are identified by name. According to Israelowitz (1996) the Patriarchs' grave sites are actually located 18 meters below the synagogue and mosque level. They are sealed off. The shaft leading down to the grave sites is marked by a brass plate in the Hall of Isaac.

A History of Hebron

The magnificent building housing the Tomb of the patriarchs was built by King Herod about 2,000 years ago, in the second Temple period. It is the largest building in Israel preserved from that period. Every stone seems intact. When the Byzantines, and later the Crusaders, captured Hebron, the building became a church. During the subsequent Moslem period, the church and structure was turned into a mosque. The parapet was added to the facade during the Mameluk conquest. During Jordanian occupation starting in 1948, until after the Six-Day War in 1967, Jews were not permitted to enter the Tomb of the Patriarchs.

The *Qur'anic* version differs quite significantly from the Judaic-Christian view as to the significance of the people memorialized here.   There is no recognition given to the Patriarchs said to be buried here other than Abraham. According to the *Qur'an*, it was Ishmael, the son of Hagar, the second wife of Abraham, who was "saved" from the sword, not Isaac as recorded in the Book of Genesis. The *Qur'an* describes the line of Arab Moslems as issued from Abraham through his second wife, Hagar, who begot their son, Ishmael. The matter of descendent and inheritor of the land and the matter of birthright of Ishmael and Isaac are seen in a much different manner than that of Jews and Christians. The resulting cognitive dissonance aroused by recognition of the issue presents a major problem to Moslems leading to a different perceptual reality of the significance of Hebron. For this reason Hebron is a flashpoint between Moslems and "non-believers," Christians perceived as contenders, and Jews now widely perceived as "occupiers" and "aggressors."[7]

As Bible study is to Jews and Christians, the *Qu'ran* is to Moslems. Jews study the balance of the Old Testament, Talmudic literature, and a host of associated and secondary literature.   Christians also study associated and secondary literature depending upon denomination.   In the case of Shi'ites, interpretation is less the responsibility of the individual than that of the responsibility of the *Imams*, clerics. But for all Moslems, the predominate focus is the *Qu'ran*.

Mohammad reported visions and dreams about matters reported in the Bible. Being illiterate, he expressed what he had gotten from these experiences and reported them to contemporaries, known as "Companions." The group listened to his ideas and determined he obtained such ideas and images through revelation. These companions put these ideas into a single volume, The *Qu'ran*, written in Arabic, often in poetic form.

The Companions of Mohammad rapidly formed a military-political-theological system that came to be known as Islam, "submit" to the will of Allah. Mobile military units were developed and dispatched through the Middle East to spread the Islamic system, including where we are now -- in Hebron.

The disparity between the text of the Bible and *Qu'ran* is quite apparent in the way people conduct their lives here.   Much of everyday life here is influenced though the teachings of the *Qu'ran*. Though much of the *Qu'ran* is poetic, there is substantial contradictions to the text of the Old Testament as well as omissions on matters quite critical to Judaic and Christian views. Much of the everyday customs of Moslems provide them with a reminder of their divergence in the theology from Judaic-Christian philosophical views and practices. There are differing and often contradictory views between Moslems and Westerners including Jews and Christians on many existential, political and practical matters. As states become more Moslem controlled, there is more adherence to the more fundamental tenets and axioms of Islam. Along with this

---

[7] The matter of "occupier" and "aggressor" is an important contemporary issue brought up by Palestinians in their conflict with Israel. The matter is taken up later in this chapter and subsequently throughout the book.

form of state control comes a a standardization of social norms and a control of political policies that directly influence everyday behavior.[8]

The Moslem interest in maintaining the purity of its theological foundation is critical in understanding the angst experienced by many Moslems in the Middle East. Judaism and Christianity can exist and flourish with or without a sacred site. Jews and Christians can share religious sites without much compromise. Moslems apparently have considerable issues to "work out" to share sites, a matter more than just a mere compromise. These issues are partly psychological, theological and political. Some of these discriminatory practices have continued throughout the entire 1,300 year long history of Islam. Moslem leaders typically continue to promote an unwillingness to recognize facilities of other religions and not share religious sites with a non-believer.

The events said to have happened here at this place in Hebron thirty five hundred years ago are taught from one generation to the next. The Old Testament and *Qu'ran*, though contradictory to one another on this and other issues, are not only aids for the transmission of events but in the case of Islam is by far the primary source. The habits and beliefs in connection to the patriarchs and matriarchs buried here are deeply entrenched in the consciousness of all observant Jews and many Christians. To Jews, the city of Hebron and the Tomb of the Patriarchs offer a spiritual, religious, symbolic, and a connection between present Jewish life and a three thousand year presence, almost continuous. To Christians, the city is one of many places connected to Jewish History and as such is seen as having roots for Christianity and the Tomb of the Patriarchs is an important historical place, once being a church. To Moslems, the city of Hebron is one of many cities perceived as Arab and Moslem, and theirs alone; The Tomb of the Patriarchs is a mosque. Below is buried the same Abraham, but no recognition is offered to other patriarchs nor any matriarchs.

In biblical times Hebron was known as *Kiryat Arba*, District of the Four, also the name of the nearby settlement. The "four" refers to the four married couples who are said to be buried there in the cave: Abraham and Sarah, Isaac and

---

[8]Changes in behavior, as demonstrated by social psychologists in the 1940s, can strongly influence attitude. When groups of people are drawn into situations where group behavior is modified, so do measurements of their attitudes. We see this in the world of sports, organizations, businesses, in politics and in the military. Participating in a group act tends to produce cohesive goal-directed attitudes shared in common.

Rebecca, Jacob and Leah (Jacob's wife, Rachel is buried near Bethlehem), and Adam and Eve. Oral tradition has it that Adam and Eve lived in Hebron after their banishment from the Garden of Eden.

The first Jews were the semi-nomads described in Genesis 13:18 and 35:27. The area was involved in the campaigns of the southern tribes ascribed to Joshua in the late 1300s B.C.E. It is here that King David lived in the capital before moving onto Jerusalem. During the 800s B.C.E., Rehoboam spent years fortifying the area of the southern kingdom. The city is mentioned during the Babylonian exile. Following the Roman destruction of the Temple and the Bar Kochba revolt, southern areas in Judea were destroyed. It was in Hebron where it was said that Jewish slaves could be bought for a horse's ration (Ben-Sasson, 1976).

Four cities were maintained by Jews as holy cities and places of refuge, Jerusalem, Safed, Tiberias, and Hebron, the first Jewish city. We had read from Abba Eben (1974) "a thin, but crucial line of continuity" had been maintained by a small Jewish communities and academies in Jerusalem, Safed, Tiberias and Hebron. Ben-Gurion (1974) reports that following the demise of the Crusaders during the Mameluk period 1260-1516, 15 Jewish communities existed: Jerusalem, Mitzpeh, Lyda, Ramleh, Gaza, Safad, Beit She'an, Gush Hlav as well as Hebron. The largest Jewish communities at the time were that of Safed (300 families) and Jerusalem (250 families). Because of lack of infrastructure, water viaducts, cultivation, drought, natural disasters and lack of support from occupying powers, much of *Eretz Yisrael* was void of community life.

We surmise that Jewish life persisted in Hebron from the Mameluk days as well. According to Avi-Yonah (2001) entry to the Tomb of Patriarchs were strictly forbidden to Jews and Christians. The Jewish Quarter, a courtyard surrounded by stone houses, was not abandoned until the Arab massacres of 1929.

Jews often took refuge in Hebron from pestilence or persecutions elsewhere in Palestine, especially from Jerusalem. In the 1600s a small Jewish, Karaite commuity had been established. In1619 we learn of a plague that ravaged Hebron. Jews of Italy came to its aid. In 1652 there were two Hebron yeshivot that endured for several generations as a center of Jewish intellectual life. Rabbi Gedalia of Semiaritz arrived there in 1700 and noted 40 householders. According to Ben-Gurion (1974), Hebron was in a precarious state during the early 1800s. Immigrants were slow to come to Hebron, though occasionally new settlers moved in. In 1819, for example, a rift between rival rabbinic schools caused fifteen Chassidic families to move to Hebron from Tiberias. By the 1840s there were 1,500 Jews residing in Hebron.

In 1882 the Jewish population of Palestine was estimated at 24,000. About half lived in Jerusalem and nearly all the rest in Hebron, Safad, Tiberias, Jaffa and Acre. In 1907, some 80,000 Jews lived in Palestine, with 1,000 Jews in Hebron. The Arab riots and pillaging that swept Palestine in 1929 had its impact. At the time there were about 700 Jews residing in Hebron, of which 69 were murdered. According to Israelowitz (1996) were it not for many of the Arabs that hid the Jews, they all would have been slain. This incident was one of several Arab attacks going on throughout Palestine at the time. Hebron was the only community that was not defended and the only one that resulted in large amounts of killings. A second anti-Jewish riot occurred in 1936. It was more thorough. Hebron remained without Jews until the Six Day War in 1967.

Though continuous for hundreds of years, the Jewish population for the last 2,000 years had been relatively small. Obadiah arrived in Palestine in 1488. In addition to his letters regarding Jerusalem he found about 20 householders in Hebron, all of them Rabbinite at the time, half were the Spanish speaking who had recently arrived (Ben-Gurion, 1974, Ben Sasson, 1969). Hebron continued as a Jewish center with movement between, during the growth of Safed in the sixteenth and seventeenth centuries.

The historical Jewish Quarter of Hebron was established in 1540. According to Israelowitz (1996) it was built around a courtyard, with the grand Avraham Avinu Synagogue at its center. There were nine synagogues in Hebron, two religious schools for children, three yeshivot, religious courts, the Beit Hadassah Hospital (established in 1893), a mikveh, two guest houses, two bakeries, inns and other public institutions. According to Ben-Sasson, in the very early 1800s there was an increment to the small numbers of Jews in Hebron, as there was in Jerusalem, Safed and Tiberias. In all of Palestine, he points out, there were very little people, because of the weaknesses of the Ottoman Empire, plague, disease, earthquakes and drought. By the 1840s there were several hundred Jews in Hebron. According to Ben-Gurion (1974), Jews have had a continuous presence from Mameluk days. In Hebron today, under Palestinian Authority control there are now about 5,000 Jews in the area, largely in the settlement of Kiryat Arba.

The Turks controlled the area from the 1500s to the establishment of the British Mandate in 1917. The U.N. partition provided Arabs with Samaria and Judea for an "Arab state" in 1947. We recall Jordan immediately disregarding the U.N. proclamation and forcibly entering and occupying Samaria and Judea, including the area where we now stand. By this time, the Jews had been forced to leave and had abandoned the area.

The Jordanians occupied the area up through 1967 when they suddenly withdrew their troops. Israel found itself suddenly required to occupy Samara and the Judea. Unlike Jordan, Syria, and Egypt, Israel did not annex these territories but set the territory aside under the auspices of the new Palestinian Authority established earlier in 1964 with Arafat as their leader. Statehood would result once the infrastructure for responsible government could be developed. What happened, was that instead of using funds for developing the superstructure, i.e. a responsible governing government body with schools, hospitals, highways, water and power, they continued to spend considerable energy of time and what wealth they had accumulated in confronting their new occupier, Israel, a practice continued to date.

Spokespersons for the Palestinian side of the Arab-Israeli conflict consistently refer to the cause of the trouble in Palestine as stemming from the "occupation," implying an entitlement to the land. The Arab media promotes the theme that Israelis are "occupiers" and refer to Israel as the "aggressor." We think the Arab conception of the word, "occupation" is different than our western view, as is their use of the word, "aggression." We conclude the terms have Islamic religious connotations stemming from numerous tenets stated in the *Qu'ran*, e.g. the Sura on transgressors, 2:190, on dealing with aggressors, 2:191, 2:193, on overcoming the dislike for fighting, 2:216, on dealing with the rewards in the after life for fighting aggressors, 4:74. 4:495, on dealing with the non-believers or infidels, and 4:102, on the matter of character of their enemies and their incompetency in battle, 59:14

To the Arabist in Palestine, the word, "occupier" implies an administration that is not Moslem oriented. To Arabs, such a term also signals the history of western intervention including the Crusades in 1000s through the 1200s and later colonialism on the part of more major powers including the Turks, Russians, British and French through to recent times. Surveys of residents in Arab Middle East nations by Pew Research Center (2002) and Gallup (2001) reveal a fear anticipating U.S. hegemony into the Middle East region. Arab leaders are closely following results of such surveys as they have expended much energy sending out information without means on the part of the readers to question or correct false information once out or published. On the issue of "occupiers," we do not recall any reference in their rhetoric toward Syria or

Egypt for their occupation of Palestine following the U.N. partition in 1948. Nor have we heard of protests against the Jordanian occupation of the West Bank Territories, of East Jerusalem and the Old City from 1948 to 1967. There seems to be no recognition at all on the part of Arab media, including those living in Hebron that Jews have resided here for over 3,000 years, and unlike themselves, Jews had lived in the area for centuries under their own rule.

The behavior of two Arab teenagers reflect a perceptual reality different than ours. These two youths are desperately attempting to preserve perceptual habits, working hard to cover up, conceal and suppress connections between old and newer adaptive ways of behaving. This egotistical masquerade is at the risk of their lives as well as others. Their hostility and discharge of anger comes about as a byproduct of denying historical facts and of truths as we see it.[9]

As far as Hebron is concerned, there appears to be lapses in the account of Jewish presence and times when the number of Jews residing there appear quite small. Nonetheless, it can be said with a very good measure of accuracy that Jews have lived in Hebron for three thousand years.

5:00 PM: We return to Jerusalem

With much on our mind, we make the short drive from Hebron to Jerusalem. Though the area remains continuously hilly, the land becomes more developed as we drive north. There is always a mixture of the old and new structures. The old is very old and the new is very new. As we approach Jerusalem, traffic picks up, yet it remains flowing fairly well. We readily pass through a checkpoint as we pass a number of turn-offs and on-ramps as we approach busy Jerusalem from the south.

---

[9]Distress occurs when new responses or habits are called upon to replace older and established ones (Margolis, 1991). No one is immune from this kind of distress. When a new habit is beginning to replace an older one, distress always occurs, only the strength varies. When the connection between the newer habit, and the habit that is to be displaced is unconscious and when there is no awareness of the relationship between the two, anxiety occurs (an emotion unlike that of fear because one is not consciously aware of what is causing the emotional arousal). In the case of the behavior of the two misguided teenagers, the denial of history, the struggle dealing with reality of the connection between the present and the past and the ensuing angst appears projected onto the Israeli soldier.

Chapter 5
Jerusalem and Northern Israel

March 20, 5:30 PM: We return to Jerusalem

We make the short drive from Hebron to Jerusalem. We opt to stay at the Sheraton Hotel. We are pleasantly surprised to find the hotel staff dressed in costumes of various sorts, mostly historical and humorous. Ben Yehuda Street Mall, the Bourbon Street or Hollywood Boulevard of Jerusalem, is filled with young adults, most with funny or weird costumes. The area seems like an adult Halloween Party.

March 20 -22, Monday - Wednesday: Jerusalem

The days in Jerusalem are spent largely walking about. [11] The hotel breakfasts continue to be remarkable. Much of the staff at the hotel are dressed in conservative costumes. The first morning, the dining room waiters and busboys are dressed in Moroccan attire with the characteristic red fez hats with tassels. Tourists at nearby tables seem to enjoy their befuddlement by it all. Humor and jest is everywhere, not just in the hotel, but also on the streets and malls throughout the city.

The Pope is seen flying above us as we watch the flight described in Hebrew. On the front page of the *Jerusalem Post,* alongside an article about the Pope's intended visit is an article with a large caption, "Christians puzzled by Purim." I overhear Americans occasionally asking one another, if this is an Israeli Halloween. It is, indeed, good times here in Israel.

The evening of Purim is spent walking about the city through the Ben Yehuda mall. The odors of food is great as we walk about the closed street. Many of the youths are in costume, some in the style of ancient Persia and Babylonia, others comical but most are just plain weird. While on the mall we chanced Colonel Sanders Fried Chicken; Kosher indeed, as was McDonalds. Most of the

---

[11]Because we return to Israel the next year, and it was not our intent at the time to study the matter of continuos Jewish presence, some of what we see and learn is reported and noted as such in context of our site visits in the next section of the book.

eateries were small family run semi-fast food sit-down and take-outs. Many people are eating as they are walking.

The next day, Purim, is spent visiting the Old City. First through the Jaffa Gate, a walk through the Armenian Quarter and a visit to the Jewish Quarter and *Ha'kotel,* the remaining western wall of the first temple mount. On this day, a number of Catholic youth groups are visiting the area and are seen dancing in the area before the wall. Such groups tend to wear colorful sweaters indicating the nature of their group. All are enthused and excited being in the Old City of Jerusalem at this time during the Pope's visit to the Middle East at time of the second millennium. Many of the youth are sporting sweaters with "K2" printed on one side or another. A small number of Christian groups are sporting sweaters claiming the coming of the end of days. All are speaking languages from over the world. Many exhibits and stores in the Jewish quarter are closed on this day.

The Israel Museum area occupies us for another full day. In its dimensions it is quite similar to the British Museum in London and Royal Canadian Museum in Victoria. Here, there is a year long special exhibit on early Christian history. We also take an interest in the large and extensive exhibit on neolithic history in the area and various exhibits on Jewish life throughout the western and eastern world. Little is offered on the matter of Jewish presence in *Eretz Yisrael* .

March 22-25: Northern Israel

Wednesday morning we head north without objectives other than to experience the northern part of the country. Traffic is swollen. We understand there are about 100,000 tourists, mostly associated with the Pope's historic visit. As we pass Tel Aviv on the freeway, we see little airplanes flying low as on approach to a landing field. Knowing there is an airfield in the area of Herzylia, I am drawn off the freeway to head for the airport. Maybe a local flight is in the offing. Though I try to find the airfield, I simply get lost. I see no posted signs that hint of a nearby field. I look to the skies, but see no light aircraft. We give up and feel lucky we can find the northbound entry back to the freeway.

Haifa is busy. We decide to head northeast, hoping to avoid traffic in the more rural and agricultural parts of the country. The highway climbs somewhat in altitude as we leave the coastal plains heading into the interior of the country just several miles now south of the Lebanese border. The area now becomes similar to the chaparral seen on the lower northeast slopes in southern California, very richly green with plants that only look similar from a distance. A transitional forest marked by scattered oaks and pines are reached as we approach the heights of Mount Meron appearing above us at about 4,500 feet. The slopes of the mountain are pine forested as is much of the area higher than the road, now at almost 3,000 feet. The historical city of Safed is near. Soon appears a more richly forested area that has been assisted by man to become a transitional forest. Pine trees were planted here a few years ago and cultivated to blend well with the existing chaparral. Before we can digest all this, we see the turn off to the historic city of Safed. We decide to look for accommodations.

We feel fortunate to find the historic Ron Hotel where we feel lucky in finding a room available for the evening, a room in which we must leave early. The hotel is otherwise completely booked, mostly by a group of Italians coming to celebrate the Pope's visit to the Galilee. We too briefly acquaint ourselves with the old city, enjoying getting lost, but wanting to come back.

The next day we head farther east to the Sea of Galilee, pass Capernaum and find we are soon in the Golan, the highlands to the northeast of the Sea of Galilee. It is cool, damp and foggy, occasional light rain with visibility is limited to about a mile or so. The hill tops and mountains are obscured in fog. The hills are much like southern California in Spring, very beautiful now with deep green grassy knolls dotted with deciduous trees separated by wet ravines and cattle wondering about freely. We stop at the visitors center in Katz'rin and inquire about accommodations and sites. We find a listing of available sites including one with an available apartment in the rear of someone's home.

We inquire and find we are pleased to stay there and welcome to spend a couple of nights there, including *Shabbot*. While there we soon become familiar with the Tel family. Samuel and Leah have a two story home with a small basement and two upstairs bedrooms converted into small apartments. They were converted upon their children growing up and leaving home and entering military duty. Samuel was exploring our interest in coming to Israel. In explaining the personal nature of our trip, we came to the conclusion together of the nature of our interest in Jewish history, particularly the matter of our developing preoccupation with the matter of continuous Jewish presence. It turns out that Samuel is employed with the Department of National Parks, took an interest in our outdoor activities and was quite pleased to offer a number of suggestions and pointers to help us in this endeavor. As a result, we visited a number of sites in the area, noteworthy in the outdoor aspects, but also in terms of Jewish history.

March 23, Friday: Ancient Katz'rin

Nearby, a mile or so south on road lies ancient Katz'rin, a national park featuring an extensive archaeological site, revealing the remains of a large ancient Jewish community. The Jewish nature of the ruins was first recognized by Shemaryahu Gutman during a survey following the 1967 war. Excavation started in 1971. More excavations occurred in 1975-1976 when the modern town of Katz'rin was built.

Ancient Katz'rin is one of 27 ancient Jewish settlements throughout the Golan. All of these towns contain a luxurious synagogue (Israelowitz, 1996). The dig covers several acres. Last year, at leisure, we walked through the area and saw for ourselves the nature of the residences, workshops, warehouses, numerous mikvot, cisterns, olive presses, tools, "appliances" and the large synagogue. We were impressed with extensiveness of the ancient city. there was no indication of walls or fortification. The area did not look destroyed through battle, but moreover seemed to have had a 'natural" demise, perhaps an earthquake.

The excavations of the village reveal how the city changed and how the people fared over the years. During its initial phase in the 300s, its plan consisted of domestic units with large open spaces, most likely courtyard areas. With time, additions were built to each structure – according to the needs of the occupants. The domestic quarters expanded inward, resulting in ever-increasing density. By the 700s, the village was made up of crowded quarters separated from each other by narrow pathways.

We were impressed with the quality of life and the advanced architecture and tools, particularly the olive press. Last year we had visited the British Museum

Table 2 Jewish Presence in AncientKatz'rin	
Year	Estimated Population
100	?
200	1,000
300	2,000
400	1,000
500	1,000
600	1,500

in London. We compared similar exhibits of everyday life during the same period in England.

Although the perimeters have not been explored, we conclude the town probably served as an agricultural and trading center for much of the Golan area, probably serving a permanent in-city and nearby population of well over 1,000 people for many years. The figure would climb to perhaps 10,000 if one considers residents in the nearby fertile areas.

Macoz (1988b) concluded the first synagogues were built in the late fourth and early fifth centuries, C.E. A century later, at the beginning of the 500s, several synagogues were reconstructed on a larger scale and more were built. Cumulative data of excavation and surveys indicate that most sites in the Golan, including the Jewish settlements, were abandoned at the end of the 500s and beginning of the 600s as a result of military invasions and the collapse of law and order and the economy brought down by the Byzantine regime. Some habitations continued through the end of the middle 700s, mostly in the southern Golan, but some also continued in the central region including the Jewish village of Katz'rin. There is some indication the city was severely damaged in the earthquake of 746. Subsequently, a much reduced occupation occurred for a short time in the Abassid period, approximately 750-878. The Jewish communities in the town of Fiq in the southern Golan and Nawa in Batanaea, continued at least until the middle Ages.

Shabbot, Saturday, March 24

We had learned the night before that Samuel was rescued from Germany and came to Israel during the war. His wife, Leah, is from Russia. They have two teenagers, one of them now serving in the IDF somewhere in southern Lebanon.

As we are sipping drinks and eating snacks in the comfort of the early afternoon in their back yard, a somewhat older distinguished man comes walking into the back yard as we are comparing impressions of the flora of the area. Samuel stands up, strokes his long beard, smiles and introduces him to me as "Abba."

I say, "your father?"

"Yeah, but he's not my father. I call him Abba because he came with me to Israel from Germany."

The gentleman explains, "He was only seven years old. I was only eleven.

I wanted to help him."

"Wow, unbelievably wonderful!"

Samuel explains, "He later came to Israel and we eventually met. I have always called him Abba."

The conversation soon turns away from their encounters to other pleasantries and to the nature of our trip. I explain, "We are from California and this is our first trip to Israel, a personal tour to be together and experience the country and see history."

As Samuel is a naturalist with the forestry and park department, he takes an interest with my trekking experience along the Pacific Crest Trail in California. He tells, "Here in this part of Israel, occasionally people in a religiously inspired mood unwittingly enter the forests and get lost, some not surviving."

"In the south part of California, there are illegal immigrants that attempt to cross over the mountains, some of them not surviving."

The conversation goes on and on. Hannah and I are quite impressed with the background of this family that seems so quintessentially European Israeli. It seems their family tells the story of the meaning and significance of Israel for European Jews.

We tell of our visit to the ancient city of Katz'rin, the museum in town, the drive up to the snow and our visit to the ski lift on Mount Herman and nearby Nimrod's Castle. Tomorrow, we will attempt to visit some more interesting sites including the National Park at Gamla that not only contains a beautiful reserve of flora and fauna, but an ancient Jewish city and fortress destroyed by the Roman Legion.

March 25/26

We visit Gamla National Park, the reserve at the Banyas, a semi-tropical area at the head of the Jordan River, some places without names that we know of, much too briefly. Too soon, we have to leave Israel to come back home. We head southwesterly on Highway 65, passing through Afula and the rich Jezreel Valley. The day continues to have low overcast skies and very light rain. We nevertheless concluded that the Jezreel Valley appears as fertile with its dark soil and richness of crop as any area we have seen in the United States, including Iowa. We connect with the coastal Highway 4, staying on the freeway passing through Tel Aviv to Ben Gurion Airport. We return the rental car, check in at the airport and soon have a long but uneventful flight back home.

As anxious as we are to get home, we feel inspired to return, especially to Jerusalem and visit northern Israel, Haifa, the Galilee and the Golan. We have ample time during the travel home to discuss our impressions of the land, the ways of its people, their personal history and aspirations and of the nature of unimpeded Jewish life. We experienced some new ways of looking at history and as a result arrived upon a number of facts and insights that we agree are divergent from that we had learned over the years. Much of what is learned this last two weeks will require some time to digest. We have much to reflect upon and much to ponder as we look down on the frozen expanses of North America on this otherwise uneventful flight home to Los Angeles. Before returning to Israel, I commit myself to study the matter of Jewish presence in the area.

AUGUST-SEPTEMBER, 2001

PROLOGUE
A troubled Year

We arrived back in Israel the following year in late August, 2001. This time I was prepared to see for myself the evidence, or lack of it, for an unbroken Jewish presence in Israel from the days of the Roman occupation. It seemed quite important to verify the evidence for myself, especially at this juncture of time when Arabs, Moslems and Palestinians claim an unpaired entitlement to the land. The project by this time had taken on direction, but because of events which were to occur during this second trip, the project had not reached its present form.

Like others before us, our view towards Israel and the Middle East had taken on more clarity since our first visit. During the passing year we read specifics on Jewish presence. We became more involved in local Jewish life as well as more supportive of Israel. We accepted a self-paid opportunity to join a small contingent of Los Angelenos for an Israeli Bond tour, August 24-28, 2001. We anticipatied meeting with Israeli leaders on current concerns and to serve afterwards as volunteers on an archeological dig-site in northern Israel.

Because of the attenuation of news hype we get from Israel on news related to the Palestinian-Israeli Conflict and our growing sensitivity to the news, we had decided in advance to take note of events covered in the *Jerusalem Post*. Upon leaving for Israel, we asked our son, David, to collect and save our daily issues of the *Los Angeles Times*. We had planned, upon our return home, to compare the coverage of the *Times* to the *Post*. The front page news accounts and leading stories of both papers are offered for each day of our travel throughout Israel.

The narration in Chapter 6 begins telling of our experience with the Israeli Bonds Tour, a series of fascinating lectures and discussions on matters of local and international interest. The meetings take place in Jerusalem and at a number of significant sites. The next three chapters tell of life in the Old City as we visited a number of historical sites. The enduring Jewish presence in

Jerusalem is summarized in Chapter 9. Subsequent chapters cover visits to historical sites in northern Israel.

Unlike the year before there was much concern with violence and terror attacks. The front pages of local newspapers carried text and images of destruction, killings and terror attacks, claimed by Hamas, PFLP and Al Aqsa Brigade. We heard explosions, rifle fire, the rat-a-tat-tat of machine guns, artillery and tank firing every day. The night skies reflected distant flashes of light.

Chapter 14 tells of hearing about the terrorist attacks in the United States, its impact upon us and Israelis we met, of our early fulfilment of our project, our return to the Old City of Jerusalem, our trip to New York and back home to Los Angeles.

The final chapter of Part I, Chapter 15, "Jewish Presence in *Eretz Yisrael* "recaps points made regarding the continuous Jewish presence and of our estimates of Jewish population throughout the centuries in *Eretz Yisrael*.

Chapter 6

Jerusalem and The Israel Bonds Tour

August 25, Saturday, 8:30 PM

Our son, Joel drops us off at the entrance to the Bradley Terminal at LAX. Moments later we approach the El Al desk and find representatives of the Los Angeles Office of Israel Bonds who confirm our flight and tour for our first three days in Israel We are routinely interrogated by Israeli security agents. We were asked who was in the house when we packed our bags,

"Our sons."

"Son's good."

Check-in goes quickly. We wait a bit at the gate for our 12 hour non-stop flight. Time permits us to review matters that otherwise might be considered trivial.   We talk of the security measures, the quietness of this Bradley international terminal at LAX. The Weekly reading, from the Prophets of Isaiah, "Awake Jerusalem" seem to relate to current events. We talk somewhat of news events that captured our attention.

Los Angeles Times

> (1) President Bush states that added Pentagon funding will not mean dipping into the Social Security surplus, (2) California Representative, Gary Condit is being engulfed with more criticism, (3) Egyptian reaction to a movie on Anwar Sadat that is running on its sixth week reveals that those who were against Sadat when he was alive are the same people that are against peace with Israel today, (4) Jewish Settlers fired on again in Hebron

We discuss the news, especially the news of continued troubles in the Middle East where we expect to be tomorrow. We recall our visit last year in Hebron by the Tomb of the Patriarchs, whereupon we came quite close to being involved in a confrontation between several teenagers and an Israel soldier. We discussed whether we should venture again to Hebron for further answers. As to Condit, we feel the matter should be left to the voters of Fresno. As to U.S. defense posture, we agree that our defense posture is in need of change away from Cold War strategies.

August 26, Sunday, En-Route LAX to Ben Gurion
Israel Bonds Tour, Day 1.

The plane is crowded. Hannah sets her watch. The time seems weird; though it is now eight-thirty in the evening after Shabbot over Los Angeles, it is six-thirty in the morning in Israel. From now on English is not the national language. Soon into the flight, we see a tiny dog peering at us from below the seat in front of me. Moments later, we see four flight stewards looking for the dog. " There he is! Kaleb, Kaleb" I call out. Everybody laughs. There are times when we doze off. We can follow our flight on the screen before us. Our flight path takes us over Lake Tahoe, North Dakota, Lake Superior, southern tip of Hudson Bay, Tip of Greenland, Great Britain, Balkans, Cypress. Now ahead are the lights of Israel, Tel Aviv! People to our rear, upon approach to landing, sing out lines of the song, *Avino Sholom Aleichem* in Hebrew. A clapping of hands. We wonder whether it is a celebration of being in Israel or whether it is an applause for the pilot who finishes a long uneventful flight with a smooth landing. While trying to shake off the drowsiness, we find ourselves in the Airport still in the middle of the night. We claim our baggage.

The tour group assembles. About a dozen of us climb aboard a tour bus. The tour guide soon describes the impact of history on this route from the Mediterranean to the mountains. He also describes sites we are passing, a huge contemporary cement factory, several communities, and the kinds of agriculture seen along the way. We arrive at the David Citadel Hotel (Formerly Hilton Hotel) in Jerusalem, a half mile from the old city.

August 27, Monday: Israeli Bonds Tour, Day 2: Jerusalem. 1.0

We arouse ourselves in preparation for our breakfast meeting in the hotel. We find the *Jerusalem Post* by our door. There's little time to digest or discuss the news. We must shower, get dressed and head downstairs for our breakfast meeting. But it is apparent that the events happening here in Israel are being captured in our home town newspaper, The *L.A. Times*. What differences may exist in coverage, emphasis, and slant, we hope to find out when we get home.

Listening and watching to television as we get dressed we learn of current activities and events going on in the Middle East, particularly Israel. The leading stories on television this morning reveals the preoccupation with the conflict with the Palestinians. We soon learn there is much interest on the nature of positions taken by representatives of other countries, both in the middle east as well as major powers in Europe, North America and the far east. Much is made of world reaction and opinion on television today.

> *Jerusalem Post:* (1) IDF tanks shell positions around Ramallah, (2) Three Israelis fall victim to road ambush, (3) PM's Office warns against Peres-Arafat meeting, (4) Israeli shot in Green Line terror attack, (5) IDF planes, tanks hit Palestine targets.

> *L.A. Times* leading stories: (1) Storming of Israeli Outpost: Palestinian commandos stage daring predawn raid on base guarding settlement in Bedolah, three Israelis and two Palestinians killed. (2) Parents of a suicide bomber grieve for their son near Gaza strip; they feel more anguish than Pride; Hamas claims the act (3) A tobacco settlement fund diverted by States.

9:00 AM: Breakfast with Natan Sharansky, Minister of Construction and Housing

After too short of a sleep we start our day with breakfast, fish, cheeses, breads, spreads, sweet breads, and beverages. We become alert after a cup of coffee, when quietly enters a short unassuming man, who joins us for breakfast. He is Natan Sharansky, a leader of the Knesset and a leader of the growing Russian community in Israel.

He explains he was imprisoned for eight years in Soviet Union.

The secret of Jewish success is our solidarity....I knew little of Judaism..... The movement leading to my freedom was connected to the dissolution of the USSR....The trial brought the matter to the whole world....To help mankind, one must identify with one's country, one's people...a lesson learned from the Bolshevik revolution. My father and others thought communism would bring freedom and rights....Rather it turned into a cruel regime....Some Jews were active in the Bolshevik revolution....[I] had been accused of being an American spy. When I was in prison in solitary confinement, I found out what was inside....I arrived upon a solidarity with all Jewish people....It is important for people of all different views to be united. For never has a democracy faced this unique kind of terror...like the Kamikaze....there is a sacred right of our people to this land....A dictator (Arafat) needs an enemy. What the Palestinian people need is a Marshall plan, not dictators....Sharon rejects the Camp David Agreements.....Democracy is being attacked by terrorism and the world should understand this....Dictators require a common enemy....Get connected with your people and your religion....We can change the relationship between the Palestinians and their leaders.

There is no time at the moment to digest what this interesting man had to say. We are asked to appear outside in twenty minutes where we will board a bus for the Old City. We head back to the room where we gear up for the day's journey. A glance at the paper indicates another wave of Palestinian attacks is underway throughout the country. Soon, we're on the bus to visit a new excavation and historical exhibit of the First Temple at the southwestern corner of the grounds of the Temple Mount.

10:30 AM:. The Old City: A Tour of the Davidson Visitors' Center

Here, we walk on the same stones that had formed a road about the temple grounds and touched the stone structures of over 3,000 years ago and walk too fast through a wonderful exhibit depicting styles of life during the time of the First Temple.

11:30 A Visit to the Western Wall *(Hakotel)*

Soon after emerging from the depths where the Temple lay, we step over to the Western Wall. There was little time for prayer or reflection as we were adroitly collected and escorted to where a bus waits for us. We are now told we are expected to appear shortly with the Minister of Foreign Affairs in his briefing office in the heart of New Jerusalem.

12:00 PM: A Meeting with Shimon Peres, Foreign Minister

We go through another security clearance. It is very similar to that at the airport. Israeli agents look into your eyes and study your facial expression while they ask a few questions. The area resembles a temporary college with classrooms in wooden barrack style buildings. The windows are barred and each surrounded by a rose garden. We were ushered quickly from the bus through a very small security room, down a path through a garden into a room which was filled with a 'cabinet' style meeting table. Water and juice drinks were served. Journalists and photographers almost outnumbered as they stood behind us. Shimon Peres was introduced as the " Ministry of Foreign Affairs, holder of the Nobel Peace Prize, involved with Israel for fifty years."

First, he asked about our flight. "Oh, uneventful, the way it should be." He did not have a prepared speech, nor did he wish to speak formally to us. Instead he asked us to be free to ask any questions or make any comments as we so please. The reporters with video cameras seemed more anxious than us to hear from the Minister of Foreign Affairs. Soon after we began our discussion, an aide comes in and hands a note to the Minister of Foreign Affairs. He glances at it hesitates for a brief moment and continues on with the conversation. We will discover later from television and the *Post* that he received word during this meeting about the missile attack that killed Zibri, the terrorist leader.

When asked a question about his relationship with the Prime Minister, he answered, "Unity is not very Jewish," which was followed by a round of laughter. In answer to a question about his dialog with Arafat he stated "It was not a romance...but it was necessary to maintain communication." A question is asked about the 'settlements,' towns or temporary residence where Jewish communities in Israel have been set up. He responds to the question in terms of the history of Israel:

Jews were a people without a land. He stated "It was not known that Jews continued living in this ancient land when Zionism first started.... Before the Zionists came, there was nothing.... On the international front, the subject must be terror....Our struggle is not against people, but terror....We want to bring the topic up of how to end the fire (referring to Arafat)....Relationship is what will make a difference.

I address Perez. "This morning we were fortunate to hear from Minister Natan Sharansky. One point he made was that Palestinian terrorist attacks are indeed an attack on Democracy."

Perez answered, "Ah yes, Natan Sharansky. On that matter he is correct."

The meeting lasted a little bit longer than expected. Most of the group were dropped off at nearby Ben Yehuda Street to seek out lunch. We opted to be driven back to the hotel for a quick lunch, a time for us to debrief and a needed nap. We felt the meeting was a bit tense characterized by a general sense of estrangement from the attendees of our group from some of the positions taken by Peres. We also felt disappointed with the viewpoint that there was "little here, before the Zionist movement." Perhaps he misunderstood the question. Yet, we were impressed with his verbal and non verbal manner, the strength of responsiveness to his English speaking audience and frankness of his answers. He doesn't seem to dodge issues.

Afternoon Meetings

We arrive just missing the introduction. A man stands up and begins to address the group.

3:15 PM: Nachman Shai, Chairman of the Israeli Broadcasting Authority

It is not enough to win an armed struggle. We need to win the hearts of the world. There also should be concern at the cabinet level for voices for Israel. The people with the Palestinian organization seem to know how to present the Palestinian view.

Shai presented his request for a special ministry to integrate the communication of Israeli policy. He pointed out that Palestinians /as a whole tend to be very limited with English. But their spokes people are quite fluent and take advantage of the media.

We plan to not negotiate with Palestinians until the violence stops...It is hard to explain how and why we kill the leader of terrorists. The matter is...if we don't hit them first, they will hit us first.

4:15 PM: Panel:

Yehuda Raveh,

Mr. Raveh is connected with a law firm. He momentarily checks with his panel members, then elects to limit his topic to the impact of the Intifada on tourism.

Israel is a good country to live and invest in...despite the Intifada..

Raveh discusses the Israeli economy. He invites us to come to Israel and make a living here.

....Israel has the sole advantage of being an associate member of the European common market as well as classified as a member of the U.S. preferred group. There are a lot of tax breaks....However, with the U.S. State Department warnings not to travel, there has been an impact on the tourist trade. In the hotel industry, 15,000 people have been laid off and Jerusalem hotel occupancy rate is 28%, a casualty of the Intifada. However, movement of cargo in and out of the country is up, and people are making more money than before.

Marc Michaels, Banker

Mr. Michaels is connected with banking in Israel. He also focuses in the impact of the Intifada on tourism, but stresses some of the problems arising from the media.

The strength of the Shekel against the dollar is maintaining it's value....

He points out the situation throughout Israel is serious, but the overall future is bright.

Daily life is of concern to all, but it is not that bad....Cargo is up, but passenger travel is down, as reported by Lufthansa....Yet purchasing and vacations continue....There are psychological problems as there are no new commitments for long term investments. Bombs go off in other parts of the world; for example Madrid, but it is not publicized.

Avi Rosenthal

Mr. Rosenthal is President of the Hotel Association and has a background in foreign trade and investment.

The high tech industry here is second to California. Tourism in 2000 reached a record 2.7 million. Since October of last year, the beginning of the latest Intifada, 15,000 employees of hotels were laid off. The hotels have 28% occupancy. No one sees the end. Yet the Dead Sea and Eilat are doing OK. Here, are seen tourists from all the three major religions. There are 4,000 hotel rooms at the Dead Sea area with 70 different languages spoken. Dead Sea and Eilat doing OK. But hotel occupancy in Nazareth is down 97%. Yet there is a 15% increase in rental properties. Long term investments in real estate continues to be promising. *Aliyas,* immigration is down from the mid 90s....No one sees the end [of the downward trend.]...All major religions come to visit. Seventy different languages are heard. Good will comes from Israeli visits to the U.S.

There is little time to discuss matters presented. For us, it's back to the room. We have some time to put together what we are learning, collect our notes, read the paper, catch a bit of news on television. After another brief nap and time for a shower, we prepare for dinner downstairs.

8:00 PM Dinner with Ehud Olmert, Mayor of Jerusalem

The mayor enters the room with an entourage of two. He immediately goes around the table introducing himself and warmly greets everyone personally. He speaks well but leaves early as there was tank activity and fire in the southern part of the city. We learn he had been with the Knesset for 25 years. He was first elected in 1993, re-elected in 1998. He aspires towards unity. He meets with Bonds Groups regularly.

There is now shooting in Gilot. The IDF reported killing a top leader of the Popular Front, at the highest level, a head of a sub-group, like a deputy to Arafat. The missile went through a window into his desk and killed him." He further went on to say that "I think this is the best way - avoiding civilians. He was in charge of sending suicide bombers.

He went on to say that Arafat is personally responsible and that Israelis will not talk to him until the violence stops (in Gilot). This year, he is glad to say, there have been no confrontations between the 200,000 Palestinians and Israelis in Jerusalem.

There are professional protesters and rioters throughout Europe....They are sought by other Palestinians to come here....The Arabs want Israeli control in Jerusalem

The mayor stressed the point that the Palestinians in Jerusalem want Israeli control. He also said there is evidence that the terrorists are prompting an Israeli retaliation that will inadvertently kill or wound Christians. He ended up indicating that Israeli-Jewish solidarity is critical to overall world understanding for it is necessary for Israeli to conduct itself in a way that is understood.

The Mayor was asked about how it is that the Arabs in East Jerusalem want Israeli control. He explained that like most people they really want peace and harmony, opportunities for themselves and their children to live in an environment that is secure. According to Olmert, they feel the PA is corrupt, cannot presently offer any of the above features, do not seek out violence, appreciate the Israeli infrastructure and prefer keeping up the existing commerce among Palestinians, Arab Israelis and Jews. This statement by the Mayor was great to hear. As was the case with the Mayor before him, Teddy Kolleck, we are also impressed with his style, knowledge, respect for all the populace and his over-riding optimism. Apparently when someone in the city becomes a victim of violence, which he says has been rare, he visits the family regardless of whether they happen to be Jews, Christians or Moslems.

We are quite impressed with all the speakers. There seems to be a close connection between the national and international problems and everyday life here in Israel. We are quite stimulated by the discussions, the news and the fast pace of the Bonds Tour. As we are still dealing with jet lag, we are not really up to par in giving much time as we would like to discuss the issues as they are brought up. We continue to feel the need to settle down early and catch up on our sleep.

August 28, 2001, Tuesday: Bonds Tour, Day 3

> *Jerusalem Post*: (1) Yesterday the IDF struck the office of Mustafa Zibri, Head of the Marxist Popular Front for Liberation of Palestine through the use of two helicopters that fired missiles through the window killing him. The paper includes Palestinian reprisals resulting in a death of a civilian, age 38. (2) IDF retaliates for 7 slain Israelis, (3) Israel weighing attendance at the Durban parley, and (4) Bush's words buoy Israel, ruffle Arafat.

> *L.A. Times:* (1) West Bank in Turmoil After Assassination, (2) School's Diversity Plan Dealt Setback (affirmative action), (3) NIH Identifies Stem Cells Sets Okd for Funds, (4) Unmanned U.S. Plane Missing in Iraqi Territory

Much of the *Post*, much of morning television and conversation among the people at the hotel are taken up one way or another with the violence throughout the country. A sound of a siren or sight of an emergency vehicle sets off more of a reaction than normally so. The atmosphere has become tense. Israel is a small country. When national news like this occurs it is close to home.

9:00 AM: Breakfast

> Naomi Blumenthal, Deputy Minister of Infrastructure, Likud Leader

Today, peace seems be far away....All in Israel want peace.... Many had initially seen the Oslo agreement as disastrous because even back then it appeared that the peace as discussed would come about being associated with defeat on the part of Israel....Israel is a democracy that is currently sharing the most difficult days; the atmosphere is similar to that before the Six Day War. But terror is a different war. Israel has no place to go and has to believe in its own ability. They will not throw us into the sea as we will not leave this place. There are problems on the northern border, not with the army of Lebanon, but with Hezbollah. There is more unity in Israel now. Peace, she says, is a long way off. The Oslo agreement led to funding and approval of a Palestinian force of 50,000.....Even should Arafat leave, there is no clear idea of what the future brings to their next government.....The people that initiated the Oslo agreement did so behind the back of the Prime Minister.

10:30 AM Visit to Intel Electronics in the northern part of Jerusalem

The bus takes us to the north side of Jerusalem to the Intel plant. More security checks. Following a group presentation by one of the engineers, we toured the plant including the library, offices of the engineers and the "clean room" where 2.0 mHz chips are assembled and checked. We return to the bus. We drive through an IDF defense perimeter, pass a military checkpoint and drive up to the top of a hill to a military base.

12:00 Noon. Military Headquarters, Central Israeli Command

We stop at the largest building, the Central Command Headquarters. We learn we will have an immediate lunch along with troops assigned to the base. Soon, we find ourselves participating in a kibbutz-camp-military style dining room. It even smells kosher! The servings were placed in the middle of the table. A delicious array of foods, including a kind of carrot soup, various salads, a choice of vegetables with entrees of pasta, chicken or lamb. A different arrangement than I experienced in the U.S. army enlisted section! Here, officers and enlisted men and women share the tables and are presented with the same options with the same ambience.

After lunch we were quickly gathered, then ushered into a conference room with fruit, water and coffee on the table before us. Briefing us was Major General Yitzhak Eitan, the Commanding officer of this one of the three commands throughout Israel. I am sitting next to him. The room is full of maps in files and some on the wall. The general is in constant communication by telephone or radio. Messengers come in and drop off notes. He glances briefly at the incoming messages, hesitates, and then with but little affect, sets it down and continues on with the briefing. Sitting next to him as I did, I noticed that he had a script to follow for such an occasion. He glanced at it briefly as he did with the messages, then set it aside. Instead of the routine or back up speech, he addressed current military and political issues as if we were governmental parties familiar with the general situation.   He explains extemporaneously,

> It is an armed conflict organized by the Fatah's leadership with a small amount of terrorists....It has been necessary to block Palestinian roads as there is a problem of shootings on the highways.   There are ambushes close to the roads and a need to protect 1,500 kilometers of highway....The suicide bombers come from inside Israel....The plan is to build zones around each of the communities.   The problems are with the communities that are half Jewish and half Arab....We want to minimize mistakes. For example to kill a small child is also damaging to the cause....We need to act quickly and not have interference of international organizations, for example the UN.   For the first time since the Oslo Agreement the army is in [sensitive] areas....The tragedy is that children are sent into the firing areas....The main terror groups are Hamas, Islamic Jihad and Fatah....There are psychological problems as there are no commitments for long term investments.

As pointed out yesterday by Marc Michaels, General Eitan also mentioned the bombing in Madrid, Spain.   He expressed the sentiment that here in Israel, when something like that happens in another country, though important, it makes little news as compared with such an event in Israel where it is covered in much of the world's newspapers.   The group limits comments and questions as all of us sense he is quite busy, has a lot of responsibility along with his authority and is obviously tired.   We retire from the area and soon we are back on the bus heading for the center of Jerusalem.   We make a stop near the walls of the Old City.

3:00 PM Museum on the Seam

In the center of Jerusalem near the walls of the Old City is located in a two story small building used as a bunkhouse following the War for Independence, on the "Green Line" between Israeli and Jordanian held land that divided Jerusalem from 1948 through 1967.   The museum provides a "peace" program that seems way out of touch with what is happening here today.   Here, movies and multi-media presentations are presented of violent scenes. Israeili soldiers are firing into crowds, protesters crying out in anguish. American GI's appear firing towards civilians in Viet Nam. There are other historical images of violence going back to the Second World War. A young lady meets with us to discuss reactions to such violent scenes. We are asked of our impressions. I explain, "I find it all disgusting and see it going nowhere."

We pass through the center of Jerusalem and told, if we like, we can stop over at a small non-profit organization and have a meeting with Mr. Carmon, who is doing work with translating Arab media into Hebrew and English. We agree.

4:15 PM Meeting with Yigal Carmon, MEMRI (Middle East Media Research Institute)

We sit around a table and again are served cookies and drinks. Mr. Carmon compellingly explains the need for a circulation of Arabic media to Israel and to Western countries. A packet of such publications covering the last year was passed to the group. All were impressed with the consistent and strong anti-western rhetoric, the illogic and distortions of historical facts.

7:00 PM: Dinner with Zvi, Minister of Regional Cooperation

Zvi, Member of Knesset. was an attorney with Mossad. She has been a member of the Knesset since 1997, now, Minister of Regional Cooperation. She has been known for her interest in the status of women. Interestingly enough, she will be replaced tomorrow.

What we are witnessing is a fight for the existence of the Jewish State. When Arafat discusses, "return," he means going back to 1948, not accepting the partition....It is the only position he can take to obtain funds from other countries....It is easy to show and easy to stop. They want to take the conflict to be that between Moslem and Jews....Maybe Arafat needs to justify the debts accumulated....

Time was allotted for group members to express their sentiments, reactions and suggestions. Most of the reaction on the part of the group was how it is that she is being "replaced." We are all impressed with the informality of the Israeli leaders.

August 29, Wednesday, Jerusalem: Bonds Tour, Day 4, David Citadel Hotel

Upon opening up the door to our room we pick up today's *Jerusalem Post*:

> *The Jerusalem Post*: (1) Mortar shell crashes into central Gilo, (2) Terror victim being buried, (3) Zibri was 'marked' after Dolphinarium bombing, (4) Eliminating the middle leadership of the terrorist groups, (5) Peres defends upcoming meeting with Arafat, (6) Settler population up by 17,000 since Intifada began.

> *L.A. Times*: (1) Villagers Trapped as Israelis Vow to Stay 'as Long as it Takes,' (2) Alleged Mastermind in LAX Bomb Plot Indicted: forging a holy war against the U.S. with Bin Laden, (3) Eyes Meet in Death Dive's' last moments.

Following Breakfast, we board an armored bus for Ariel. This bus is used to transport school children in the West Bank. School is scheduled to start next week. Upon reaching the plains to the east, the bus turns north on Highway 4, alongside the Via Mars, which was the ancient North/South Highway that cut through the area. Left of the highway, about a mile away are extensive population centers of modern cities, whereas to the right are the desolate hills with sparse and low growth resembling the driest of chaparral seen in southern California.

11:00 AM: Mazor

We make an impromptu stop at Mazor, a Roman Mausoleum comprising of an intact stone structure and nearby cistern. Stepping outside the air conditioned bus, we realized how protected we were from the hot and humid environment here. As we stepped inside the structure we immediately felt the coolness on this hot humid day. The structure was so designed, we were told, that family could visit and spend the day in the area.

12:00 Noon: Tour of Ariel

Our bullet proof school bus soon turns east towards the West Bank areas. We pass an Israeli-Palestinian checkpoint. In about a mile the bus pulls over to the side. The bus comes to a stop in a rather exposed area. Waiting for us is Ron Nachman, Mayor of Ariel and another man standing beside a small car. The Mayor steps onto the bus. He exchanges a few words with Mike, our guide, then as the bus lunges forward, he turns around, faces us and explains his role in developing the "settlement."

In this way we toured the city of more than 20,000 people. The Mayor points out the commercial industrial areas, some of the local schools along the way, the numerous residential areas, nearby parks and playgrounds. The bus comes to a halt in a parking lot. We disembark and are given a personal tour of the rehabilitative workshop which provides sheltered employment in fabricating electronic equipment and packaging them for shipment. The workers were a mixed population with physical and mental disabilities and senior citizens; but all are busy at work. We are impressed with the goals, the morale of the workers and their productivity.

We are ushered onto the bus and tour more of the area. The mayor addresses us while directing the driver where to go. We drive by more residential sections. We head for the top of a hill where we drive around a liberal arts and technical college. It is quiet as school starts next week. We later stop and visit a pre-school and elementary school. It seems as though each of the elementary schools have some kind of "magnet" aspect, specializing in one or another aspect of society. We stop at one such school. We met with the children attending a workshop on robotics. Each youngster presented his robotic project demonstrating scientific principles using *Lego* play materials, robots that were quite delightful to watch in operation. The children speak with foreign accents revealing their newness to the country. They were born in the former Soviet Union in such places as Turkestan, Uzbekistan and Kazakstan. Though the Mayor has seen these demonstrations of projects by the children many times, he seems to get as much delight of their action as any of us. He takes full advantage of his status to interact quite well with the kids and obviously feels much pride as he thoroughly enjoyed his mayoral position and interaction with the kids.

We visited the city's radio and television station where a recording took place with the Mayor participating in a panel discussion. This was the only time the Mayor seemed to sit quietly as he listened intently to the others on the panel. We also had a demonstration of the city owned radio and television stations.

The city is surrounded by video cameras which assist with security concerns. There are two Arab villages on either side of the community. One aspect of the video system involves security surveillance in a similar way to that of the monitoring of streets and alleys in Old Jerusalem.

We drive by the College of Samaria and Judea which were in between sessions. The college is developing the technology to process micro chips with laser beams. We drive some more around this self contained city of over 20,000 people tightly contained. We stop at a middle school which is powered by solar power. The mayor states that this technology would be able to help California with its power problems.

A senior chorus, about the size of a hundred are waiting for us in one of the large recreation buildings. They sing songs in Russian, English and Hebrew. Mostly comprised of women, there were a few men, including the leader who managed to communicate the essentials in English despite his thick Russian accent.

The center of the community has a green belt spotted with parks and playgrounds. Because this community lies in the "territories" the government will not pay for its development. To finance the parks, e.g. a water reclamation project was developed. The community does not receive more water than the Arab neighbors, but the water is recycled several times resulting in the appearance of much greenery. Also, for the same reason, the UJA will not finance development and the mayor seeks funds from private individuals including the Israeli Bonds and some Christian organizations.

We have lunch at the Eshel Hahomron Hotel in Ariel. Here, we sit next to the mayor. He never tires of answering questions. On the matter of terrorism, he proclaims, "The answer to terrorism is tourism." Our pleasant and delicious luncheon too soon comes to an end. We must leave for Tel Aviv for a visit at the U.S. Embassy. We now drive directly to Tel Aviv.

6:30 PM American Embassy in Tel Aviv.

Daniel C. Kurtzer, U.S. Ambassador to Israel was transferred from his position as Ambassador to Egypt, in Cairo, July 16. He has a B.A. from Yeshiva University and a Ph.D. from Columbia. He started off with the note:

There is no positive improvement in the Middle-East situation.....Israel has still to define as to what is a Jewish State...with equal rights. Faith and nationhood immediately arise with the word, "Jew"....There is no sign of positive improvement in the mid-east situation....Bush is looking for ways to negotiate....All that is necessary is to stop the violence. Israel has approved assassinations and targeted killings.

He speaks out against Israeli incursions into Area A, Palestinian controlled sections.

Israel should avoid economic closures; related effects are hurting the economic integrity....There is a 21 Billion dollar excess of exports....There should be a balance of trade... more imports into Israel from the US....There is co-development of a program where Israel helps the security of the U.S....We look forward to space ventures....Arafat is the elected Chairman and we rely upon him....We don't know if he can do the job....All provisions of the Egypt-Israel treaty has been implemented without incident since 1982....The dialogue has now become tense between Egypt and Israel....One of the greatest threats is coming from the rising Islamic fundamentalism.

He seemed rushed and skipped about topics. Yet, we got a good glimpse of his views. We learn he keeps a kosher kitchen and tries to observe Shabbat. We climb into the bus again and head for Ben Gurion Airport.

8:00 PM Back by shuttle to the David Citadel hotel

Once at the airport, most of the group departs the bus where they will await a flight back to the U.S. We remain on the bus to return to the hotel. The tour is over. Once at the Hotel, we are on our own. We decide to spend this late night here and leave for the old city tomorrow, with enough time to try to come up with a place to stay.

August 30, Thursday, 9:30 AM: The David Citadel Hotel: Update on the News

We have now learned how to observe and experience the news as reported in the news media in Israel. Each day we review what news we can get. We rely heavily upon the English version of *The Jerusalem Post,* generally available throughout Israel. English reports on television include the European version of *CNN,* British *Skynews,* and short morning daily reports in English on radio and television. There are numerous places throughout Israel, including the Old City where there is ready access to the Internet. In this news-hungry country, there are non-translated foreign language reports in German, Spanish and French available that I can understand more readily than Hebrew. Although we catch some of the Israeli (Hebrew) accounts of news, we still miss most of the important subtleties. We listen to what people tell us in English of their experience during these troubled times. We speak with Jews with varying political and religious views as we do with Christians and Moslem Arabs who we meet from day to day.

We discuss the news during a quiet breakfast at the hotel.

> *The Jerusalem Post* (1) Israeli murdered in restaurant near Green Line, (2) IDF pulls out of Beit Jala, (3) Truce paves way for Peres-Arafat talks next week, (4) Palestinians fear that Arafat may be a target, (5) Israeli Arab leaders, peace activists demonstrate outside Orient House., (6) U.S. Poll: The *Post* reports a new survey of 1,000 likely voters.

> *L.A. Times*: (1) Durban: Under pressure, Israelis Pull out: (2) Both sides steadily escalating punishment: Sharon is gaining some international tolerance, (3) U.S. avoids falling into a recession, (4) Chechen blast shows risks facing Russia: A deteriorating situation.

The survey catches our attention as does the current human rights meeting in Durban, South Africa. The paper seems to catch the mood around here in Jerusalem: war and peace both seem to be occurring just around the corner. The survey was commissioned by an Arab-American lobby group of roughly 1,000 likely American voters: A majority of these Americans, while supportive of a Palestinian state, have an unfavorable perception of the Palestinian Authority and PA Chairman, Yasser Arafat. Twenty-nine per cent had a favorable impression of Sharon and 20% unfavorable. Forty-eight percent were unfamiliar with him. Asked about the PA, only 16% were favorable, 63% unfavorable and 16% unfamiliar. Sixty percent were favorable toward Israelis and 39% favorable toward Palestinians

We are not surprised by the results of the opinion survey taken throughout the United States. We note this poll was funded by an Arab-American group. It is as if terrorism is measured by the impact it has on American attitude. We find it interesting that the price we Americans are paying for being "fair," to avoid picking sides, is inspiring the Palestinians to support the terrorism that we now find close to us. We find the accusations and protests from Durban in regards to Israel preposterous in light of what we observe in Israel and the lack of human rights as exist among those nations behind the accusations.

Israel society is highly sensitive to news coverage. They are self conscious. There seems little doubt that the Israelis, Palestinians and terror groups associated with their cause are closely tuned in to world opinion. The expression of fear among Palestinians that Arafat may be a target directly follows the result of the Arab-American sponsored poll. The local papers and television focus on this kind of stuff daily. But it is the slant of the news and the way it is reported that gets the attention here in Israel. We learned from speakers familiar with media styles on our Israeli Bond Tour that there is a concerted effort to develop an organization to develop a single voice representing the Israeli government and to de-program the impact of the Arab propagandists.

Much is on our minds as we have breakfast and prepare to leave for the Old City. It is apparent to us that much of purpose of the terrorist action here in Israel is to impact attitude, not only here among Israelis, but also throughout the world. Interestingly, much information is based on myths or falsehoods, some of which we had earlier reported. We had learned from our meeting with Nachman Shai, Chairman of the Israeli Broadcasting Authority and our visit with Yigal Carmon, of MEMRI that much of the media in Arabic is not translated into English. Much is full of distortions and continuation of myths that incite readers to violence as a solution.

At the moment, Israel does not have a single voice in the world media. The freedom of press in Israel is quite similar to that we experience states-side. Although efforts are now being made in Israel to translate foreign media into Hebrew and English, there is no way yet to integrate the information in terms of counter-propaganda and communicate it to the world. For several months now, MEMRI has a web site that provides translations of Arabic news releases, www.memri.com.

11:00 AM: A Visit to the Jewish Quarter of the Old City

We hop in a taxi in front of the hotel. We ask to be taken to the Old City. It turns out the driver knows our friends who live in the Old City. He takes us directly to the Jewish quarter, as close as he can get to their home. We stroll down a narrow main street and allow our senses to experience the sounds of Hebrew, the smells of pizza and bread baking. We observe the bustling activity. We are looking for the hotel that friends had recommended. We inquire in a police station, but the uniformed office doesn't know of the any hotel at all in the Old City. We go into a gift shop and purchase some postcards. We inquire where we may find a hotel. She points out the location of the Hotel Kotel. She directs us to continue on the same street, turn at the palm tree, and go through an alley to a square where Mama's Deli is located.

We look in the direction of Mama's Delicatessen. Cooking, serving food, and running the cast register is a lady who resembles the face in an advertisement hanging above the entrance of a small sidewalk café. She speaks in a good English (We later discover that she is able to speak seven languages). We explain we are looking for a hotel room. We soon realize Mama runs a hotel. We are led by a young Arab boy who speaks no English, only Hebrew and Arabic with gestures enabling communication. We follow him down a couple of narrow streets and he leads us through an unmarked entryway, opens a door with one of the keys, and we go down a few steps to our new home for a few days.

The suite had been prepared for the observance of the Sabbath. There are candles, grape juice, dishes, and cutlery ready for our use. We are told, when the owners replaced the flooring to this suite, artifacts were found relating to *Cohanim*, priests responsible for operating the Temple. We take note we are indeed within a couple hundred yards of the Western Wall area. Could this structure have served as residences for *Cohanim* that served the *be'it hamikdash*, the central Jerusalem temple. This area, where we will eat and sleep for a couple of days, was re-constructed during the Crusader period. Here we see a Roman type arch between the bedroom and dining area.

We find the street where our friends live and head for their house. Chaya is up on the roof which can be seen from the street. There are grape vines growing on the roof. This a Jubilee year when no new planting is done, so this harvest is special. Some of the harvested grapes are being made into wine. A contractor happens to be there as our friends are remodeling the roof area to accommodate dining.

Driving in Jerusalem is a unique experience. Chaya drives her car out of the parking which serves the Jewish quarter of the Old City. She adroitly negotiates the turn through the Zion Gate, which obviously had been constructed long before introduction of cars. Most of the streets are narrow and crowded; and all the time she is talking on her cell phone! They drop me off at the David Citadel Hotel. Hannah assists her in looking up numbers in an electronic Rolodex; the whole purpose of all of this phoning is to arrange that all Americans are accommodated for Friday night dinner and Saturday lunch at someone's home. They go to a flour store where organic wheat is hand ground. This store is around the corner of the pizza shop which was destroyed by a suicide bomber. This shop is covered by plywood which has murals with patriotic themes. They go to a butcher shop; when Hannah offers American money, he refuses with the statement, "My boss wouldn't like it." He also refuses her credit card and gives her the herring free. They also go to a natural food store.

Throughout the day we hear the shofar sounding; the shofar is a ram's horn which had been used in ancient Israel as a summons and in modern times still is used for certain religious ceremonies. However, we couldn't think of any reason that it should be sounded at this time. Our friends offer that people are crying out for the messiah to come because of the crisis that Israel is in now. The hotel, the Old City and the stores Chaya visited are all within blocks. Before being dropped off at the hotel, we learn that while Chaya is on the phone she had arranged for us to have Friday evening supper with a Jewish family residing in the Old City.

Back at the hotel, now knowing that lodging in the Old City is secured, Hannah and I have a leisurely dinner out in the hotel's open patio overlooking the pool while discussing the events of the day.

August 31, Friday, 9:00 AM: David Citadel Hotel

Over breakfast we try to make some sense out of the news. We again realize, without the perspective of the past, it is difficult to understand the present. Here, in Israel, time takes on a different dimension than what we are used to back in California. Much of our taught history began in 1492. Records in California are rare before the 1800s and didn't take much form until after the Spanish and Mexican influence of the mid 1800s. In Israel, extensive records of life goes back thousands of years. What happened among cultures centuries ago is felt today. What happened a decade ago affects the current mood as does politics of the last week.

> *Jerusalem Post*: (1) Truce paves way for Peres - Arafat talks next week, (2) Modi'in man slain in Palestinian restaurant, (3) Israel sends low-level envoys to Durban, (4) Terror suspect nabbed in north Jerusalem, (5) High alert in North for Hizbullah attack, (6) Most schools open as scheduled; Arab schools stay closed in three-day protest

> *L.A. Times* (1) Suspect in six killings caught in mother's yard, (2) Army shifts to Asia: Troops may follow, (3) Israeli pays with his life for a faith in coexistence, (4) Racism protesters (Durban) stand disunited, (5) Judge backs Florida ban on adoptions by homosexuals

We have some time to reflect on what we had been learning. We had met with the Minister of Foreign Affairs, Shimon Peres just days ago. We learn that the meeting with Peres and Arafat could take place, perhaps while we are in Jerusalem. We concur that even if this unlikely event were to take place, it probably will not make much of a dent towards a peaceful resolve of issues. We are impressed how difficult it is for Israel to make peace with constituencies that do not respect their existence. We recall how different the situation was with Egypt, the first Arab League state to recognize the existence of Israel. Sadat wanted a real peace in 1982 and came with outstretched hands recognizing the state. These negotiations came back alive to us last year as we stayed in the same hotel suite last year where he and his entourage resided while the treaty was negotiated in 1982. We think a small proportion of people in the U.S., but quite vocal, take positions in regards to the middle-east, as it they did with regards to discussions in Durban: to take care to offer a measure of fairness to both sides. Show impartiality! In only this way can we be fair! This axiom seems to hold true regardless of who is "right" and who is "wrong." The matter at the Durban Conference is continuing to frustrate Israelis.

We see that schools are being opened for registration here in Jerusalem. In fact it is quite hectic. Small kids being escorted to school, perhaps to sign up for the year. We share our thoughts on matters of gay marriages – how ridiculous.

We wonder why not just co-habitate and make up an agreement. But not a marriage contract; it's hard enough to maintain a workable marriage! The article in the *Times* about the "killing" refers to an Israeli that ironically had spent much of his time with fellow Arabs in hope of keeping cross cultural ties alive. We later discover that the incident of the Israeli slain in the restaurant was covered in the *Los Angeles Times,* but not as a headline article.

After a leisurely breakfast discussing this news we pack our gear, checkout, and prepare to return to the old city. We hope to travel north to the Galilee and Golan, we take note that there is an alert in the northern part of Israel for attacks from over the border.

Chapter 7

Contemporary Life in The Old Jewish Quarter of Jerusalem

August 31, Friday, Noon: Jewish Quarter, Old City, Jerusalem

A taxi takes us to the Jewish Quarter where we laboriously carry and roll our luggage to Mama's Deli. We purchase a newspaper from the corner grocery store and retire in our room. The suite remains prepared for the observance of the Sabbath. There are candles, wine, etc. ready for our use. We still try to grasp how it might have been living here during the time of the Second Temple and during the Crusade period.

Excited just being here, we are anxious to speed up the period of getting acquainted with the layout of the quarters. Much is to be done to prepare for the coming of Shabbat. There is an immediacy to it all. Regardless of whether one participates or not, there is no stopping it. It will start in a few hours with or without us. The small streets are crowded and it is hard to navigate the area. Others are having this same trouble. People are picking up their pace attempting to get that last bit of purchase before the stores close. The stores are beginning to close. Some stay open til the last moment before dusk. Most of the stores have variable closing hours, adjusting to their personal needs as well.

We discover how self-contained the quarter is for residents in the area. We could get along here for weeks meeting our basic needs through the local grocery stores, Laundromat, computer and Internet establishments, libraries, book stores, gift shops, bakeries, fast food eateries, sit-down and take-out restaurants, news stands and active religious sites. All this exists along with museums, ruins of old synagogue, archeological sites, ongoing digs and religious and historical attractions. All of this, including The Western Wall, is all within ten minutes walking distance from our apartment.

Friday night services are at the Western Wall. Families are walking together. Yeshiva students are following their rabbis, some marching in cadence and singing along. The Chassidic groups are seen singing and dancing to joyful strains. Security is present requiring all to pass through metal detectors, and people not appearing to be there for the purpose of religious observation are being stopped and questioned. But all hurriedly pass through.

For most, Friday night services are at *ha'kotel,* the Western Wall of the Temple. After lighting the Sabbath candles, there is no longer any vehicle traffic. Everyone is more dressed up, some in festive dress. Families are walking together; *yeshiva buch'ers,* religious school students, some in characteristic attire, are following their rabbis. *Chassids,* religiously inclined men with characteristic dress and beards are singing and dancing joyfully to musical strains in minor keys. Security people make their presence felt throughout all of the Jewish quarter.

As men and women approach the large plaza before *ha'kotel,* they go to separate sections. On the men's side small groups of religious services, *min'yons,* groups of at least ten men, are formed. There are probably a couple dozen *min'yons* going on at the same time each at their own pace, lasting about twenty minutes. The larger ones tend to conclude with song and dance, joining hands forming a circle or line meandering near the wall. Meanwhile, the women *dov'n,* read prayers individually; for it is said somewhere that it takes the spirituality of ten men to equal that of one woman. Small children dart in and about the worshipers in both sections, and some of the women step back into the plaza to chat with each other.

We are invited for an evening meal and respite with a family who has an apartment with a balcony overlooking the Western Wall. He is from the United States and she is from Great Britain; he is a retired businessman. They are writers, she is a botanist whose column on plants appears in the *Jerusalem Post* which we will read later. Two other guests, students from Hungary, are studying for the summer at a local university. They claim they are here to discover their roots as they know little of their *yiddishkeit,* Jewishness. They seem to be reaching out to be in touch with their heritage. It is indeed a magical moment dining in the moonlight within the sights and sounds of *Yiddishkeit* manifesting itself so brilliantly among the three monotheistic religions. We pleasantly dine overlooking the lights playing on *ha'kotel,* now only two hundred yards away. We leisurely go through the several courses: an array of salads, chicken soup, roast chicken and vegetables. Dessert is a homemade ice with fruit. We engage in some short blessings and then review, with help from Eshkial, some aspects of the weekly Torah portion.

We note the crowd before the wall has lessened but continues to have a large number of people congregating throughout the area. We take note that the men tend to congregate together, now in larger groups whereas most women tend to be by themselves. After sharing niceties, we find we are not quite recovered from our recent jet lag, and too soon take leave for our own quarters for a well deserved sleep.

September 1, 2001, Saturday: Old City, Jerusalem

We sleep late; but there is a tranquility in the air. There is only foot traffic; almost all movement consists of going or returning from *ha'kotel* where religious activity dominates the day. The *Jerusalem Post* is not published on Shabbot. We have no access to news today. The leading stories in *The L.A. Times*, in order of their place of importance, reconstructed for this day is as follows.

> L.A. Times:(1) Deputy slain as gunman sparks siege, (2) Blaze kills 44 in Tokyo adult district, (2) Obstacles abound for racism forum, (3) Palestinians believe that Israeli settlers killed their livestock, (4) Arafat not a target, Israeli official vows, (5) Afghanistan closes aid groups offices, (6) U.S. jets hit radar site in south Iraq.

We attend lunch with our friends and some very interesting people. We engage in some questions of war and peace and a religious-ethnic way of looking at the matter from the perspective of being in Jerusalem. There are a dozen people at the table; we are all Americans. It is a leisurely meal with a fish course, meat course, and desserts. There is discussion of the Torah portion for that week; All are concerned with the current unrest. Everyone had known someone who had been a victim of a terrorist attack. One woman described her friend's eleven year old daughter who had gone out for a pizza with a friend and her family who was struck with so many pieces of metal in her body that the doctors were unable to remove but some of them. She still had to stay in the hospital, but her family had taken her home for this Sabbath in hopes that being with family and friends would cheer her up. There was smoldering anger. One woman described a conversation she had with an Arab workman who had been employed for a number of years by their family. When she asked him if he would ever do anything to harm anyone in her family, he did not vocalize an answer but his eyes indicated to not go there. Almost everyone there had children. They were upset in the way the Palestinians were using children as instruments to be placed in the direct line of firing.

Being here, in the midst of the unrest, puts matters in a special perspective. Each person has something to offer on this matter. Yet we concur we find things safe here in the Jewish Quarter of the Old City. The area is highly guarded. We find little interest on the part of others in our project of visiting the sites associated with continuous residence of Jews in the land of Israel. Quite likely they already accept the notion of a continuous Jewish residence in *Eretz Yisrael*, are trying to blot out the preoccupation with the continued violence which our topic seems related, or are disinterested in this topic time because today is Shabbot.

We feel resigned that if something were to happen to us here in the Old City, it would follow from our choice to be here. We tell each other how unlikely it is, even in these times, that someone would strike out with a violent act at a place that is the center of three major religions. We have also come to note the entire Old City seems heavily guarded with police and automated video surveillance. If someone were to cause trouble, they would likely be identified. In any event, we rationalize by saying that a hostile strike here would backfire.

We come to view the violence occurring on all sides about us in a historical, philosophical and religious way. It seems too close, yet so very distant. We remind ourselves of the brief conversation with a visiting landscaper from nearby Gilo that describes the sounds of firing in his neighborhood. We recall the description of the injuries inflicted on a young girl following a suicide bombing attack just a few hundred yards from the Old City. We continue to hear firing. There is a prevalent feeling here of more troubles to come, and soon.

September 1, Saturday Night: The Jewish Quarter of the Old City, Jerusalem

In the evening we explore the Jewish quarter on foot. We find a section of a very old looking wall. The wall is associated with the time of the First Temple. We then walk on a restored ancient boulevard, the Cardo, built by the Romans several hundred years later at the time of Second Temple. We note that after all these years, this old city remains a place of active life with children riding bikes, people shopping, eating, and groups of students walking and socializing.

Almost every building in the old city is of historic significance; there are plaques describing the historic events from the fighting during the Six Day War to a building's use during the time of the Crusaders and of times much earlier.

Also marked are buildings used as a hospice for travelers over the intervening years. Even some of the remodeled and newer buildings have plaques on them.

September 2, Sunday Morning: The Old City

The morning is spent resting, putting together our thoughts, participating in life in the Jewish Quarter and taking note of what we see. Sunday is the first day of the work week here in Israel. The Old City is no exception. Kids, teenagers and adults are streaming by with backpacks and new clothes to classes on this first day of school after the summer.

The *Jerusalem Post* is not currently published over *Shabbot*. The Post is circulated on Sunday, but they have been sold out. There is no Sunday paper for us to read or discuss. Below are leading stories from *The Los Angeles Times* in order of their place of importance.

> *L.A. Times*, Sunday, September 2, 2001 (1) Congress girds for battle of priorities, (2) Mexico curbs migrant flow, (3) U.S. seeks to placate China on missiles, (4) On fringes of racism forum:, some believe in miracles, (5) Gaza car blast kills top aide to Palestinian security official: Israel denies involvement,(6) Three Arabs die in West Bank violence.

Hannah joins Chaya to attend classes at a women's *yeshiva*. The classes are conducted in English, but part of the work involved the translation of the original Hebrew. The instructors are all women.

September 2, Monday: 8:00 AM: Life in the Jewish Quarter

Before we set out to complete our notes, we peruse the morning's *Jerusalem Post* over breakfast in our apartment as if we are home.

> *Jerusalem Post*:(1) Annan: 'Zionism is racism' - a dead issue, (2) Palestinian group claims Khatab killing, (3) High Alert in Jerusalem, North, (4) Efforts to set Peres - Arafat meeting in high gear, (5) Pending attacks or preventive hysteria?

L A Times: (1) Bush and Fox are Intent on New Era, (2) Zionism Issue Roils Racism Talks, (3) It's Back-to-School for Israeli Children on Gilo's Front Line, (4) Hopes Slim as Sharon Plans Talks with Putin, (5) Is Jet Lag All in the Mind?

We agree with Annan, perhaps not for the same reason. We also note there always seems to some clandestine group that seems eager to claim responsibility for an attack on Israelis. Quite likely they are competing with one another for the rewards that they perceive might come once the Palestinian territories become a state. At the same time, we suspect, they are making a claim for a higher interpersonal status for themselves. Though the northern part of the city is a couple miles to the north of here, we hear more sounds of firing in that direction as well. The sounds of firing and distant explosions are now becoming more routine, and thus we find ourselves somewhat desensitized to a fair proportion of its sounds and news accounts.

With such a national concern and preoccupation with terrorist acts, we wonder how Israelis can go along now in the direction towards peace? If anything, the sentiment seems to be the contrary, to strike back. There is indeed a strong sense to have peace. But this time around the sentiment expressed is "peace" must be followed with security.

The area around Jerusalem seems heavily guarded by Israeli troops and police. The country seems geared for a long struggle and more military moves. We are aware that many civilians are in the reserves and know what it means for a "call-up." Our impression is that much of the citizenry are simply "fed up" with the inaction of their government to strike back effectively. At the same time, Israelis feel they are carrying on the burden for the West and take note that western powers do not seem to recognize that Israel is where their front line exists between Arab holdover, Islamic growth and that of Western economy and culture.

Being in the Old City of Jerusalem creates a heightened state of awareness of the worldly interest in the Middle-East. It is here, where we stand today, that is the focus of the world. It is in Jerusalem where much of the beauty and flaws of world culture can be seen, where both distant and recent history make its impact on everyday life.

Before Hannah and I start out to take notes on historical sites, I attend a couple of classes at a local yeshiva geared towards English speaking students, with Ron. The method of instruction is classic. In a rather large room with other small groups of two to four students, we are a group of four with a rabbi guiding us through classic literature. First comes a reading of Talmud in the original Hebrew. Then comes a translation of the sentence, word by word. Then comes interpretation from the group and an agreement as to what meaning is derived. Then comes a reading of the secondary literature by Rashi prepared by the rabbi and another passage from even more secondary literature. The example covered today was relating to when a kernel of wheat can be considered edible, and under what conditions can be considered *Kashrut*, and then what conditions enable it to be suitable for Passover.

September 2, Monday Afternoon: The Old City

We are adapting a Mid-Eastern schedule. Napping in the afternoon. In the late afternoon we become further acquainted with the Jewish quarter, taking notes pertaining to Jewish presence in Jerusalem enjoying sauntering through the narrow streets.

While Hannah catches up on her reading, I manage to spend a couple hours at the laundry store getting our clothes done. The same small store also has an Internet section, one of two or three Internet centers in the Jewish Quarter. They are busy. The stereo is playing contemporary rock, some from the U.S.A. Mostly young adult students are seen sitting before the ten computers. Some are playing games. Others writing notes as if for class or journals. Here, e-mail is sent and received. Local and international news can be had, including *Ha'Erez*, the *Jerusalem Post, CNN, USA Today*, the *L.A. Times* and *New York Times*. The computers all seem fairly fast. The cost is nominal for use. Printing a page costs equivalent to ten cents. I note the international news is similar, both in content and in the form in which it appears, from one paper and media to the next. There seem to be no translations of Arabic papers available. The weather forecast for Israel is for clear, pleasant weather, a good omen for the week to follow.

September 2, Monday: 6:00 PM: An Evening in the Jewish Quarter:

In the evening we meet with the hotel's owner who everyone calls 'Abba.' His family had lived in Jerusalem for many generations. He speaks of the time when the Turks controlled Palestine. There were no quarters then; Jews and Moslems lived side by side. The Islamic religious structures, he says, had to be the highest; so when Jewish congregations needed to expand, they dug deeper into the ground. During the War of Independence when the Jordanians invaded the Old City, there were seventy synagogues. There was a deliberate governmental policy to destroy and desecrate Jewish holy places. Abba tells of sixty-nine synagogues that were destroyed. One remained. Its name, *Tifferet Cohanim*, The Priest's Crown. This synagogue was saved because the Arab caretaker would not let the soldiers onto the property to destroy it. Though leery because of the recent violence, we want to see it.

6:30 PM: A Visit to the Moslem Section

An employee of the hotel was recommended by Abba to be our guide. The young man was born in Israel and is Moslem; he speaks Hebrew and Arabic fluently. He attempts to gain our confidence by showing us the video cameras and the security people patrolling the streets with cell phones. But we remain nervous; the atmosphere in the Moslem Quarter feels completely different than the familiar Jewish section. It is past sundown. The appearance and ambience of the old city is changing. Whereas the streets of the Jewish Quarter are often wide and open to the late afternoon sky, the streets and passageways in this section of the Moslem Quarter are more narrow and tighter. The illumination becomes dependent on electric lights. Clusters of young men not apparently engaged in any enterprise are in the streets; and children run about without the appearance of being supervised by any adults. There are complaints that this quarter lacks city services. The Moslem Quarter is indeed littered with trash. In the Jewish Quarter we noted the local merchants hosing down the stone in front of their businesses each morning. In this atmosphere we feel on edge. I take out my camera to take a picture of a building having a Star of David in front. A young boy comes out of nowhere, grabs the camera out of my hand saying, "I take good pictures." He motions for us to stand together while he takes our picture.

7:00 PM: *Tifferot Cohanim*, the only synagogue in the Old City not destroyed by the Jordanian army

Our guide leads Hannah and I to an unmarked alley way leading perpendicularly from the narrow street. We turn right onto it and find a stairway leading upstairs. The guide asks Hannah to wait there. The guide and

I walk up a short flight of steps to a platform. All is dimly lit and getting darker as night approaches. When we begin to step up to a second landing, we are confronted by an armed guard on the roof above peering at us through barbed wire which circles the perimeter of the top of the building. Our guide gets into a shouting match in Hebrew with the armed guards. While I do not understand exactly what is being said, it is apparent that they will not easily give us permission to enter. Not wanting to stay in such a situation for long, especially as Hannah was downstairs, I head down the darkened stairwell to return. Besides I don't like the idea of guns pointed in my direction. Once downstairs, away from the weaponry, I noticed the area was grimy and the paint was peeling, a sign of trouble maintaining the building or a passive effort to be made to assure the venerated structure fits in with the grubby environment, thus drawing little attention to itself.

One of the yeshiva's students comes down the stairs and explains that I would be welcome to study with them, but Hannah would not be admitted as it is a men's school as well as place of worship. I return upstairs with the guide as Hannah waits below. A small crowd of men now gather at the tiny store across the way. The men seem agitated and our guide shouts back to them in Arabic. Hannah turns her back to them. She does not understand a word they are saying; but the language of men leering is a universal one. The guide goes across to the store and brings back a kitchen stool. He explains that the men wish that she sit down. She requests that he thank the men for their thoughtfulness.

While Hannah is waiting downstairs, I was escorted beyond the first landing up a short flight of stairs to a third landing which has a small unmarked door to the left with a *Mezzuzah* on the door post and a guard's nest ahead. I am asked by the guard beyond the barbed wire to pass through the door. Here, I have an opportunity to observe what is inside.

The interior is quite identical to the Centennial Street Shul I attended just off Temple Street in Los Angeles during the 1930's and 1940s. The shul had the same characteristic dark wood with carved art work, a central and eastern raised platforms for reciting and chanting. The tapestries, seats, their arrangement and method of book and carpeting seem altogether similar. What is different is that there are group of about twenty or so men studying together in small groups of two, three and four. A few take notice of me, most don't.

While I am still upstairs, the men across the way disperse. The guide climbs up on a nearby ledge of the building. Our guide appears agitated by the tension in the atmosphere and states, "It is not good for women here." He explains his frustrations to Hannah. He wishes that the whole Middle East conflict would be over. He was born in Israel and claims that he doesn't want to live any other place. He is going to school and working. He is unsure of his future. He would like to travel, but he is not able to go into any of the Arab states.

7:30 PM: A stroll through the Christian Quarter

We choose to walk back through the Christian Quarter of the Old City of Jerusalem. We walk up Via Delorosa on the way to the Church of the Holy Sepulcher, splendidly lit up and brightly open in the still night illuminating the immediate area revealing the cleanliness of the Christian Quarter. All businesses in the Christian section at this hour are closed. The only people we see are security patrols and guards. It is now dark, lonely and eerie as stroll towards the Jewish section.

It is a relief to be back to the well lit Jewish Quarter. Groups of people are congregating, eating and talking. Some people have musical instruments and are singing. We explore a little on our own, walking about the several levels; and just enjoying the ambiance of the place.

We remain apprehensive about venturing further into the Moslem portion of the Old City. To be sure, we are also reluctant to visit some parts of Jerusalem and its environs. Certainly, there are areas within Israel, particularly in the West Banks of the Jordan River, Samaria and Judea where the danger is even greater for travelers. We conclude there are plenty of significant sites which are likely to reveal the continuity of Jewish life in areas that are safe. In any event, there are more than enough sites to fill our allotted time this year for the project.

Chapter 8
History of Jewish Presence in Jerusalem

Overview

The location of historical sites in the Old City can be visited in very short time if one were content to briefly walk by. Doing so is hardly a difficult task as the entire perimeter is typically no more than a half mile wide by and a little more long. From distant corner to corner, the longest of any straight line through the Old City would be less than a mile, actually 7/8 of a mile. The perimeter is contained by the Turkish wall built in the 1500s, the entirety of the city of Jerusalem since the 1500s. During most of this time, if one lived immediately outside the walls, they were not living in Jerusalem, but nearby, as was the case of some Jews that for no other reason than that they were Jewish, were not permitted to live inside the wall.

Except for a short corridor to the Western Wall, from the center of the Jewish Quarter, all points within the quarter are within 200 yards. A direct line from the center of the Jewish Quarter to the Western Wall is about 700 feet. The streets of the Old City are generally north and south and east and west. To get anywhere in the Jewish Quarter from any other place in the quarter required us to do an easy stroll of about five or ten minutes, including the stairs. In many cases, the sites outlined below can be reached next door from one another, across the street, or around the corner.

The sites and locations are listed in chronological order, are captioned by the historical period of the power of occupation with the general time frame given.

THE FIRST TEMPLE PERIOD: ca 1000 B.C.E. - 587 B.C.E. (423 YEARS)

Hezikiah's Tunnel

The Gehon Spring, below the summit, is the main reason offered as to why the Jebusites settled on the low Ophel Ridge rather than to have chosen the adjacent higher ground. There is believed to be enough water from this source today to support, at that time, a population of about 2,500 people. The tunnel was constructed in about 700 BC by King Hezekiah to bring the water of the

Gihon into the city and store it in the pool of Shiloah, or Siloam. Its purpose was to prevent invaders, particularly the Assyrians, from locating the city's water supply and cutting it off.

City of David

Here is the oldest part of Jerusalem, the site of the city developed by King David. The excavations are the result of work, still ongoing, that started in 1850 and dating beyond. The only part of it we were able to see was an excavated wall lying within the more southerly part of the quarter, near the external wall of Jerusalem at the time of the First Temple.

Near the later built Roman Cardo

Within the Jewish Quarter, on the eastern side of the current "Cardo" walkway, about a hundred yards lies a recent digging about 75 feet down, an area of about 50' x 50'. There is lighting from above behind a grated fence and gate permitting an unimpeded view of the depths below. Beyond the gate lies a temporary stairway/ladder that leads down in a spiral manner. We saw no sign indicating restrictions. Opening the latch releases the gate door. We now descend step by step and venture down to the lowest level. At the partially illuminated bottom we step on or near the ancient road that led to, and perhaps was part of the First Temple, built by King Soloman, 3,000 years ago. We are standing now about 300 feet or so in a direct horizontal line to the outer perimeter of the Temple Mount.

The Siebenberg House

With limited hours for visiting, we pass by the Siebenberg House. When the Siebenbergs began renovating their home in the Jewish Quarter after reunification they found artifacts laying about which were found to date back 3,000 years. Water cisterns, mikvehs, royal burial chambers, and mosaic tiles were among the artifacts.

Near the Current Chabad Shul & Yeshiva

In the northwest part of today's Jewish quarter, along the busiest west-east streets, Chabad Street, just west of the Chabad House and Cardo, lies another recently dug archeological site, imposing, but not well marked at all. Down an elevation of about 35 feet, with no entry way, lies a structure, the remains of a building. Quite likely it was some kind of structure adjacent to the entry to the First Temple.

GRECIAN AND ROMAN INFLUENCE, 536 B.C.E. - 324 C.E. (860 YEARS): THE SECOND TEMPLE PERIOD, 445 B.C.E. - 70 C.E. (505 YEARS)

The Second Temple was built after the fall of Babylon, in 536 by Cyrus, King of Persia, who became overlord of Judah. He issued his declaration, which allowed those desiring to return to *Eretz Yisrael* to do so and to rebuild the Temple on its historic site. This construction was done gradually as the surrounding nations were hostile to this activity. It was completed in 515 BCE to remain almost empty. According to Cohen (1984) the city was attacked once again, its wall breached and gates burnt. In 445 BCE an appointed governor of Judah was given the responsibility to oversee the rebuilding of the city. It was Ezra the Scribe who was responsible for the restoration of the authority of the Mosaic Law and for making Jerusalem the undisputed religious center of Judaism. At the time of destruction of the Temple itself, the area was already a world center. According to Keter (1973) its area had increased to one square mile and its population was estimated at 120,000. Such a figure indicates a high density of people. The figure seems highly inflated as were the figures reported by Josephus in his treatise, *The Jewish Wars,* written in Rome not long after its destruction. According to Israelowitz, the city remained in ruin for 61 years. According to Haral (1974) Jews lived on in Jerusalem and worshiped amid the wreckage of the Temple. Anti-Jewish decrees were not enforced. Synagogues were established in the 200s on Mount Zion in Jerusalem itself as well as throughout Galilee.

Kobler (1952) reports a letter recovered from the *Genizah* in Cairo revealing a communique from Philadelphus, King of Egypt in Alexandria, to Eleazar, the High Priest in Jerusalem dated sometime in the first half of the 3rd Century B.C.E. The content provides an idea of numbers of Jews involved in the movement south into Egypt and what was their fate. The king reports giving liberty to more than 100,000 captives, paying their owners at the proper market price and making good wrongs suffered through the passions of the mob. Many were drafted into the army; some attached as offices of state. Another letter in this period pertains to the Egyptian requests of translators to assist in translating the Hebrew scriptures into Greek so as to meet the needs of the large Greek-speaking Jewish colony in Egypt. A group of scholars were dispatched to Egypt for such a task.

Much of the material describing the Bar Kochba Revolt, 132-135 C.E., comes from Roman sources. Dio Cassius wrote of the destruction of 50 fortresses and 985 villages, and the killing of 580,000 men. We think these figures are also highly exaggerated. Though Judea was ruled by Pagan Rome, the first generation of this Roman rule (138 - 235) saw the cancellation of the anti-Jewish decrees, but nevertheless with continued populations moving away from Jerusalem.

Perhaps not as traumatic as it has been believed, the view now is that anti-Jewish decrees at the time of the destruction of the second Temple were not enforced. Synagogues were established in the third century on Mount Zion, in Jerusalem itself.

The Burnt House

Next to the Quarter Café, southeast of the Hurva Plaza is the reconstruction of a luxurious house in what was the Upper City of the Second Temple era. It is believed the house was destroyed along with the Second Temple. One can see the burnt condition.

The Roman Cardo

The most readily seen, and perhaps the most spectacular site revealing the immensity and significance of the role of Jerusalem in this period is the uncovering of the Roman *Cardo Maximus*, a commercial section of Jerusalem built by the Romans. Dominating the site is a 72' foot wide boulevard consisting of a flattened stone promenade, a roadway of 36' and a colonnade of 18' on each side. Remains of porticos and shops can be seen along the way. Excavations, meticulously done reveal a small but substantial part of the boulevard that had extended from the Damascus Gate to the Zion Gate, a distance of about a mile and a half

The Davidson Center

This new excavation and exhibit lies on the south and western corner of the grounds of the Temple Mount. Descending a spiral staircase takes us back in time where we find ourselves at the same elevation of a street inside the Second Temple. Too quickly we passed through artful exhibits depicting the life and times during the period of the Second Temple. We walked on the same stones that had formed a road off the temple grounds and touched the stone structures that lined that road. Here are displays of the artifacts of the period and a description of the life and times of the people who resided in the area during the Second Temple period.

BYZANTINE PERIOD, 324 - 637 (313 YEARS)

During the build-up of rising Christianity, and for a time, Jerusalem was the only city in the land with a Christian majority. Helena, mother of Emperor Constantin, visited Jerusalem in 326. Some Roman structures were reported to have been destroyed. Constantin erected the Church of The Holy Sepulcher on the spot where the Temple of Venus lay (Keter, 1973). Quite likely the city had a Christian character. A prohibition against the entry of Jews was renewed, with the exception of the 9th of Av, when they were allowed to lament on the Temple Mount. Yet there is evidence that Jews continued to reside in the city albeit, as a minority. In 333 The Traveler of Bordeaux wrote of the stones on the Temple Mount where Jews went to Pray. According to Keter (1973) the Emperor Julian reverted to the ancient Greek religion and favored Judaism. Subsequently he ordered the reconstruction of the Temple. A sanctuary was indeed built on the Temple Mount in 362, in the attempt.

Jewish life continued in Jerusalem through this transition period. The Cairo Genizah hosts a letter, dated 438 from somewhere in the Galilee inviting Jews to celebrate the Feast of Tabernacles in response to news from Rome indicating the re-establishment of the Jewish Kingdom. But development was halted due to a fire in 443. The emperor had just started on his Persian campaign. The work then stopped. Nevertheless, heartened by the goodwill of the empress Eudocia, Jewry begin to redream the Day of Redemption. Jews were being permitted to dwell peacefully in Jerusalem.

The governments and church during this period were amazed at their failure to Christianize the land. Despite their efforts, there were comparatively few Christians throughout Palestine, even by Christian sources. Jew and Samaritans remained in majority. According to Ben-Gurion (1974) there was a respite during the 400s related to a change in the polemics of the Church which led to a number of new synagogues built in Jerusalem and restoration of others. St. Cyril of Scythopolyis records that St. Sabbas journeyed to Constantinople in 512 to persuade the emperor to exempt the poor of Jerusalem from taxation (Haral, 1974).

In 614 Persians handed the city over to the Jews, who ruled it for a while. Later, in 629 by order of Modestus, the Persians handed the city back to the Christian powers interested in the area. Jews were then banished for a while (Keter, 1973).

PERSIAN PERIOD, 614-629 (15 YEARS)

Upon the Persian conquest of *Eretz Yisrael*, a pact was concluded between the Persians and its Jews, one mutually desirable: the Jews would have a Jewish administration and worship without prohibitions. But in 629, the Byzantine emperor Heraclitus seized the city and decreed the expulsion of Jews to a distance of three miles. In 638, it fell to the army of Caliph Omar (Haral, 1974).

THE UMAYAD CALIPHATE, 629 - 750 (121 YEARS)

The townsfolk of Palestine consisted of Jews, Arabs, Persians and Samaritans, all living side by side - in Tiberias and surroundings, in Dan, Haifa, Jaffa, Hebron, and Eilat. Jews flocked to Jerusalem after the Muslim conquest. Jerusalem began to become the most important city in the country. Jews no longer looked towards Tiberius, but to Jerusalem (Haral 1974).

A document in Judeo-Arabic found in the Cairo *Genizah* reveals that Jews asked the Caliph, Omar for permission for 200 families to settle in the town. As the patriarch opposed the action, Omar fixed the number of the Jewish settlers at 70 families. The Jews were assigned southwest of the Temple area, where they lived at the time (Keter, 1973). According to Keter (1973) although many Arabs came to live in Jerusalem, the great majority of the inhabitants were Christian. Records of *Genizah* fragments and other Rabanite and Karaite sources concerning the earliest Jewish inhabitants of Jerusalem during the

Umayyad period is insufficient for even a general description of historical events, let alone the daily life of the Jewish community. Even the date of the transfer to Jerusalem of the Talmudic academy from Tiberias during the late Byzantine and earliest Muslim periods is unknown. During this time the Dome of the rock was being finished. Jewish families were appointed guardians of the Haram. As such it was decreed they should be exempt from tax (Keter, 1973).

According to Keter (1973), from the time Jerusalem was conquered by the Arabs in 638, it remained a provincial town and never became the seat of rich princes who had chroniclers at their court. Jewish traditions and beliefs influenced early Islam's attitude toward the holiness of the Temple Mount and its surroundings. The Dome of the Rock was finished in 691. Evidence of this interaction reveal that Jews indeed lived in Jerusalem in the early Arab period. The prevailing opinion, based on Christian sources that the Jews were not allowed to live in the holy city or its surroundings during the whole Byzantine period is not confirmed by any non-Christian source.

THE ABBASID CALIPHATE, 750 - 969 (219 YEARS)

The importance of Jerusalem dwindled by reason of its remoteness from the "metropolis" of Damascas, the capital. Meanwhile as Jerusalem was being neglected, Jewish life went on. The courtyard of the Temple Mount became a meeting site (Harel, 1974). A letter dated 835 from the Cairo Genizah from the Babylonian Exilarch recognizes that schools were still entitled to fix the days of the new moons and festivals, as they had done for centuries. It was not clear where these schools were located. What is clear, however, is that in 921 there is record in the Cairo Genizah of Aaron ben Meir, who appears to have been head of a school in Ramlah, who proclaimed a revised calendar in a ceremony from the Mount of Olives in Jerusalem (Kobler, 1952). Another letter from Joseph, the King of the Khazars, dated 965, acknowledges Jews residing in Jerusalem.

THE FATIMID CALIPHATE, 969-1071 (102 YEARS)

Fatimid first ordered the synagogues and churches to be destroyed, but in the end relented and Jews were permitted to rebuild them. The Seljuks took Jerusalem in 1071 in an assault of unbridled devastation. As the Seljuks and Fatimids fought, the citizenry in Palestine drew less and less. The population of all groups apparently dwindled (Haral, 1974). A north African Jew described the economic conditions, as poor and indicated the community had to draw its livelihood from gifts sent from the Diaspora or what was offered during the pilgrimages to Jerusalem (Keter, 1973). This period also saw the western slopes of the Mount of Olives serving as the main gathering places for Jewish Pilgrims. Nevertheless, letters reveal Jewish activity going on in Jerusalem during this period (Kobler, 1952).

According to Genizah sources, the majority was still non-Muslim and had a number of churches. The Jews had two quarters, one southwest of the Temple area and one north of it. By the end of the 900s, the Christians were still the strongest element in town. According to Salmon ben Jeroham, the Moslems and the Christians persecuted the Jews and tried to diminish their rights (Keter, 1973). But Jews were present.

Jerusalem was weakened prior to the Crusader invasion due to revolts, punishments and struggles between the Seljuks, Iraq and Persia. The decline of Ramleh in the middle 1000s and the increase of Christian pilgrims from European countries gave sorely afflicted Jerusalem another chance.

Economic life in Jerusalem was generally impoverished. Jewish religious activity was invigorated by charity from the Diaspora during much of this period. A letter from the Cairo *Genizah* in the 1000s refers to a letter from Soloman the Younger, head of Jerusalem's Yeshiva of the Pride of Jacob, thanking the Jews of Fostat for their generous support. Sasson (1974) noted a letter sent from the congregation of Salonika to another community lying on the route to Erez Yisrael in the 1000s which read:

> ...who hails from the community of Russia and has been staying with us....He met a relative who came to our Holy Jerusalem and who told him of the splendors of Erez Yisrael. His spirit has moved him to go likewise and prostrate himself at the Holy Place (Ben-Sasson p 395).

CRUSADER PERIOD, 1099 - 1260 (161 YEARS)

The city was besieged for five weeks, June 6 to July 15, 1099. Jews and Moslems defended the city. One of the religious attractions for participating in the Crusades was the belief of complete absolution from their sins. This theme of Christian afterlife can be seen in much art work.[12] According to Ben-Gurion (1977), the country was overrun with rapacious hordes, who had received religious sanction to murder and rob. Jerusalem was ravaged and the Crusaders slaughtered Muslims and Jews without discrimination. The city was largely depopulated. The first years of the Crusaders' rule were marked by insecurity and economic difficulties. The Crusaders transferred Christian "Arab tribes" and settled them in the former Jewish Quarter.

As a matter of course, Jerusalem became the capital of the Crusader Kingdom. Jewish communities in Judaea and those in villages near Jerusalem suffered the same fate. Contemporary notes obtained from Haifa, the city of the Sanhedren tell of the destruction of Jaffa, Ono, Lydda, Hebron, Usafiya on Mount Carmel, and Haifa (Beb-Gurion, 1977). The situation in the north, as it was 1,000 years earlier, was better in Samaria and in the Galilee. There were accounts of people killed, but no mention of a general massacre. The relative survival rate seems related to the lack of fortification and armed response. Caesarea surrendered and the Jewish population was spared. By Crusader accounts, Haifa was attacked with all of its defenders put to death.

According to Benjamin of Tudela, ten Jewish communities were seen to be active in the year 1170. These including Tiberias and Safed. The largest communities were in the coastal cities of Tyre, Acre and Caesarea.

The Crusaders' rule invigorated Christian religious life. Many Muslim shrines were turned into churches as was the Dome of the Rock. The new Church of the holy Sepulcher was dedicated in 1149. Most of the inhabitants were of European origin, except for the Eastern Christians. Muslims and Jews were not permitted to reside in the city; however, Muslims came into the city for business purposes and some Jews settled near the Citadel (Keter, 1973). Benjamin of Tudela (1170) reported there were about 200 Jews living below the Tower of David at the limits of the city. One of their enterprises was a dye factory, which the Jews rented yearly from the king. No one other than a Jew was permitted to do dyeing work in Jerusalem (Haral, 1974).

Following the fall of the Crusader Kingdom to the armies of Saladin in Nobember of 1187, and due in part to the influence of Maimonides (1135-1204), a court physician at the time to the Egyptian Sultan, Jews once again returned to Jersualem. The Western Christians were banished. The next four decades

---

[12]The Huntington Museum in Pasadena houses an exhibit of stained glass depicting three scenes, the first, of Crusaders marching to battle, the battle itself, while the theme of the third glass work depicted soldiers arising after death, to heaven.

witnessed more Crusades. Worse still, in 1244 a horde of Kwarizim Turks rampaged through the city, and only sixteen years later Jerusalem was sacked by the Mongols.

MAMELUK PERIOD: FALL OF CRUSADER JERUSALEM 1260 - 1516, (256 YEARS)

The Mamluks had taken over in Egypt. The Mongols invaded the Near East and penetrated into Eretz Yisrael at the beginning of 1260. The inhabitants fled when the Mongols swept over the country sacking the towns and villages. When the Mamluks succeeded in September, 1260 in defeating the Mongols at Ayn Jalut (En-harod), Jerusalem, along with all of Eretz Yisrael, was annexed to their kingdom and remained under their rule until the Ottomans conquered Syria and Egypt in 1516 (Keter, 1973).

After the Battle of Hittin in July, 1187, Saladin and his successors besieged all Christians. Except for Easterners, all were forbidden to reside in Jerusalem. Most of the churches were restored as Muslim shrines. Mosques, like the dome of the Rock were restored. Saladin favored the Jews. Jews, Moslems and Eastern Christians resided together in Jerusalem. Alharize (1170-1235) recounts that "three hundred rabbis" from France and England came to live in Palestine. Jews from North Africa, accompanied by Muslims, came to live in Jerusalem (Harel, 1974). Ben Gurion (1974) listed the existence of 15 Jewish communities throughout Eretz Yisrael. Jerusalem consisted of 250 families.

Later, when Nahmonides (1194 - 1270) arrived in Jerusalem in 1267 he found ruins. The following is an excerpt collected in the *Genizah* pertaining to what Nahmonides reported about Jewish life in Jerusalem to his son.

....Great is the solitude and great the devastation, and, to put it briefly, the more sacred the places, the greater the desolation. Jerusalem is more desolate than the rest of the country: Judea more than Galilee. But even in this destruction it is a blessed land. It has about 2,000 inhabitants; about 300 Christians live there who escaped the sword of the Sultan. There are no Jews [prosperous Jewish communities in Jerusalem]. For after arrival of the Tartars, some fled while others died by the sword. There are only two brothers, dyers by trade, who have to buy their ingredients from the government. There, the ten men meet, and on Sabbaths they hold the service at their home. But we encouraged them,

and we succeeded in finding a vacant house, built on pillars of marble
with a beautiful arch....For the town is without a ruler. Whoever desires
to take possession of the ruins can do so.

Abba Eben(1984), p137f

Nahmonides later goes on to say how he helped promote their well being,
how he located a Torah scroll from Schechem (Nablus) and how it was that
people continually crowded into Jerusalem, men and women, from Damascus,
Zobah (Aleppo) and from all parts of the country to see the Sanctuary and to
mourn there. The suggestion arises that a small contingency of Jews resided
there serving the visitation of larger populations that would regularly come
through. According to Israelowitz (1996), Nahmonides renovated an ancient
synagogue which dated from the Gaonic period, still in use today. Jews lived
in Jerusalem and quite likely were supported by the visitors. According to
(Keter, 1973), he succeeded in getting some to return and rebuild the Jewish
community.

Letters in the Genizah of this period reflect the difficulties in traveling to
Jerusalem, but also suggest a Jewish presence in the period immediately
following departure of the Crusaders. That travel was difficult is apparent upon
reading letters of this period. One in 1286 and the other in 1321 tell of
harrowing experiences in attempting to travel to Jerusalem.

The situation of Jerusalem in the years after the retreat of the Mongols was
very depressed. Muslims and Jews were permitted to live at least in the hilly
parts of Palestine. The ban on Jewish residence in Jerusalem was formally
lifted. When Rabbi Obvadia of Berinoro (1415-1510) settled in Jerusalem,
things improved for the Jewish community. At this stage the Ottoman conquest
of Constantinople, marking the end of the Byzantine empire and their expulsion
of Jews, marked a turning point in the history of Jewish activity in the land of
Israel and signaled the onset of a trend for entry (Haral, 1974). At the end of
the 1400s, the areas about Jerusalem probably had no more than 10,000
inhabitants. The Dominican Felix Fabri, who was in Jerusalem in 1483,
reported there were 1,000 Christians. The Jewish community numbered 100-150
families (Keter, 1973).

According to Keter (1973) the role of the Jews in Jerusalem was very modest.
Until the end of the 1400s the numbers were apparently quite small. In the
beginning of the 1400s, immigration of Jews from European countries began in
earnest. In 1428 the Pope stopped Jews from sailing to Eretz Yisrael. That

Jews resided in Jerusalem in 1435 is clear from a letter from Elija of Ferrara to his sons, he writes of a great plague ravaging Egypt, Damascus and Jerusalem. He writes that ninety victims perished in Jerusalem. He describes the situation between Jews and Moslems in Jerusalem as cooperative as they work side by side, with no jealousy between them resulting.

The Mamluks harassed the Jews and in about 1440 imposed a heavy tax on them to be paid yearly.   Many left.   Meshullam of Volterra, who visited Jerusalem in 1481, spoke of about 250 Jews residing in the city. In 1488, Rabbi Obadah of Berinoro, complained of the poverty and oppression. He reported seeing no more than 70 Jewish families and many +widows in Jerusalem. In 1495, following immigration of Spanish exiles, about 200 Jewish families were living in Jerusalem (Keter, 1973).

In 1488 we learn from a letter from Obadia Hare da Berinoro to his father of Jerusalem of a Jewish community in Jerusalem:

.... though for the most part still in ruin (Jerusalem) has about 4,000 families,of which there are about 70 families of the poorest class (of Jews), scarcely a family that is not in want of the commonest necessaries; one who has bread is called rich. Among the Jewish popuation there are many aged, forsaken widows from Germany, Spain, Portugal and other countries, so that there are seven women to one man.

(Kobler, 1952), pp 297-309.

A year later the tax for Jews had been modified;   hope had arisen that Jerusalem could be rebuilt. In 1495, a letter reveals that 200 families were seen, "who abstain from every sin, and fulfill the commandments of the Lord with great zeal. All people gather in the evening for prayers (Kobler, 1952, pp312-318). Gurion (1974) concluded that according to letters, there were 1600 Jews in Jerusalem in 1455.

The Rambam Synagogue

The synagogue was later established in 1400. In 1588 the Jews were banned from worship and the synagogue was converted to a workshop. It is active today. We saw it and heard the commotion of activity from the nearby Rambam Yeshiva, a half block down from our apartment in the Jewish Quarter.

OTTOMAN RULE, 1516 - 1917 (401 YEARS)

According to Keter (1973) even before the Ottoman conquest there were many indications that Jewish Jerusalem was growing from its lethargy. At the beginning of the 1500s it attracted the kabbalists who were awaiting the imminent redemption. Suleiman rebuilt the walls in 1537, restored the Citadel of David, and improved the city's water supply. But the Ottomans introduced no changes in the composition of the Muslim population of Jerusalem. After construction of the wall, Jewish life grew. Jewish physicians were employed at the royal court. Spanish refugees continued to come and contributed to the rising population throughout Palestine. Then, the community in Jerusalem began to contract as a result of burdensome taxation and confiscation of property, until only the poor were left (Haral, 1974).

Four Sephardic Synagogues

South of Hurva Square on Hatu'pim Street are four repaired and restored Sephardic synagogues. They were built in 1586 by Jews fleeing the Spanish Inquisition. In accordance with the law of the time, synagogues could not be taller than neighboring buildings, a measure that saved some of the buildings from complete destruction during the bombardment of the quarter in 1948. The buildings were then looted by the Jordanians and used as sheep pens. The Sephardic Educational Center, next door to this synagogue now has possession of much of the area.

Hurva Synagogue

Plans to build the synagogue began in 1700 when Rabbi Yehuda came from Poland with hundreds of his students. It was unfinished. The structure was rebuilt in 1850 and totally destroyed by the Jordanians in 1948. All that remains is a restored solitary white stone arch. An American architect, Louis, Kahan, was commissioned to design a new Hurva Synagogue following the Six Day War. Plans were put on hold since his death in the early 1970s. All that is seen now is a solitary arch. Much of it now forms the tree-shaded social center of the Jewish quarter, where Mama's Deli faces.

Population Surveys by the Turkish Administration

Cohen and Lewis (1978) reported, surveys of Jewish population taken by the Turks to impose special tax revenue. The reports indicated more than a thousand Jews were residing in Jerusalem from 1525 through 1568. From 1572 through 1595 the population decrease, reflected by the movement towards Safad and Tiberius, cities competing with Jerusalem as being the center of Jewish activity. Jews resided in three sections, Sharaf, Maslakh and Risha. Christian households increased from 119 to 303 between 1525 and 1533 (Keter, 1973).

Movement of Jews within Palestine

After a decline of Safed at the end of the 1500s, the Jerusalem's Jewish population increased. In general, the situation improved, but the tax burden and other impositions were not eased. From the end of the 1600s there were about 300 Jewish families, with nearly 1,200 persons. This number exceeded the quota and served to cap the growth (Keter, 1973). At the end of the 1600s, the Jewish community numbered approximately 1,000 persons. A quarter of them were scholars and rabbis. The remainder were craftsmen and small businessmen.

Table 3 provides a glimpse of the population of Jerusalem for the years 1525 - 1587. Interestingly, they reveal the movement of Jewish population to Tiberius and Safed which became the centers of Jewish activity competing with Jerusalem. Later, when Safad experienced its troubles, many Jews moved back to Jerusalem.

Table 3.
Jewish Population of Jerusalem

Number of Persons
According to Turkish Survey

Survey Year	Number of Persons
1525	1194
1538	1363
1553	1958
1562	1434
1567	1050
1572	690
1584	870
1587	816

Cohen and Lewis, *Population and Revenue in the Towns of Palestine in*

After the massacres in the Caucasus in 1648 and 1656, Jews made their long way to Palestine from Russia and Poland. According to Keter (1973), before their arrival, the population was around 1,200, about a sixth of them, Ashkenazim. The Hurva synagogue was rebuilt in 1837. In the 1770s Rabbi Mendel of Vitebsk brought 300 of his followers from the Ukraine, Lithuania and Rumania to Safad and Tiberius, then to Jerusalem. By the mid 1700s, wealthy Jews from all parts of the Diaspora were contributing to the establishment and maintenance of Yeshivot. At the end of the 1700s there were approximately 10,000 Jews in Jerusalem.

The New City of Jerusalem

The small Yemin Moshe neighborhood can be identified immediately by its windmill, actually the first Jerusalem structure to be built outside the secure confines of the Old City about 1860. It was part of a development led by Sir Moses Montefiore, an English Jewish philanthropist who wanted to ease the overcrowding within the city wall. He built the block of 24 apartments, a development known as Mishkenot Sha'an'anim (Tranquil Dwellings) and the windmill was to have provided the basis for a flour industry.

After Montefiore visited Palestine in the mid 1800s, the condition of Jews in Jerusalem became better and the area of settlement wider. Yitzhak Ben-Zvi wrote "There were periods of devastation and ruin in Jerusalem....[illegible]...but was never abandoned even for a short period, as in Tiberias, or even for a few years, as in Safed. During the tribulations which befell Safed, several times in the fourth decade, many people began to leave the town and move to Jerusalem where conditions for settlement had improved.

The Hebrew Press of Israel Bank moved from Safed after the 1837 earthquake, publishing its first book from Jerusalem in 1841. Newspapers were printed. Montifiore established a clinic in Jerusalem in the early 1840s. The number of Jerusalem's inhabitants in 1845 have been estimated at 15,000, including 7,100 Jews. (Keter, 1973, 112-114).

The year 1860 marked the beginning of the "new city" and the relative decline of the Old City. In the 1870s, cabs and carts began to make their appearance in the streets of new Jerusalem. By 1863, there were three newspapers competing with one another until closed down by the government. In 1868 a Jew opened up the first modern bakery. By 1865 the city was linked to the coastal plain by the Turkish telegraph. In 1864 the first Jewish school for girls opened. By 1865 the Jews became a majority in the city. The British consul reported in 1865 that there were approximately 18,000 residents in the city, of whom 8-9,000 were Jews. In 1875 a scientific demographic survey counted 20,500 inhabitants in Jerusalem, including 10,500 Jews. The Me'a She'arim quarter, just outside the Turkish walls to the northwest, was established in 1874. In the 1880s Jerusalem gradually began to acquire the

Table 4
Settlement in Jerusalem in the 1800s and 1900s

Year	Jews	Muslim	Christians	Total	% Jews
1844	7,120	5,000	3,390	15,510	45.9
1876	12,000	7,560	5,470	25,030	47.9
1896	28,122	8,560	8,748	45,420	61.9
1905	40,000	7,000	13,000	60,000	66.6
1913	48,400	10,050	16,750	75,000	64.3
1922	33,971	13,413	14,669	62,578	54.3
1931	51,222	19,894	19,335	90,053	56.6
1948	100,000	40,000	25,000	165,000	60.6
1967	195,000	54,963	12,646	263,309	74.3

Statistics compiled from the *Encyclopedia Britannica* (1970)

character of a "Western" city. Road links were established with Nablus and Jericho. By the end of the 1880s, the population numbered 43,000 including 28,000 Jews, 7,000 Muslims, 2,000 Latins (Catholics), 150 Greek Orthodox, 510 Armenians, 100 Copts, 75 Abyssinians, 15 Syrian (Jacobites and Malkites) and 300 Protestants. According to Ben Gurion (1974), in 1880 there were 7,750,000 Jews in the world, nine-tenths of them in Europe – the majority in Tzarist Russia.In 1907, 80,000 Jews lived in Palestine: 45,000 in Jerusalem, 8000 in Jaffa, 8000 in Safed, 2000 in Haifa, 2000 in Tiberias; and 1000 in Hebron. There were 30 Jewish villages with a total population of some 6000 as well as 8000 or so Jews on undeveloped land.

At the turn of 1900s, the population of Jerusalem was estimated at 45,000, including 28,200 Jews (15,300 Ashkenazim), 8,760 Christians, and 8,600 Muslims. The number of Jewish residents did not increase because of difficulties for Jewish immigration. Nevertheless by 1912, the population was estimated at more than 70,000, including 10,000 Muslims, 25,000 Christians (half of them Greek Orthodox) and 45,000 Jews (Keter, 1973, p 138).

Impact of the First World War

The development of Jerusalem came to a halt after Turkey's entry into the war at the end of 1914. Epidemics, famine, arrests, and expulsions wreaked havoc among the inhabitants. By war's end, population was reduced to 55,000. The city recovered upon occupation by the British on December 11, 1917.

BRITISH RULE, 1917 - 1948 (31 YEARS)

The King David Hotel

As the Savoy is to London, Raffles is to Singapore, so is the King David to Jerusalem. It was designed in 1930 by a Swiss Architect, Emil Vogt, for an Egyptian Jewish family. The hotel has been given its seal of approval by a stream of kings and queens, prime ministers and presidents including our last five. George W. Bush has not yet had the opportunity to come to Jerusalem.

Old Yishuv Court Museum

At 6 Or Ha'Cha'im Street, west of the Cardo, is a reconstructed house in which each room illustrates an aspect of Jewish life in the quarter before the destruction ensued as a result of the 1948 Israeli War for Independence.

Recovery after the First World War

The city slowly recovered from the setbacks caused by WWI. The 1922 census showed a population of only 62,578, of whom 33,971 were Jews, 14,699 were Christians, 13, 413 Muslims, and 495 others. In 1931, the total population was 90,503, 51,222 Jews, 19,894 Muslims, 19,335 Christians, and 52 others. In 1948, the population was estimated at 165,000: 100,000 Jews, 40,000 Muslims, and 25,000 Christians.

JERUSALEM DIVIDED, 1948 - 1967 (19 YEARS)

In 1948 the population on the Israeli side (West Jerusalem) was estimated at 69,000, including 931 Christians and 28 Muslims. In 1949 the population on the Jordanian side was set as 46,000 which continued in that range as late as 1956.

East Jerusalem

The Old City and areas generally on the east side of Jerusalem were occupied in May of 1948 by the Arab Legion. Its first act was the destruction of the Jewish quarter, including almost all synagogues. The ancient cemetery on the slope of Mount of Olives was desecrated. East Jerusalem turned to the east bank of the Jordan through which all its relations with the world at large were conducted. Water supply remained poor. The number of inhabitants never surpassed 65,000, of whom about 25,000 lived within the walls of the Old City. According to Olmert, the Mayor of Jerusalem, there are currently about 200,000 Moslems living in the environs of East Jerusalem.

West Jerusalem

The cessation of hostilities and the conclusion of the armistice agreement with Jordan left the Israel sector of Jerusalem situated at the eastern extremity of a "corridor" that was almost devoid of Jewish settlements. To the north, east and south, the city was surrounded by hostile Arab territories. At first the population was diminishing and its political future obscure. The Jewish city began to recover quickly, however, when it was proclaimed as the seat of the Knesset and the capital of the State of Israel at the end of 1949. Water supply was resumed, at first through emergency pipe and later through pipelines of considerable capacity. An immense water reservoir was built in the southwest of the city. Soon, the first train since the war arrived. A landing strip for light airplanes was built. By 1961, the population of West Jerusalem was 166,300,

Table 6
Jewish Presence in Jerusalem

Year	Rule	Highest Jewish Presence in Jerusalem	
B.C.E.			
1000	Jewish	2,500	First Temple Constructed
800	Jewish	2,500	
600	Babylonian	2,500	
400	Jewish	5.000	Second Temple Constructed
200	Jewish	4,000	
C.E	Jew/Roman	4,000	Destruction of Temple, 70
100	Roman	500	
200	Roman	500	
300	Roman/Byzn	500	
400	Byzantine	100	
500	Byzantine	1,000	
600	Byz/Persian	100	
700	Umayyad/Ab	100	
800	Abasid	500	
900	Abasid/Fatim	50	
1000	Fatimid	500	
1100	Crusader	Trace	200 Jews near city limits
1150	Crusade	1,000	
1200	Crusader	1,000	
1250	Crus/Mamlk	500	
1300	Mamluks	25	Mongols overrun Palestine
1350	Mamluks	Trace	
1400	Mamluks	600	Pop: 8,000; 1,000 Christian
1450	Mamluks	1,600	
1500	Mam/Turks	1,500	Turkish Wall built 1537
1550	Turks	1,900	
1600	Turks	1,200	
1650	Turks	2,000	
1700	Turks	6,000	
1750	Turks	10,000	
1800	Turks	7,000	
1850	Turks	47,000	Development of new city, 1867
1900	Turks/Brit	45,000	
1950	Israel	100,000	
1975	Israel	200,000	
2000	Israel	750,000	

including an estimated, several hundred Muslims and over 1,000 Christians. In 1967, the number of inhabitants was estimated about 185,000.

THE SIX DAY WAR AND RE-UNIFICATION

For Jerusalem, the six day war, despite its name, was in fact only a three day war, from Monday morning to Wednesday afternoon. The two parts of the city were officially reunited on June 28. East Jerusalem was connected to the Israeli water supply.

A glimpse at Table 6 gives the overall picture of the growth of Jews in Jerusalem and Palestine from 1833

		Table 5	
	Jewish Population of Jerusalem as a proportion of Jews in Israel		
Year	Jerusalem	Eretz Yisrael	%
1833	3,000	-	
1856	5,700	10,500	54
1895	28,000	47,000	60
1913	45,000	85,000	53
1916	26,000	56,000	46
1922	33,970	83,800	41
1931	51,220	174,000	29
1934	64,500	300,000	21
1939	80,800	475,000	17
1946	100,000	625,000	16
1967	200,000	2,500,000	8

Government Census of Palestine
Encyclopedia Britannica (1970)

through 1967. We believe the figures are higher than that reported for that of Eretz Yisrael and will take this up later. Note the population decline associated with the First World War, the growth of relative population outside of Jerusalem, the rapid increase in population following the second world war and the impact on growth by the establishment of the State of Israel. Table 7 displays my current estimate of the presence of Jews in Jerusalem over the centuries. The reader may refer to Appendix A for the varied sources of my population estimates.

Our visit readily reveals how the city of Jerusalem has maintained itself despite religious and economical sanctions, pain of death for entry and widespread havoc by outsiders. Jews have always believed that they were maintaining something of great importance, that at times had been taken from them by force.

The most recent desecration in Jerusalem occurred in 1948. Bier (1976) writes of the devastation of the synagogues during the 19 years of Arab rule from May 1948 til June 1967. A few retained their external structure, though pillaged from within. He tells of one synagogue that remained intact, in the Moslem Quarter, which included a Jewish district until the 1929 Arab riots when the district was destroyed. The synagogue was guarded by a hired Arab watchman in 1929 after prayers had ceased to be held there. My visit to this synagogue was described in chapter 7.

Road Map of the Golan
Tourist Map, Golan Tourist Association, Qatzrin, Israel

Chapter 9
The Golan

September 4, Tuesday, AM: Jerusalem.

We will leave Jerusalem with an improved perspective on our Jewish presence here. We are anxious to get the rest of the story in northern parts of Israel. Before we leave, we purchase a paper and leisurely eat breakfast in our suite before leaving the Old Quarter.

> *Jerusalem Post*: (1) Suicide Bomber rocks central Jerusalem (2) US, Israel quit Durban, (3) Four bombings in 7 hours shake Jerusalem, (4) Tight race in today's Labor primary, (5) Hebron clashes leave 3 Israelis wounded, 2 Palestinians dead, (6) NY Jews protest Durban resolution

> *L.A. Times*: (1) U.S. & Israel Quit Forum on Racism, (2) Computer Giant to Buy Rival Compaq, (3) Gov. Davis Doing Too Much, Energy Critics Say, (4) Libya Offers Millions in Aid to Islam Nations, (5) Suicide Bomber Hurts 11 in Jerusalem

We conclude there is quite a bit of news coverage of events occurring quite close to us. Indeed, being in Jerusalem, we seem in the midst of it all. We find we have become somewhat desensitized to the violence occurring about us. There is a sense of safety so long as we in the Jewish Quarter. Adding a measure of security is the knowledge the Old City is heavily secured by automated closed circuit television of the alleyways and streets, numerous patrols of police and Israeli solders in armed pairs.

10:00 AM: Leaving Jerusalem

We readily find a taxi that drops us off back at the David Citadel Hotel, across the street from the Traffic car rental office. We find ourselves behind the wheel of a new Opel, heading towards north Jerusalem looking for the highway to take us eastward and downward to the desert junction with H 90. We readily get lost. We take advantage of the situation to purchase fair sized ice-storage cooler. We discover, while at the store, we must be in a heavily populated Russian section as the clerks and customers are speaking a combination of Russian and Hebrew.

We shortly find a ramp leading to the main road heading east down towards the Jordan River Valley. The design of the major highways take into account security problems throughout this part of Israel. It is difficult for tourists like us to find an on-ramp. Should one be missed, it may be a few miles before the next one turns up. We head east down the long grade to the depths of the Jordan River Valley. Once at the junction, we are but eight air miles from the Dead Sea.

As we leave the outskirts of the city and descend to the east of desert divide we find conditions rapidly becoming more arid, almost as much so as the driest areas of southern California. It seems we are back home in the reaches of the Coachella Valley.

We are approaching Area A, Palestinian controlled land. We soon pass checkpoints and find ourselves dropping more and more in elevation in quite deserted and desolate areas. There are occasional Bedouin encampments with goats or sheep foraging on grass we cannot see. There are nearby dilapidated temporary housing looking like shacks. Perhaps on a clear day one can look southward and view the Dead Sea or across the Jordan River into Jordan. But today, like the days of last year, the visibility seems limited to about six miles in a kind of sandy Dead Sea haze that permeates the whole area.

We make out the indentation of the Jordan River. It looks similar to the riparian growth throughout dry parts of southern California where a small stream cuts through the desert with green on each side for a few yards. Here, the green stretches become more wide as we drive north.

September 4, Tuesday, Noon: A Blockade: The IDF Surrounds Jericho

Soon after turning northbound at the junction of H90, abeam Jericho, to our left about five miles, we see a small group of soldiers have set up a blockade. A few cars are stopped ahead of us by barriers. They recognize our plates as Israeli. As we approach the soldier, he leans towards us, looks inside the car and tells us, "There is shooting up ahead."

"Really?"

"Where are you going?"

"To Tiberias."

"Ah, Tiveria."

"To make it to Tiveria, go east at this intersection. Take a round about way that will connect you back to Highway 90 a few kilometers to the north. There, the road is good and safe."

We now head east and discover we are heading straight for Jordan. We see the river ahead, a small bridge, another barricade. We are approaching the Allenby Bridge! Here, a solder at the checkpoint tells us, "Back up, then turn north and go up the military road. It parallels Highway 90. Then turn right, then turn left to get around the shooting."

We head up the narrow semi paved road, that goes up and over hills without switchbacks and after about five or ten minutes of some anxious moments, we make a turn to the right, see a smaller dirt road, then turn left. Relieved, we find ourselves back on Highway 90 going through more of Arab territory. The Arab land is desolate. After about an hour of driving we approach Israeli areas and find the landscaping and agriculture generally getting back to normal. We stop and buy some ice in one of the "settlements." About this time a terrorist incident occurs here on the road that I will read about tomorrow in the *Jerusalem Post*.

The terrain becomes more hospitable with each mile as we approach the southern perimeter of the Galilee. The Jordan widens and forms a greater belt of green. There are several reservoirs which are connected to irrigation ditches. We see more signs of cultivation on both sides of the Jordan. As we approach the Sea of Galilee we decide to turn left and head for Tiberias not knowing what we'll do when we get there. Perhaps we head that way because we told the guard that's where we're going.

2:00 PM: Tiberias

We soon find ourselves trying to find our way through the streets and residential areas of Tiberias. The streets are too busy and confusing to us to accomplish anything. What's more, the main north and south streets are one-way with controlled access to either left or right turns except at spots that the locals know about. They are congested. A lot of drivers seem to be getting lost. Could they all be tourists like us? The fact is, of course, there are not very many tourists around. School has already started. The beaches are almost all empty despite the warm and comfortable weather.

5:00 PM: Katz'rin

We decide to make contact with the Tel Family in Katz'rin where we stayed last year. But we cannot figure out a way to get through to them on the telephone. All we get are recorded messages in Hebrew which we cannot understand. We later find out that Israelis also have the same trouble. So we simply take our chances and head for their home. They remember us. Once there we find there is ample space for a few days, but a question remains about staying over through Shabbat.

We obtain an update on what had transpired in the last year. We discover their son and daughter had finished their tour of duty in the army. As many Israeli's seem to do, the son intends to travel through North America before starting on his higher education. Their daughter is studying sociology and as of now is planning to specialize in criminal justice. Samuel is now retired from Park service. Mrs. Tel, Leah, continues to teach piano. As we spend some of the evening together, I cannot permit myself not to play a ballad I wrote of my experiences on the Pacific Crest Trail in California for them. They seem to enjoy the adventure of it all. We leave for the center of town, purchase some foods and snacks and have a pleasant evening in our cozy apartment upstairs putting our concerns about troubles in Israel aside for a while.

September 5, Wednesday Morning: Katz'rin

Jerusalem Post: (1) Gov't Freezes IDF plan for Green Line buffer zones, (2) IDF reinforces Jerusalem after suicide bombing, (3) A fateful foot patrol: policeman prevents a serious tragedy in Jerusalem yesterday, (4) Ongoing efforts to change anti-Israel text in Durban, (5) Shekel set a 3-year low record NIS 4.293 by Bank of Israel, (6) Terror cell planned multiple attacks (7) Peres seeking secluded meeting with Arafat.

L.A. Times: HP deal could trigger more tech mergers, (2) Bomber posing as orthodox Jew adds to terror, (3) Reno enters race to try to unseat Fla. Gov. Bush (4) S. Africa offers proposal aimed at salvaging U.N. racism forum, (5) Taliban trial gets underway [detained Americans - preaching Christianity] (6) Older drivers found to have lowest crash rates, (7) GOP pushes new tax cuts as elixir for sagging economy

We are saddened by more news of troubles in Jerusalem and how guarded the city was when we were there just a couple of days ago and compare the situation with how pleasant it was last year. Much of our discussion today is trying to figure out what accounts for Palestinians behaving as though they feel entitled to Israeli turf as theirs, and how it is that youth are involved in suicide attacks. We wonder what may be the distortions of historical facts that underlie the prevalent hostile attitudes on the part of Arabs in this part of the world. We feel compelled to answer these questions, if only to ourselves to make sense out of the violent behavior on the part of these desperate peoples.

8:00 AM: Gamla National Park

We visited the area last year. Although we had time to wander about the forest reserve, we did not have adequate time to visit the ancient city far below on a ridge a couple hundred feet below. Arriving there in the afternoon, we were unaware of how extensive the park is and the time involved to visit the sites. Last year we overlooked the walled city and a replica of Roman battle machines used to breech the wall. Here was a Jewish city-state, about the same dimensions of ancient Katz'rin. Gamla was taken over by zealots under the leadership of the Jewish General, Josephus Flavious and fortified in anticipation of the Roman siege.

When discovered by archaeologists, the whole area was under ground. They deduced the site on the basis of Josephus's description of the site in his book, The Jewish War. The book is the only surviving non- biblical account of what Eretz Yisrael looked like, a description of the people, their activities and their military prowess. The Jewish General defected to the Romans, to become one of their chroniclers. His description of the battles, war machines and the manner of the Roman Legion and Jewish armies are legendary. Much of his writing is in obvious exaggerated style, biased in the glory of both armies; we take the military exploits and his counts of people and soldiers with more than a grain of salt.

As we approach the park this year we see a number of military vehicles and tanks being carted on large trucks. Soldiers are hitch-hiking as they did last year. This time around, we arrive at the park early. In fact we get there just before 8:00 AM when the park gates are supposed to be opened. They remain locked. We wait at the end of the spur road, about mile off the perimeter of an armored battalion, tank base. We saw some tanks, but none seemed to be firing. All is quiet.

We wonder if anything happened on the frontier to the north or perhaps there was a nearby terrorist attack. It remains very quiet as we wait. We are aware of the tank practice area off a few hundred yards to our north. We become aware of the vultures in the area. For some reason, their presence doesn't seem to help matters. Eventually the park ranger appears. He explains apologetically that he overslept somewhat and some things that had to be done around the house. He chooses to not charge us admission and offered a map and description of the area as a token of his apology.

This time around we readily opt to go walk down hill the old Roman "road" to the walled city of Gamla. The road more resembles a steep and difficult ledge trail, requiring step downs, at times requiring us to hold on to rocks at the steep hilly side of the trail. The high temperatures add some adventure as we know it will be difficult making it back up. We are impressed with the southern California-like low foothills of chaparral and intermittent streams. Here we admire the grace of the low flying vultures. The park is known as a place for their protection.

The excavation reveals much of the ramparts, walls and fortification that was laid by Josephus to offset the expected Roman attack. The Romans came prepared. Facing the walls are battle machines used to break through the wall and mechanical bows that shoot arrows with great force. The opening of the wall destroyed by the rams still exist as if it just occurred. Walking through the outer wall, we take notice of the thickness of the wall, fortified from inside, lessening the space of the rooms on the inside. The walls facing the battery were about ten feet thick of stone and mortar.

Once inside the wall our attention shifted to the kind of living arrangements and work areas. The synagogue is partially restored, as are *mikvot*, cisterns and recreation areas. There are two running streams running along both sides of the ridge which forms the base of the city. Reaching the top, we find the panorama quite breathtaking. To the west lies the Sea of Galilee and to the northeast lies the Mount Harman range. The immediate hills are all mixed with thick chaparral and deciduous trees with a few conifers. We thought of the waste of it all, because it was fortified. All that was left of the city was a big ridge and plateau covered with chaparral.

Chapter 10
Korazim and Capernaum

September 6, Thursday AM: Katz'rin

Jerusalem Post: (1) Israeli shot dead inside Green Line, (2) IDF kills two in missile attack in Tulkarm, (3) Burg scores unofficial Labor win, (4) Israel Arab terror gang uncovered in north, (5) EU weighing Durban walkout, (6) Peres - Arafat meeting next week - PA source.

L.A. Times: (1) Fox (President of Mexico) jousts for migrants pact by end of year, (2) Bomb thrown at a Catholic school for girls, (3) Iraq orders expulsion of five U.N. officials, (4) Macedonia accused on human rights, (5) Sailors cited for bravery for action aboard Cole

It seems to us that the trouble is only deepening. It seems to us that because of the capturing of many of the attackers, the Israelis must have a pretty good bead on the source, training and funding of these people. We hope that this violence can stop, and soon. We sense an impatience among people we meet from day to day. Last year we felt a sense of well being throughout the country. If the behavior and attitude of people could speak out loud, we think it would say, "Enough is enough already."

Thursday, AM: A Drive to Safed.

We drive up to Safed to return back to Katz'rin following our making arrangements for the upcoming weekend. We drive out northwesterly to connect with Highway 91 where there is a mall. We fuel up and choose a restaurant that looks promising for an American style breakfast. We enter the small stylishly modern restaurant and wonder what kind of breakfast they may have for us. They have nothing that resembles fried eggs, hash brown potatoes and toast. We settle for sharing a large lox and cream cheese sandwich on a delicious roll. Soldiers, officers are sitting next by discussing the news. Enlisted men and women are wandering about outside. One way to tell the difference between officers and the enlisted ranks is that the officers appear older and as a rule are not armed. Otherwise the uniforms seem much the same. We see in this area, a mixture of training and front line duty. We share with the Israelis, their intense interest in the news. They have access to constant news on radio and television that we cannot really understand. We appreciate having the English *Jerusalem Post* which is available in one place or another in each community.

We leave the mall to descend southward on Highway 90 for a few miles before turning westerly towards the mountains of the Galilee on Highway 89. We climb out from below sea level through agricultural areas and a couple of small communities. We soon find ourselves climbing up the steep mountain side, but on a well graded highway which at times slices through the mountains. The exposed hillsides are covered with chaparral similar to that seen in southern California. Climbing higher at an elevation of about 3,000 feet we find a transition area between chaparral and low level of montane forests in the more protected areas. There are no streams to be seen near the road, only gullies that look like they might have an intermittent and perhaps a wild flow during the wet season. Now, in September, all is dry. This is a second consecutive drought year. The grass is quite brown. The low growing flora seem to be waiting for their renewal that should come soon with the rains.

Safed lies spread out on the top of one of several hills, at about 3,000 feet. The general terrain of the area is one of a low transition between chaparral and pines. The old city lies on the highest of hills in the vicinity and is generally forested, especially so on the sides of slopes protected by the heat of the afternoon sun.

We make reservations for the upcoming weekend at the Ron Hotel. We re-acquaint ourselves with the old city and drop by the Visitors Center and the Old Government House in the old city of Safed. A description and the historical significance of both the Ron Hotel and the old Government Center, along with other sites, are presented in Chapter 11.

Korazim and *Kfar Nahum* (Capernaum)

On our way back to Katz'rin we make an impromptu stop at Chorazim National Park, a partially restored site of a Jewish city dating back to the first century. The site is ten air miles to the southwest of Katz'rin and ten miles due west of Gamla. We find it is similar in size to that of Katz'rin and Gammla with no sign of fortification. The site reveals a large number of buildings including a synagogue. The synagogue has more decor than others we have seen, reflective perhaps of the culture of the area at the time, Greek, Pagan and Roman. The proximity of the Mikveh and the synagogue appears distinctly Jewish.

The center of Korazim lies only several hundred yards to the north of the Sea of Galilee. Part of its activity was associated with products of the lake. The area in the immediate surroundings to the north is grassy with rounded hills and occasional chaparral. There is now but little tree growth in the immediate area. Quite likely the area grew following the diaspora from the south following the Bar Kochba revolt in 135. According to Hellender (1999), records indicate the town was in ruins by the 300s.

We pass through *Kfar Nahum*, Capernaum, a pleasant site on the upper banks of the Sea of Gallillee. According to Hellender (1999) some believe there was a strong Christian presence here in the 100s. Other Christian scholars, e.g. Horesley(1995), had concluded that there is no evidence of anything Christian throughout all of Palestine until after the 400s. There are nevertheless several references to the town in the New Testament. Here is where Jesus is said to have rendered sermons in the synagogue on getting rid of the *yetzer hurrah*, the evil spirit, the curing of Peter's step-mother and the "walking on the water." Nearby, Jesus is said to have delivered his "Sermon on the Mount, " a round grassy hill overlooking the Sea of Galilee a few hundred yards to the south.

Table 7 Jewish Presence Capernaum and Korazim		
Year	Occupier	Population Est.
C.E.		
0	Romans	500
100	Roman	2,000
200	Roman	5,000
300	Rom/Byzan	2,000
400	Byzantine	1,000
500	Byzantine	1,000
600	Byz/Persian	1,000
700	Ummayad	1,000
800	Abbasid	
900	Abandoned	
1000	Abandoned	
1100	Abandoned	
1200	Mameluk	1,000
1300	Mameluk	500
1400	Mameluk	500
1500	Turkish	500
1600	Turkish	500
1700	Turkish	500
1800	Turkish	500
1900	Turk/Brit/Isrl	1,000
2000	Israel	1,000

By 300s the area expanded to cover the surrounding hills. After the Arab conquest, 700 C.E., the area was destroyed, uninhabited for 300 years.

According to Keter (1996) Jews appeared to have flourished and prosper in the dozens of towns throughout the Galilee and Golan in the early centuries of the common era. Being free to do so, they built synagogue s. A beautiful and well reconstructed one is in Kfar Nahum. Buildings there, like that of Korasim, were built of the black basalt rock so typical of the area. According to Keter (1996) the Jewish community was wealthy enough to build the synagogue with imported shimmering Jerusalem white limestone. It was highly polished to resemble marble. The foundation stones were made of the local black basalt stones. The Capernaum synagogue was partly restored by the Franciscans in 1894.

According to Tsvika Tsuk (1999) the earliest occupation was in the first or second century, C.E. The town grew in the Mishna and Talmudic periods and spread southwards. The town was restored in the 400s or 500s with many repairs and changes including the synagogue. The next period of growth was in the 700s during the Arab period where additional changes were made. After a hiatus of several hundred years, settlement was renewed in the 1200s A small population occupied the site from the 1400s to the present time. The *Genizah* reports a traveler passing through the area in the 1500s reported Jewish fishermen living in Korazim.

We return to Katz'rin and purchase a *Post* and settle down for another evening in our pleasant apartment, elaxed knowing we have accommodations for the weekend in Safed. Our thoughts are soon interrupted by the roar of large canon fire that shake the doors and windows. The next morning we learn of routine tank training taking place an hour or so before midnight a few nights a week.

September 7, Friday AM: Katz'rin

> *Jerusalem Post*: (1) Officer killed, 2nd hurt in ambush, (2) Security cabinet to discuss seam plan, (3) IAF wounds top Tanzim leader, (3) Peres given 'full mandate' for Arafat talks, (4) Out of an anti-racism conference into a trap, (5) Israel signs $2.5 billion F-16 deal.

> *L.A. Times*: (1) Justice department drops effort to split up Microsoft, (2) Bush to weigh residency for illegal Mexican immigrants, (3) Health

benefit costs soar 11% on rising drug prices, (4) Delegates still at loggerheads as racism meeting nears close, (5) House slams Hanoi but also votes to normalize trade, (6) Israelis kill Palestinian militants, (7) Peres announces meeting with Arafat next week

The matter of the "seam plan" seems critical as it is indeed something visible the Israeli government can do in response to the terrorism occurring throughout their land. We assume the sentiment is strong for the plan that would seal off the Palestinian areas. Coming up with such a plan underscores the seriousness of the matters at hand. We have a strong sense that the Palestinians are bringing much trouble upon themselves. Should this seam plan be implemented their plight will further increase.

The terrorism in Israel appears highly related to its propaganda value in the minds of the leader/s who provide support its perpetrators. The propaganda value can be measured by opinion surveys around the world. The *Jerusalem Post*, August 30, reported results of a survey commissioned by an Arab-American lobby group of U.S. citizens searching for changes in attitudes among U.S. voters towards the Palestinian cause and current stance towards Israel. Supporters of the violence in Israel are probably keeping a keen eye on such measures. We also think normalization of trade between and among countries of the Middle East with western and eastern nations is desirable. We have seen the good it has done for Europe. We saw in Eilat the benefits such trade has for Jordan, Egypt and Israel. Not only does trade develop stability and economic progress, but also lessens the need for securing political boundaries.

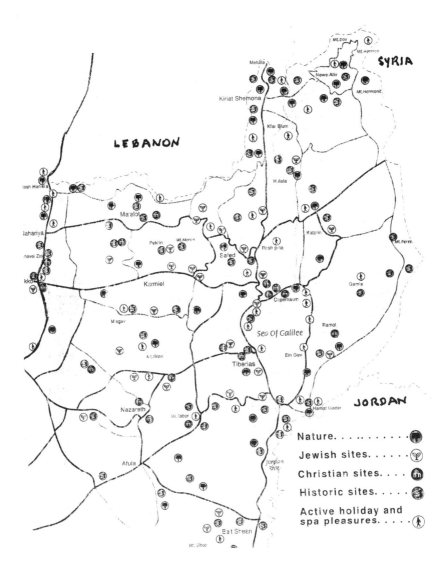

Map of the Galilee Area

From *Go Galilee*, Corazin Publishing, Rosh Pina, Israel, 1998

Chapter 11
Safed

September 7, Friday AM: To Safed

We leave in the morning again for Safed. This time we take an alternate route to Highway 90, closer to the banks of the Sea of Galilee. The area is quite barren. The sparse chaparral and brown grass had long dried. The lake level appears low reflective of the drought conditions over the last two years. Heading up the hill from the large lake, our second time in two days, we are more aware of archaeological sites, memorials and ancient synagogues. We attempt pulling off the road, but find the dirt roads too hazardous to attempt in our rented car. Arriving in Safed a few hours before dusk, we readily find the Ron Hotel, set up our room and opt for a short walk to the nearby old city and purchase some historical material about the area.

The Ron Hotel

The Three story Ron Hotel sits on the northeast protected side of the hill. Above it lies The Citadel, reached in a few hundred yards by way of a narrow, winding paved road. Though moderate in size, the three story hotel has beautiful grounds with a large lawn and swimming pool in the rear nestled in the forest below the Citadel. The building was at one
time a school and served as billeting for troops during the War for Independence.

The Government House

Upon walking up and down the small streets in the old Jewish quarter, we obtain information from the Visitors Center nearby. The information center is housed in a distinctive three story building resembling what comes to mind what a Turkish embassy from the late 1800s may have looked like. The building was built by the Turks in 1886 as a government house. The three story building is U-shaped. The two wings extend to the rear with a large courtyard in the middle which extends by concrete and lawn further to the rear of the property. The building was turned over to the British following the Turkish defeat in the First World War. The British used the building as an active governmental house during the British Mandate, 1917 through 1948.

An inscription on the building describes Arab riots here in 1929, the same year that Hebron endured its massacre. The British informed the Jews of the community of an impending attack by the Arabs. The British rounded up the Jews and interned them in this courtyard for "their protection." The Arab population knew the location of Jewish businesses and where Jews resided. Upon hearing the Jews were rounded up, they looted the stores and vandalized their homes. Wherever we go in Israel we run into surprises and gain new insights into the nature of historical events and discover for ourselves the many perils experienced by Jews residing in Palestine, up to recent times.

Shabbot in The Old City of Safed

Shabbat will soon happen. We find ourselves in the large dining area on the main floor in the hotel where a *Shabbaton* is starting to get underway. There are several groups, each engaging in their style of observance. Singing among the individual groups break out. There is a subtle element of competition among tables. Before nightfall, a small musical group plays outdoors before a mixed group of thirty or so semi-observant young people from Jerusalem. The band plays contemporary popular music. Dancing breaks out. The young ladies and men dance separately. But soon the band stops playing. There is a stillness that pervades the entire area. It is has become Shabbot.

With the approaching of Shabbot, businesses close and the streets become almost entirely empty. The city, as viewed from our window, becomes quiet. Breaking the quiet are occasional sounds of shots being fired, perhaps a half mile away and though the ground is still, some howitzer or cannon fire can be heard far away echoing through the hills. But inside the dining room, the sounds of conversation, prayers and singing drone out whatever sounds that may be outside.

September 8, Saturday: Safed

The *Jerusalem Post* is not published on Saturday.

L.A. Times: (1) Jobless rate in U.S. jumps to 4-year high, (2) Bush aide sees drain on social security, (3) Stock market drops sharply on jobs report, (4) U.S. won't invoke law against Israel [use of U.S. weapons used against Palestinians], (5) disputes prolong conference on racism, (6) Condit still considering reelection run, (7) Jobs: unemployment rate hits 4.9%

Following a more modest breakfast we stroll to the old city. It is Shabbot. Life remains slow. No automobile traffic or bustle around. We walk uphill in the middle of the road upward of about 150 feet to the park on top of the hill. We see from atop the semi-conical hill that the old part of Safed lies immediately on all the down hill slopes of this somewhat conical hill. The top of the hill forms a plateau of several acres, serves today as a playground, picnic area, and an overlook of 360 degrees. Though the playground for toddlers is well maintained, much of the improved landscaping and pools seen along the extensive walkway on top are neglected. The railing is in need of repair, as are many of the wooden benches along the way. Today the area on top of the old city is a park. It wasn't always a park.

The Citadel

The area now serving as a park is also called The Citadel. The top most recently served as a British garrison prior to the War of Independence of 1948. Before them, the Turks. Before them, a number of occupiers. The structures are gone except for a strange concrete building that looks like it may have served as either a bunker or warehouse for ordinance by the Turks and/or British. After the War for Independence the building served as an entertainment center. Recent signs and posters indicate that during the fifties, it might have been a night club. But by the appearance of things inside and out, it looks like it had been vacant for about five or ten years.

Safed was fiercely contested because of it's strategic position at the heart of the northern Galilee and being midway between centers on the Mediterranean coast and garrisons in what is now Syria. At the Citadel there are no placards other than memorial plaques to soldiers killed in the battle for the city during the 1948 War of Independence. All 12,000 Arab residents fled as Israeli forces took over the city.

We can see much of the city of Safed from this vantage point. We have view of the Sea of Galilee about eight miles to the southeast. Opposite the shore we see the hazy heights of Golan; Syria lies another ten miles to the east. Looking to the south, we can see Tiberias along the banks of the large lake. To our west, beyond the downward slopes of the ancient cemetery, lies a canyon and a rise to a wide plateau with a transitional forest that rises gently to the eastern forested steep slopes of nearby Mt. Meron, 3,962 feet, but five miles away. The mountain and ridges block the view to Acre, twenty-four miles away. North, seven miles beyond exposed slopes of sparse chaparral and 2,000-3,000 ridges lies unseen Lebanon. Northeast, beyond the green Hula Valley, ten miles away, lies the summit of Mt. Herman, 9,232 feet, obscured by haze.

To someone interested in walking or backpacking, the area about Safed is quite appealing. Tiberias looks like it is only half days walk downhill, even with a pack of 30 pounds. Coming back from Tiberius to Safed probably requires a full day hike with such a pack. There is a liklehood there would be water available along the way even at this time of year. Heading down the mountains, one could pick up the Nahal Ammi'ad (Amiad River) that follows a canyon down from the bottom of the immediate eastern slopes of the old city where it soon crosses Highway 85. From there it is quite direct to the Sea of Galilee where one would find themselves on Highway 90 about five miles north of Tiberias. Ami'ad, Capernaum and Korizim and Tiberias all seem to be within a day's walk should there be foot trails. Perhaps they all could be reached within a day.

History of Safed

Safed was founded during the 2nd Temple period. According to Hellender (1999) it existed as a city in the 2nd Century, B.C.E. It was a fortified by Josephus in 66 C.E. in anticipation of Roman attacks. It is recorded in Mishnaic and Talmudic literature, following the Roman occupation, as a seat of influence of the *Cohanim*, temple priests. During this period many rabbis and sages settled here. Because of the height and central location in northern *Eretz Yisrael*, new moons were announced here (Israelowitz, 1996 p 72). People we talk to about this matter believe the reporting the new moon had been going on for many centuries; how far back no one hazards to guess.

There has been no organized archaeological study of the area. Little is known beyond what can "be seen" by foot. Little is also available to us as to the population before the 1400s. That there is an ancient cemetery tells us little.

There continues to be difficulties in determining who was buried, and where they actually had died.

On the basis of what we saw in nearby areas in nearby Golan and lower Galilee, Capernaum, Korazin, and Kat'zrin, there indeed was an influx of Jewish population during the first 200 years of the Common Era. The movement of peoples was directly related to the destruction of the Temple and, of more significance, the catastrophe of the Bar Kochba revolt of 135-137 throughout Judea, in the south.

Safed may have been without a Jewish presence for several centuries while Crusaders and Arabs captured and recaptured Safed (Israelowitz, 1996). But there is no certainty, and some can argue that Jews were active there at the time. Meanwhile Jews began to return around the beginning of the 1200s. According to Ben Gurion (1974) Meshuman in 1481 reported finding in Safad and the villages within the city bounds, "a pleasant community of 300 householders."

The town of Peki'in, ten miles to the west, was mentioned in 1522 in the travel memoirs of Rabbi Moses Bassola. Tax registers taken by the Turks for 1555-56 and 1572-73 listed 45 Jewish householders. Israelowitz (1996) points out in his guidebook that Peki'in has an unbroken chain of Jewish habitation from the time of the Second Temple. We hope to visit Pek'in in a couple of days.

Many Spanish Jews, following their expulsion of Jews from Spain in 1492, settled in Safed. One of the synagogues hosts an original Torah that was brought over from Spain during the Inquisition period. By the 1500s, Safed became known as a commercial and religious center, particularly as a resource of Jewish mysticism.

Internal war between rival rulers in the 17th century undermined the economic and spiritual life of Safed. This decline continued until the end of the 1700s. At that time a new wave of settlers arrived. The *Baal Shem Tov* arrived in 1778. In 1837, the entire city was leveled by a powerful earthquake. The Jewish population was reduced, but at the end of the 1800s Jewish presence began to increase. The increase of Jewish population in Safed coincided with the development of the *moshavim* (small agricultural villages).

During WW I, famine and cholera devastated the Jewish community. The area became predominantly Arab. Jews and Arabs coexisted amicably until 1929 when Safed's Arabs participated in anti-Jewish riots sparked by Hajj Amin al-Husseni.

Saturday Evening: Ron Hotel

We return to the Ron Hotel after our stroll anxious to read more of the local history. We hear from outside our window and immediately down below, the musical group striking up again. The music is a combination of Israeli folk music, European Klezmer, Carlbach and Western Rock. It is too loud to try to do anything in the room. We head downstairs to the deck below. Just as we become inspired to join the group in dancing, the group disbands. The group of thirty youths immediately head for their bus under the eye of an armed youth serving as guard. They head out back to Jerusalem. We choose to have another quiet night. As we gaze out the window we see and hear the people in the streets. Shabbot is over and the everyday busy style of the city has re-emerged for another week..

September 9, Sunday Morning

> *Jerusalem Post*: (1) Gov't satisfied' at Durban Outcome Israel, (2) Bush - Arafat meeting likely this month, (3) IDF hits Tanzim base in El-Birehj, (4) Powell: Israel's use of US arms not illegal, (4) PA is a 'kingdom of terror' Sharon tells 'NY Times', (5) Jewish Museum opens in Berlin, (6) Slovaks to hold nationwide Holocaust commemoration today, (7) Christian prisoners plead innocence in Taliban court

> *L.A. Times*: (1) Divisive U.N. race talks end in accord, few satisfied with result, (2) Utah paying high price for polygamy, (3) Jewish history: a new star in Berlin [a caption of the Jewish Museum], (4) 8 Foreign aid workers attend Taliban hearing in Afghanistan "We have not converted anybody", (5) Israeli army hits offices of Arafat's Fatah party

We review and discuss the news of the day and hope that something good might come of the meeting between Peres and Arafat, but agree that because of the continued violence, it is unlikely that such a meeting will even occur. We are reassured that parts of the European community still memorializes the holocaust. Here, among the Arab population there continues to be much discounting of the significance of the Second World War and a denial that a holocaust resulting in the killing of Jews even took place in Europe during the war. This attitude is reflected in the rhetoric of the Arab media. We take note that the Taliban government, through their courts, are taking aggressive steps towards Christians, especially Evangelists and wonder what this kind of approach will lead to.

The Ancient Cemetery of Safed

Driving through the older parts of Safed and on top of the ridge we see overlooking the area to the west, immediately below, is a large expanse of downhill slopes. All is the ancient cemetery. The site is huge. The dimension is greater than of the Mount of Olives in Jerusalem, and larger than that of any cemetery we have seen including Mt. Sinai, Forest Lawn, Edan and others in the Los Angeles area. It covers the entire hill to the west side of the old city down to the floor of the canyon. From on high is an elevated white walkway so one can readily traverse the hilly area and avoid contact with the ground. We later approach the site from across the canyon and overlook the site. Despite the size, very little seems known about the dates and who lies below the turf. That Jews are buried there is not an issue, but at the moment, the cemetery does not seem to hold much immediate promise for determining the years of the Jewish presence.

Beit Heimari (The Hameiri House)

The *Beit Heimar* is a restored household of an observant family typical of the late 1800's, lying in the heart of a former neighborhood of the mystics. From the house are views of the ancient and contemporary cemeteries. The museum is a typical house of the late 1800s, furnished as such with the everyday appliances and artifacts of the period. The building was originally established in 1517 by Jews exiled from Spain. In the 1500s it served as a center for the activities of the Kabbalists. In the earthquakes of 1759 and 1837, the building was partially destroyed. The chief Sephardic Rabbinate and the Sephardic Court of Law were situated in this house during the years preceding the First World War. The first school in which the language of instruction was Hebrew was situated on the top floor. During the Arab riots of 1929 and 1936-1939, parts of the building were burned. The occupants were killed and the building was abandoned and destroyed. The building was restored during the years 1959 - 1980 and refurbished well into the museum in which it is today. The kitchen, bedrooms, and other living areas are all in decor of what may be expected of an observant Jewish family living in the1880s.

The curator happens to be there. We inquire about the nature of Jewish presence before the 1500s. She explains that there has been no attempt made yet to uncover what exists below the ground. She believes that there was indeed a Jewish presence since the days of the Second Temple, but there is little record of it in the literature. She points out the reference made by Josephus in his book, *The Jewish War,* suggesting an enduring and continuous Jewish presence in Safed.

We drive and walk around the old city discuss what we are learning, including our reading of Rosoff's book on the history of Safed struggling to find answers to our many questions on Jewish presence in Safed.

September 10, Monday, AM: Safed

The Post: (1) Five killed as terror hits nationwide, (2) PA was repeatedly asked to arrest suicide bomber, (2) 'There was utter pandemonium' (3) Rumsfeld backs Israel's retaliation, (4) Expert: Bomb wake-up call to Israeli Arabs, (5) Durban racism parley ends tumultuously, (6) Hamas: Sharon gov't to blame for terror.

L.A. Times: (1) DWP exceeded profit it reported, (2) Some Israelis hoping for a concrete line in the sand, (3) 5 killed: heavily armed man sought in Sacramento, (4) New Mideast attacks put truce talks in doubt, (6) Afghan opposition leader hurt in blast

We become disheartened as we hear of more terror attacks and wonder how it can end. We assume the Peres-Arafat meeting will not be held. We are encouraged by hearing of U.S. support from the U.S. Secretary of Defense. Hamas seems to be posturing. Perhaps what we are seeing is the vying for political recognition as leaders of a pan Arabic and Moslem cause. We are also getting more insight now as to how Israeli's must feel. As we feel! Anger, frustration and an interest in seeing something done about the security of people.

How is it that the Palestinian leadership cannot condemn suicidal behavior. Opinion surveys of Palestinians indicate support for the terror attacks and resistance to recognizing Israel?. They continue to perceive Israel as the "aggressor" and "occupier." Unfortunately, to express a public opinion in Arab

Gaza to the contrary, especially if it were in print, would likely lead to big trouble to the author as well as their relatives. Much of the motivation on the part of the attackers lie in the prevalent precept that by defending Islam, regardless if they are victorious or be they slain, because they fought the occupiers and aggressors, are assured an enriched existence in the life hereafter. That funds are available to family survivors of the "martyrs" provides a secondary gain that exacerbates the matter. These matters are taken up in Part II, Chapter 16 on the *Qu'ran* and Chapter 22, on motives behind the suicide attacks.

11:30 AM: Meron

Before heading to the Sea of Galilee, we decide to turn westward to look at the town of Meron and the adjacent area. Meron seems like a typical very small rural town. Mt. Meron stands nearby at 4,205 feet. On the way up is the tomb of Rabbi Simon bar Yo who hid in Piki'in for 13 year while contributing to the lore of the Zohar by starting the oral tradtion.[12] Among the great sages buried are are Hillel and Shamai. Further up Mt Meron are the remains of one of the oldest Galilean synagogues, dating from the end of the Second Temple period.

We stop at a reforestation project of which part of it is developed for a picnic area. Here we stop at a table and fire spit and eat our picnic lunch in the shade of some conifers that were planted as a project from a town in Canada. The trees are doing well. After a rest bit of sorts, we head towards the Galilee.

12 Noon: The Plateau between Safed and Mount Meron

We see a dirt road heading south on the hill-top adjacent to the ancient cemetery where we overlook the city of Safed–now from the east. The area has a maze of dirt roads meandering through the lightly forested mesa or plateau. There are ancient looking remains of walls that might be a form of fortification in a past era. The area may have been strategic serving as a barrier between the Crusader influence on the coast and the Moslem culture to the east. Better they

---

12

The Zohar is a book of mystical writings compiled in the 13th Century. Credit for writing the book is generally attributed to R. Moses de Leon (1240-1305) while he resided in Guadalajara (Eban, 1984).

fight here than in the cities. But now it looks like there may be an attempt to develop the area. If so, it would be in a pleasant pine forested setting between the Galilee and the northern Israeli coastal plain.

We know of no safe way to reach Safed by this dirt road in this rented car. We head back to the Highway and continue eastward to the Sea of Galilee. On the way, now heading eastbound, we see more signs indicating tombs and archaeological sites. But they are either poorly marked or posted with signs in Hebrew that we cannot read. We search out one or two, but quickly give up because of the condition of the dirt roads. Besides, there is the prevalent feeling that it is not smart to leave the roads in areas off the beaten track.

September 10, 2:00 PM, Ami'ad Kibbutz

Driving eastward, we pass the turnoff to Safed, continue down the mountain and soon reach the narrow plain adjoining the banks of the Sea of Galilee. We stop in at Joseph's Well Bed and Breakfast Motel at the Ami'ad Kibbbutz. We arrange accommodations for the next day or so. This classical kibbutz developed in 1947. Much of its early character remains. The community has been modernized over the years to keep up with the times. As such it maintains the flavor of the past with the convenience of the present. It is largely agricultural, but there is a plant that produces large filters. There is a dairy, horses and other livestock throughout the area among various varieties of crops and orchards including a vineyard. They grow fruit and grapes, produce and bottle their own brand of wines and liqueurs. The Ami'ad Kibbutz has its own elementary and secondary school with a host of recreational facilities including swimming pool, tennis courts and soccer field. There is a large dining room as well as a small general store that has hardware, groceries including fresh produce and a variety of fresh bakery goods. Though more is to see here, we are anxious to drive on to Tiberias in hopes of seeking more information on the continuous Jewish presence throughout *Eretz Yisrael*.

Tiberias

We drive the few miles along the west shore of the Sea of Galilee to Tiberias, then wander through the congested downtown area trying to get a grip on how to find information on key historical sites that might reveal a Jewish presence. A check into a few stores downtown finds no tourist literature available. We head for the Holiday Inn, where I get some help from the lady running the gift shop. She advises me how to get to the Information Center. There, we are fortunate in that we meet with the manager who introduces herself as K'trina. She is conversant in English and understanding of our quest.

K'trina indicates she has always believed that Jews were continuously living in the Tiberias area since it's construction by the Romans. She explains that the city of Tiberius "was moved" by the Crusaders to its present place in approximately 1,000. She arranges for us to meet tomorrow with a local gentleman who is well informed on the matter of Jewish history in the area, a retired fellow from Mogen David services who is currently studying to become a tour guide, an accomplishment in Israel. We will meet with him tomorrow here in Tiberias at the visitors center. We return to the bed and breakfast facility, Joseph's Well, in the Amiad Kibbutz. It is a pleasing compact apartment with an inside/outdoor kitchen facility.

Chapter 12
Tiberias and Ami'ad

September 11, Tuesday AM: The Ami'ad Kibbutz

A leisurely breakfast is provided in the large kibbutz dining room. The food is presented cafeteria and buffet style, moderate, but ample with a variety of choices of fish, pastry, eggs and drinks. All seems fresh and Kosher. Residents, staff, and uniformed soldiers are sitting around a number of small clothed tables. The conversation, all in Hebrew, is subdued and task oriented. The mood is relaxed. Apparently the only tourists, we catch occasional glances.

Jerusalem Post: (1) IDF says ready to strike Jenin, (2) Peres - Arafat meeting may be spoiled, (2) Government must support Nahariya suicide bomber's widows, orphans, (3) US and British planes strike Iraq, (4) Turkey: We want to improve ties with Israel, (5), Parley to fight 'new anti-Semitism', (6) Suicide bomber kills two in Istanbul, (7) Traffic congestion - above Tel Aviv - hang gliders.

L.A. Times: (1) Stock markets around world take a beating,
(2) Many security guards get minimal screening, (2) Key foe of Taliban is dead (3) Israeli Arab's set off shock waves, (4) Economists warn against new tax cuts, (6) Existing gun laws fail to halt those intent on killing

Skynews is aired on the television. United States and British planes have been reported to attack Iraq and a report of readiness for an IDF attack in Jenin. We hope the war will wait until we get back home. Our flight is scheduled to leave September 13, Thursday evening. There are signs of a military build-up here as officers and enlisted men share the facilities here. It strikes us as odd that Israel has welfare laws that provide support for the widows and orphans of suicide bombers. I suppose we, in the U.S., at least in California, have welfare programs that support families of perpetrators of crimes as well. But surviving families of the perpetrators here in Israel are provided stipends from the PA and nearby Arab countries including Iraq and Saudi Arabia. In regards to the attack in Istanbul, we are concerned that such acts may become contagious. We are getting a glimpse of the motives of individuals that use their bodies as a weapon carrier leading to the death of others and themselves. An Islamic leader condemned the attack. We wonder what the text of his speech looks like when directly translated from the Arabic. But such matters continue to allude interest in the media.

The "Old City" of Tiberias

We head out for Tiberias again. As we drive south towards Tiberias we become increasingly hopeful that today we may conclude that *Eretz Yisrael* has had a continuous Jewish presence. We are hopeful we may find the answer in the old city. At about the same moment, we pass the Sheraton Hotel on the banks of the Sea of Galilee, we note the flags of several countries waving about from the upper decks. Included among the nations friendly to Israel is the American flag waving as proudly as the others.

We follow the lead offered by K'trina, the manager of the Visitors Center. We drive up through narrow paved roads that soon become dirt roads meandering in different directions through the slopes of the barren hills just south of Tiberias where we were told the old city was established. It was in this area that it is believed that most of the Jerusalem Talmud was compiled, in the second half of the 300s. We see an area between two dry stream beds lying in an area that could likely have been a source of water for the abandoned city. We see an ancient wall by the stream bed as if forming a viaduct. Maybe a water source had dried up and led to the abandonment of this area of the old city. We envision what the old city might have looked like.

There are but little clues as to the grandness of that which was once here. The earth around the immediate area and to the northwest is slightly discolored suggesting ancient sites are below the surface. Up on the ridge, a couple hundred feet higher lies a section of Tiberias that is currently being developed. Along side of the ridge is a row of recently built residential facilities. We wander about driving up and down the hills, through paved and dirt roads that come to a sudden end. No other man made structures can be seen other than the wall.

Back at the Visitors Center we chat with the guide for about half an hour. He answers some of our questions, as does K'trina, the manager of the museum and Visitors Center. We learn from them, as well as by Hellander et. al. (1999) that the city reached a population of around 400,000 swollen by the northward movement of Jews following the Bar Kochba Revolt in Judea, in the south, during 135-137. The majority residing in old Tiberias were Jews. We are quite impressed with the figure given; such a population makes the old city larger and perhaps more significant than that of the city today.

We visit and walk through the remains unearthed adjacent to the Center. Here, near the center of Tiberias is an archaeological garden with a synagogue, an amphitheater, walkways and structures nearby, perhaps for home dwellers. The inscription on the plaque reads;

The city of Tiberias, named after the Roman Emperor Tiberias, was founded in the year of 20 C.E. by Herod Antipas, the son of Herod the Great. At the end of the second century CE, Tiberius became the spiritual capital of the Jewish People, both in Eretz Ysrael and in the Diaspora and the city became the seat of institutions of Jewish leadership, first the *Sanhedrin*, and then the Patriarcate (Neshia). According to tradition the greater part of the Jerusalem Talmud was codified in the city. Jewish institutions continued to function in Tiberias long after the Arab conquest (635 CE), until the 10th century CE. The method of Hebrew vocalization in use to the present day is named the Tiberian vocalization.

During the period of Moslem rule, Tiberias suffered several earthquakes. The most severe in 749 and 1033. During the Crusader period (1099-1247), Tiberias became the capital of the Galilee Principality. Benjamin of Tudela, in 1170, reported sizable Jewish communities in Tiberias and Safed, as well as to the west on the coast, in Tyre, Acre and Caesarea.

The archaeological gardens contain remnants of structures that cover the time period between the Roman and Ottoman Turk occupations. Jews and Samaritans were in majority. There were comparatively few Christians in Palestine. In the 300s there were 25 Christian congregations, small and almost all in the coastal or Judean towns. According to Horsely (1995), no evidence has been found of anything in the area that could be called Christianity before the time of Constantine. According to Ben Gurion (1974) both leaders of the Byzantine government and church were amazed at their failure to Christianize the land.

According to Meyers (1999) there was a sharp borderline between Jewish and Christian communities in the Galilee area. The hills along Sephorus formed a kind of barrier to the eastward limits to the appearances of churches. East of an imaginary line stretching from Fassuta in the north to Baqa in the center to Rama in the Beit Kerem Valley, not one church had been identified; however, thirty one or more synagogues had been identified. None of these synagogues have any decoration resembling a cross. West of the line, the remains of more than fifty churches and monasteries were identified being associated with the Byzantine period.

When the Persians invaded Palestine in the 600s, large numbers of Jews joined their ranks, largely from the Galilean hills - from the neighborhoods of Nazareth and Tiberias. In the 400s a Jewish majority still persisted in Galilee. During the 800s there was considerable writing coming from the area. Rabbi Ben Asher of Tiberias was active in the late 800s working on his book on Hebrew grammar (Ben-Gurion, 1974). Persia's pact was short-lived. Persian rule lasted only 14 years. Prior to the Crusaders the first center of Jewish autonomy was at Tiberias. In later periods the Jewish center moved to Ramleh and to Haifa. With the Crusader conquest of Jerusalem in 1099 to the fall of Acre to the Mamluk occupation in 1291 there were battles, raids and invasions throughout Palestine. In the northern part of Eretz Ysrael, in Samaria, the Gallilee and in the Golan, it was somewhat better for Jews and Moslems. Though there were persecutions and emigration in these areas, there apparently were no massacres (Ben Gurion, 1974).

Immediately following Saladin's defeat of the united Christian army and conquest of Jerusalem in 1187, Jewish revival ensued throughout all of Palestine. According to Ben Gurion (1977), from contemporary letters and travelogues there appeared to be fifteen Jewish communities: Mitzpeh, Lydda, Ramleh, Hebron, Gaza, Beit She', Gush Halav, and Safed. There were also a few Jewish communities in what is now Jordan (Badruh, Ajlun and Malka). As pointed out earlier, Jerusalem at the time had 250 families and in Kfar Kana, near Nazareth, there were about 70 householders. Very little seems known about the population of Tiberias at the time. Apparently, the overall population dwindled, but Jewish life persisted in the area, including Tiberias.

According to Israelowitz (1996) Tiberias laid in waste until Sultan Suleiman gave the city to Don Joseph Nasi and his mother-in-law, Dona Gracia, in the 1500s. They restored the Jewish community, introduced industry, and Tiberias flourished for a hundred years until devastated by an earthquake. It is recorded that Rabbi Horowits had fled from Jerusalem to Tiberias in 1624 to escape persecution, staying in Tiberias til his death in 1628. Earthquakes in the immediate area in 1660 resulted in the destruction of the entire city. Tiberias laid in ruin for the next 80 years.

Abulafia, rabbi of Izmir, from Damascus reached Tiberias in 1740 (Ben-Sasson, 1976). Under the patronage of the governor of Galilee (Avi-Yonah, 2001), he facilitated the construction of bath houses, shops for market days, and presses for sesame oil. Roads and walls around the Jewish quarter were built as were houses and courtyards for the Jews, and a synagogue more beautiful than any existing in the land (Ben-Gurion, 1966).

Tiberias flourished in the 1700s under the rule of Omar. The area was resettled by a group of Chassidic Jews and since then it has, with little interruption, thrived and grown into a prosperous town. In 1844 there were 50 Ashkenazaic and 80 Sephardic families, about 148 Jews. In 1887 there were 2035 Jews, and in 1895, 3,200 Jews. The Turkish census in 1911 recorded 3,389 Jews of Ottoman nationality. Today, Tiberias is Israel's most popular northern holiday resort city.

September 11, 3:00 PM: Driving Back to Joseph's Well Kibbutz

I am keen on getting more into the records and to confirm the matter of continuous Jewish presence in The Land of Israel. We agree that it would be interesting and certainly worthwhile to visit Peki'in and the Haifa area. There are a number of sites in the Haifa the area pertinent to the historical presence of Jews in the area. These include:

(1) the site of Megiddo (Armageddon and Casesarea with its Herodian ruins, (2) the Haifa Museum with displays of ancient art and ethnology: The Hecht Museum, concentrating on the subject of "The People of Eretz Yisrael" Items on the lower floor are displayed in chronological order, beginning with the Chalcolithic period and ending with the Mishnaic and Talmudic era (Roman and Byzantine periods). The upper floor is is devoted to thematic displays, such as coins, seals, weights and jewelry, (3) the Israel Edible Oil Museum, featuring 5,000 years of edible oil production, (4) Elijah's Cave, a place of pilgrimage for Jews, Moslems and Christians alike, (5) , the Beit HaGefen Arab-Jewish Center, the Railway Museum featuring collections of artifacts associated with early rail transportation in the area, (6) The Clandestine Immigration and Navy Museum featuring the history of attempts of Jews to infiltrate the British blockade of the

1930s and 1940s, (7) the National Maritime Museum, dealing with the history of shipping in the Mediterranean, (8) A museum associated with Haifa University that features a collection of artifacts relating to Jewish history before the Diaspora, and (9) Carmel National Park, covering the scenic slopes of Mt. Carmel, renowned for its vineyards during ancient times.

Haifa is Israel's third largest city with a population 262,600. According to Israelowitz (1996), Haifa had well established Jewish communities in the 3rd century and the name, according to Hellender (1999) began to appear in Talmudic literature. By the 11th century Haifa was a thriving Jewish center. In 1100, Jews joined their Moslem neighbors in an unsuccessful attempt to thwart a Crusader attack. Following its capture, the town declined and in the 18th-century the local ruler, Dahr El-Omar, demolished and then rebuilt the town with new fortifications. Nearby Acre superceded the town in importance. At the time of the Ottoman conquest of Palestine, Haifa was still an insignificant village. By the early 19th century, Haifa's Jewish community had begun to increase. With the growth of immigrants, the town expanded. During the early 1900's the population was 10,000. The modern revival got under way with the construction of the Hjejaz railway

Table 8
Jewish Presence in the Galilee

Year	Safad Area	Tiberias Area	Comment
C.E.			
	Trace*	0	
100s	Trace	100,000	
200s	Trace	300,000	
300s	?	300,000	
400s	?	300,000	
500s	?	100,000	
600s	?	100,000	
700s	?	75,000	Earthquake 749
800s	?	50,000	
900s	?	50,000	
1000s	?	20,000	Earthquake 1033
1100s	200	1,000	
1200s	200	Trace	
1300s	200	Trace	
1400s	1,000	Trace	
1500s	10,000	1,000	
1600s	30,000	500	Earthquake 1660
1700s	1,000	2,000	Vacant 80 Yrs
1800s	2,000	2,500	
1850s	2,000	3,200	
1900s	8,000	3,200	
2000	24,000	45,000	

between Damascus and Medina in 1905 and the later development of lines to Akko and the south country. Land was reclaimed from the sea to create an area of offices and warehouses. Haifa rapidly became a shipping base, naval center and oil terminal while part of the British Mandate.

The first priority though is to first drop by Pek'in and see what we can learn there of Jewish presence. Whatever time we have left before flying back home can then be spent on selecting and visiting a few of the above sites in the Haifa area and be at the airport the following day for our return flight home.

Chapter 13

The Attack on New York and Washington, DC

September 12, 4:00 PM: The Attack on New York

Back at the Amiad Kibbutz, and confident after our visit to Tiberias that we had found an important missing piece in our puzzle, we are anxious to settle down and leisurely relate our experiences and what we had learned from the ancient sites and from our discussions with the people at the Visitor Center. We settle down for an outdoor picnic meal on the picnic table outside our suite. I tell Hannah that while in the Kibbutz store, I had noticed on the small TV (in Hebrew) that there seems to be some kind of incident in the U.S., but couldn't make out what had happened. It seemed like there was an incident involving a restaurant and parking lot in an American city. The few people in the store were too preoccupied with their purchasing to view the screen. We discuss our plans for tomorrow. We will leave for Peki'in, a village to the west of Safed, on our way to Haifa, where there is evidence that Jews may have lived continuously at this place since the time of the Second Temple (Sa'ar, 1997).[13]

Before dusk, three senior uniformed Israeli officers, walk by us, in tandem order, each with a cellular phone. Without changing their gait, they each glance over at us with controlled tense affect. I sense something is up! About ten minutes later as we finish supper outside on the picnic table outside our room, a guest from the suite next door tells us that we should watch T.V. We turn on the set and find the New York attack is fully covered by all news channels.

We're stunned; a feeling of estrangement from the television set, as if this can't be true what we are now seeing live. We watch the account on the catastrophe enfold through British Skynews and CNN through the night until we can no longer stay awake.

---

[13]Sa'ar (1997) includes a photographic study by Doron Horowitz of the habits of current villagers amidst the relics and excavations revealing the various periods of habitation since the days of Roman occupation. According to Sa'ar, 76% of Peki'in's residents at the time of their visit were Druze, the rest mostly Christians. They found three Jewish Families.

September 12, Wednesday AM: Ami'ad Kibbutz

By watching television we had become aware of most of the details reported on the front page and leading stories in the *Post*. The Jerusalem Post will not be available to us until later in the day upon reaching Tel Aviv. The front page and leading stories are placed here.

> *Jerusalem Post (9/12/01):* (1) America Under Attack: Thousand die as two hijacked planes destroy World Trade Center, (2) Pentagon also hit by seized plane, (3) Sharon declares day of mourning, (4) Nightmare scene in lower Manhattan, (5) 'Now I know how the Israelis feel' (6) Sharon weighing response to attacks, (7) Israel closes air space following US terror attacks, (8) Arafat 'horrified' but Palestinians celebrate, (9) Air travel worldwide disrupted after US attack (10) Gunmen kill two border policemen, (11 IDF tanks ring Jenin, a 'center of terrorist activity', (12) Katsov expresses nation's sorrow, (13) What's yellow, a herb and a spice? Mustard.

> *L.A. Times* (9/12/01): (1) Terrorists attack New York, Pentagon: thousands dead, injured as hijacked U.S. airliners ram targets; World Trade Towers brought down, (2) In New York, a day of fire and fear, (3) A chilling voice from the sky: 'Our plane is being hijacked', (4) Real test for Bush in weeks to come, (5) large holes in U.S. security], (5) World leaders condemn 'new evil', (6) Bin Laden tops list of suspects, (7) Blasts in north of Afghan capital, (8) Shock waves echo for Arabs and Israelis: Palestinians at Shatila refugee camp near Beirut celebrate, (9) Retaliation rife with risks, hard choices, (10 Once a military fortress [The Pentagon], (11) All airline flights in U.S. grounded, (12) Muslims in southland brace for retaliation, (13) Israeli tanks ring Jenin; truce talks called off, (14) Baghdad says it downed another spy plane

I am awoken by the sound of low flying aircraft. It does not help matters to hear and see low flying single engine piston military planes and helicopters overhead. All are flying in the direction to nearby Lebanon and Syria. I realize all military presence here is gone. I wonder what may be happening nearby to the north. But we continue to feel overwhelmed with thoughts and feelings of the horror in New York. Suddenly, nothing seems more important than finding out what had happened and what other calamities might be occurring throughout the United States.

On our way to the dining room, we first walk through the motel area. All is quiet without any of the military presence that we saw yesterday. Yesterday there were a number of military personnel staying in nearby rooms. There is not a soldier to be seen. Unlike yesterday, the dining room staff are tense and tired as we are -- from staying up late and watching the terrifying news of the terrorist attacks on the U.S.A. There are no newspapers; no one is reading. Whatever conversation is going on is muted. Whereas yesterday, there was air of pleasantry and a buzz of conversation, the air seems stifled and the mood is disheartening. It is too shocking and there are too many things to think about, including what may happen right here close to the Lebanese and Syrian borders and of the soldiers that have been pulled out.

The reaction of the residents of the area seems to be of reserved shock. It is as if it happened to their cousin country. Indeed, many people have friends or relatives in the United States. As we are readily identified as Americans, people offer their quiet sympathy. Words are too hard to come by. The manager of the guest rooms tells us we are welcome to stay as long as we wish without cost. She offers us her telephone for our use. With the kind help from the manager, we get a call out to our son, Joel in San Diego. We express our gratitude to the manager. She simply nods her head and offers a sympathetic smile. Without conferring with one another, we thank her for her concern, but tell her we will leave this morning for Tel Aviv where we hope to ascertain our chances for boarding a flight home or perhaps to Europe.

September 12, Wednesday, Early Afternoon: Haifa and the North Israeli Coast:

We leave Amiad and Tiberias, heading west on Highway 65 to Haifa. We soon pass two military convoys, one sitting, the other speeding eastward, both in jeep-like vehicles with disciplined armed troops with combat banners waving in the slipstream. In contrast to the military action, we note an occasional person *dovening,* reciting classical prayers, at ancient sites along the way. Soon, we pass through the foothills and enter the more distant environs of Haifa. We head straight for Akko, avoiding what appears a shortcut directly to Haifa. We learn later, there was a drive-by killing at this intersection a bit later in the day. We try to pick up information on the radio, but it is all in Hebrew. There is talk of the attack in America as well as some terrorist killings in our vicinity.

I also learn of another drive by shooting resulting in a fatality on highway 90 about the time we passed on our way north to the Galilee.

Driving through Haifa, the radio provides news of the attacks in the United States. All is in Hebrew. Anxious to have clarification of the situation and be closer to the airport, we choose not to stop and visit Haifa. Tel Aviv offers a better opportunity to communicate with El Al Airlines and be prepared for an immediate flight at nearby Ben Gurion Airport should one arise.

Traffic is intense through the area. There are occasional stoppages on both sides of the divided highway. Most of them are on the opposite lanes. We find out later, that the drive by shooting from one car to another was near here occurring on the northbound side. Is this the way some Arabs celebrate the attack? If only we can understand the spoken Hebrew.

The Haifa area is large and diverse. There seems to be a large residential area on the hill forming a peninsula overlooking the Mediterranean to the west and the Haifa bay to the northwest. Here is a combination of residential, business, commercial areas with a rich agricultural district to the east and north of the developed city area. The growing populated area has almost replaced the agriculture along the coast line north from the Haifa peninsula to Akko, about ten miles to the north. We eventually pass through the congested center of the city, the seafaring centers, continue on the semi-freeway around the hilly peninsula protruding into the Mediterranean and soon find ourselves breaking out of traffic heading south along the coast by sand dunes as we approach the ancient city of Caesaria.

We stop at a service station center just north of Tel Aviv to have a needed snack. The mood of the people about is somber as reflected by their quiet speech and lack of affect as Israelis go about their business of ordering food and talking to one another. Many are reading one of the many newspapers strewn about the restaurant. The visible front page headlines, in Hebrew with images referring to the attack on the United States. The mood, the tenseness and lack of the usual buzz of the Israelis makes it more imperative to read informational material we can more readily understand.[14]

---

[14] We were not able to purchase the paper until after arriving in Tel Aviv, and then only after a search for a news stand. Any news in English captured our attention, not only because of being able to read and understand the events, but also because it gave us an anchor of opportunity to relate to one another of the terrible events.

Wednesday, 3:00 PM: Tel Aviv

The news on the radio remains quite terse. We can barely understand the gist of it all. Though almost twenty four hours had passed since the attacks in the United States we know very little beyond what we saw and heard this morning at Amiad on television. Our immediate problem is to find a place to rest, to get some information on the significance of the events and determine if it is possible to get across the Mediterranean or Atlantic.

We opt for the Hilton in Tel Aviv with the understanding they have a small El Al office in the hotel as well as an El Al baggage check-in service just outside the front door of the hotel. We arrive at the hotel in mid afternoon. We check in and request a day room with an overnight option so as to have the security of a place to rest. The atmosphere here at the hotel, here in the midst of the largest city in Israel, is as if the country may be on the verge of a general mobilization. At times we feel we have answers before we can think of the many questions that arise.

We find out from the El Al baggage check-in people that they cannot help us in processing our baggage for a flight out of Israel. Though scheduled to be open, we are surprised to find the main El Al office in the hotel closed. We are at a loss as to what to do at this time. We decide to stay overnight, take a needed opportunity to rest and watch the news on television, buy a newspaper. and by doing so, we hope to obtain some information on the limits of transportation out of the country one way or another.

September 13, Thursday AM: Downtown Tel Aviv

Before breakfast I stroll the streets inquiring as to the availability of an English newspaper. Eventually, I find the *Jerusalem Post* at a small grocery store on Ben Yehuda Street. The paper is now a day old.

Here we are in Tel Aviv. Though in a resort hotel, we are not able to feel comfortable. We walk a mile through busy of Tel Aviv to the El Al office. We learn, that should a flight open up, our ticket will be considered valid. As of now, all flights across the Atlantic have been grounded, anywhere to North or South America.

Having spent the last few days in the relative quiet parts of Israel, we become irritated by the sounds of the city. We start to think we can be anywhere in Israel. Where might we choose to spend the next Sabbath? Though intrigued with the hustle and bustle of downtown Tel Aviv, and though we stop for a moment to have a submarine sandwich from *Subway*, we are not in the mood to appreciate this largest of Jewish cities. We realize that we wish to be in the Jewish Quarter of the Old City of Jerusalem. Upon returning to the hotel, I am relieved to find today's issues of the *Post* had just arrived at the hotel and were still on the floor by the news stand and gift shop. We review the news in the room and downstairs over breakfast.

> *Jerusalem Post*: (1) Bush clams 'acts of war,' (2) Bin Laden seen prime suspect; White House may have been target, (3) Woman slain in drive-by shooting: 10 Palestinians killed in clashes, (4) Powell urges renewed Mideast peace efforts, (5) US intelligence's day of reckoning, (6) Massive search in New York locates 1,000 missing Israelis, (7) Israel's war is no longer its alone, (8) Saddam says America is harvesting its thorns, (9) Country mourns with Americans, (10) Blood for America [photo of Arafat giving blood], (11) Air traffic outside U.S. slowly returning to normal , (12) Toronto Jews welcome El AL passengers, (13) Canceled flights wreak havoc with holiday travel, (14) NATO, US military tighten security across the Balkans, (15) Bin Laden's link to the Palestinians widening, (16) Iranian media blame US-Israeli ties for attacks, (17) Iraqi media hail attack on 'American cowboy', (18) New US stance on Mideast seen likely, (19) Horror hits world financial centers

> *L.A. Times*: (1) 'Act of War': Bush says 'Good will Prevail' (2) Some Attackers Trained as Pilots in U.S., (3) Investigators Identify 50 terrorists tied to plot, (4) America: stunned, saddened and now ready for revenge, (5) 'Normal' travel not on horizon, (6) Travelers scramble for alternatives to flying, (7) Tragedy affects many lives in myriad of ways, (8) New York: frustrating search for tower survivors, (9) Hijackers likely took flight classes in U.S. (10) U.S. moves fast to form anti-terror coalition, (11) Europeans show solidarity with the U.S., but fear their cities will becomebattlegrounds, (12) Travelers at Israeli airport scrutinized, (13) Probes found breaches in security, (14) Israelis kill 7 in West Bank actions.

Part of getting on in age is being able to recall events that to others are part of a "historical" recorded past. Recalling important events of the past helps to anchor the significance of current events. The knowledge lends more depth to the understanding of its importance, but the knowledge itself does not ease the digestion of the facts.

Hannah and I recall the reporting of such events as they occurred in our lifetime. We recall experiencing the news of the Japanese naval air assault on Pearl Harbor, the London Blitz, the tremendous losses during the battle for Stalingrad, bombardments in Europe and the destruction of cities in Germany and Japan. These events were making headlines in newspapers I was selling on street corners. The contemporary depictions by *Movietown News* in our local theaters broke the fantasy of the comedies and adventures. We remember how we heard of news of the extent of the European holocaust following the occupation of Germany. Then the extent of the horror on islands nearest to Japan, the Kamikase attacks on our Pacific Fleet and the after-effects of the atomic bombing of Hiroshima and Nagasaki. This attack on the twin towers exacts a recall of much of the horror that has occurred in our lifetime.

We walk back and readily check out of the hotel. In so doing we now learn from the hotel clerk that the airport is "open and guests had begun flying." On the way to Jerusalem, we stop at Ben Gurion Airport to follow up on matters and to try to differentiate facts from rumors about flying home across the Atlantic.

11:00 AM: Ben Gurion Airport

We are more familiar with the layout of the airport as we had spent much time here waiting for flights. We go to the area where passengers bound for the New World depart. Eerie! No one is in the large cavernous space that usually is reserved for crowds awaiting flights to the Americas. The other side of the departure area are filled for people leaving for Asia, Africa, and Europe; it was bustling with a busy but normal look to the activity. Flights are indeed leaving for all parts of the former Soviet Union, South Africa, London, Amsterdam, and other cities in Europe. We find lines for information are heavily packed with little information nor support being offered from the beleaguered airport staff. The emphasis is apparently on security at the expense of airline passenger service.

Getting any accurate information proves to be aggravating. The person in front of me in line was screaming, "Put me in the computer, just put me in the computer." The person behind the glass kept saying that it wouldn't do any good, and then she broke down almost crying saying that she had no money or any place to stay. The person behind the glass closed the window and led her away. I step into one of many chaotic lines where windows open and shut as exhausted staff require a break.

I explain to Hannah that the lady behind the window said that flights across the Atlantic should "likely" occur soon. And "when they do, they will honor tickets and try to seat everyone on a fill-in flights" across the Atlantic. As we anticipated from the newspaper, we learn that U.S. airspace is still closed.

What we anticipate now is the uncertainty associated with waiting. For how long? For a flight that goes somewhere in North America that might fill up while we wait to be checked in? This problem occurred during happy times last year during the visit of the Pope. We also learn that should we catch a flight to New York, or anywhere else on the east coast, even if flights were available to the west coast, a connection to a westward flight would be problematical and in any event the fare would not be covered. In other words, once we land in New York we will be on our own. We have no option but to work along with these assumption. We make arrangements with our rental car company, *Traffic*. They graciously permit us to keep the car for an indefinite period.

Tension is growing as we drive on to Jerusalem. I make a wrong turn. The signs and billboards now are in Arabic; We find ourselves on a road where there had been a recent tank fire. Now, trying to avoid being disoriented, I find an empty parking lot near the Zion Gate, an easy walking distance to the Jewish Quarter. A tall man in American cowboy boots and a white Stetson saunters up to our car. In perfect American English, he introduces himself and offers to take us to the site of the Last Supper or King David's Tomb. I ask if our car is safe in that location. He points out a video camera and indicates that the lot is monitored 24 hours a day. He leads us to the dividing line between the Armenian and Jewish Quarters. He asks us if we are familiar with the Jewish Quarter. We tell him we indeed are. He turns to leave. We thank him for guiding us and offer a tip.

The streets of the Jewish Quarter are now familiar. We wander through the narrow streets toward the square where Mama's Deli is located. As we round the corner, we see both Mama and her son, Abba, standing out on the few steps leading to the restaurant. They smile broadly in a welcome recognition. We explain that we are not able to fly home. Both in unison say, "But you are home!" In true Middle Eastern hospitality, they offer cold drinks remembering my favorite mango drink. He says, one way or another, he'll accommodate us. He and I walk over to the car. People greet this popular fellow along the way. He drives the car through the narrow streets to the restaurant. Because of the potential of bomb threat, he parks the car onto the square in front of the restaurant where, should there be an inquiry, he would vouch for the occupants. We make arrangements to spend the weekend. We soon find ourselves in a similar suite in the same complex with an option to move to another suite in a couple of days.

We sit on a bench on the square before Moma's Deli. We warm in the sun as familiar people come up and greet us. To each one we explain that we are not able to fly home. Each respond, "But you are home!" Whether it is the cold drink and warm sun, the comfort of being among friends, or the closeness of the Divine Presence; the tension leaves us. We sense a feeling of peace overcome our being.

September 14, Friday Morning

We pick up the *Post* early in the morning.

Jerusalem Post: (1) 'First war of the 21st century, (2) Gulf War-Style anti-terror coalition to include Israel, (3) Anti-Muslim backlash across US, (4) IDF strikes four West Bank towns, (4) US refusing incoming foreign flights, (5) US prepares its demands, (5) Peres, Arafat to meet despite criticism, (6) Ben Gurion Airport told: No flights to US. (7) French ambassador: Arab terror differs, (8) Hundred attend terror victim's burial [Kfar Saba].

L.A. Times: (1) U.S. Readies War Options: 'We will lead the world to victory', (2) Limited air travel resumes, (3) Wounded city endures more chaos, (4) Experts differ on peril from smoke, (5) U.S. airports cautiously open for business, only a few flights come and go, (6) Activist groups on lookout for erosion of civil liberties, (7) Military effort would be perilous, (8) Calm urged as Muslims face threats, (9) Some call for lifting of assassination ban, (10) Events will alter dynamics in Mideast

The news for the first time seems reassuring. There are no further reports of terror attacks in the United States and reports of violence thus far throughout Israel. The newspapers are full of interpretations, conjectures and much of the articles are speculative in nature. The nearest television set, it seems, is a couple blocks away at a restaurant. It is a bright and sunny day, and our mood is uplifted. There is now time to take care of a number of tasks before sundown. These tasks serve well to distract us from the catastrophes in New York, Pennsylvania and in Washington DC. While having our clothes cleaned, access to the Internet provides further details of the news. E-mail back and forth takes place with our son, Joel and a couple of friends at home.

The Jewish Quarter is as a village. The obtaining of all supplies we need for the weekend is within easy walking distance. We order prepared food from Mama's Deli. We purchase other foods that can be readily prepared in our suite. We continue to run into people with whom we had made some acquaintance. We relate our circumstances of being back in the Old City. All continue to respond to our tale, "But your are home!" It begins to feel as if we are at home. Of course, we had always felt that Jerusalem was in some sense, home; as so many times during praying we face to the east. It is a memorable part of the Passover Seder to repeat the familiar expression, "Next year in Jerusalem!"

7:00 PM: Shabbot

Following a visit to the Western Wall, we return to our room with the inviting smells of the food that we had left on a warming tray. We enjoy food and wine with each other. We hear the sounds of young people singing, clapping hands, and dancing. Immediately above our suite is a yeshiva. We sleep through it all.

September 15, Saturday AM: The Old City

The meaning of Sabbath peace is evident on the streets. There is no sign of a world crisis; there is only the sound and sights of people walking, singing, and chatting with each other. We sleep late and leisurely prepare for the day.

We have a large mid day meal with our friends. Again, the table is filled with a dozen or so people; there are children, too. Most of the people at the table live in Israel; but all are Americans by background. Another family, a rabbi with his wife and kids are also "stuck" and anxious to go home. The word now is that flights are leaving Israel for all over the world, including some limited flights to New York. Airspace throughout U.S. is still uncertain. The rabbi decides to head for the airport after Shabbot to take his chances for a flight to NYC, where he will go on to his hometown pulpit in Florida. The events of the current week are on everyone's mind. Some are philosophical; others relate the sense of being here in Old Jerusalem.

September 16, Sunday AM: Arranging the Trip Home

We wake up in the morning. As there is no *Post* published over Shabbot, some time is spent going over the details of the Friday edition of the *Jerusalem Post* in more detail.

> *L.A. Times*: (1) Congress OK's use of force, (2) Suspected hijackers: 19 had quiet lives that later shattered the world, (3) Nations' many faiths find strength as one, (4) Lengthy waits at airports, (5) Rallying in defense of Islam, (6) On the trail of Osama bin Laden, (7) Israel rejects Bush plea, cancels Arafat meeting

We need to face the world and make decisions. The paper contains obituaries of Israeli citizens who lost their lives in the World Trade Center. A small item in the paper catches our eye; "Israel is planning to distribute gas masks again." The rumor is that El Al is loading up one plane after another with people who are at the airport. While being in Jerusalem is comforting to us, our thoughts are with our sons; and it seems that the best place for us, if there is a declaration of war, is with our family. We are old enough to remember Pearl Harbor, and the next day after December 7, 1941, the way of living changed completely; there was rationing of food and gas, blackouts, air raid drills, etc. And many people we knew had already elected to enter the armed services for the 'duration'.

We pack and settle our bill at the hotel. We head for Ben Gurion on the assumption that flights may be available across the Atlantic before Rosh Hashana. We arrive at Ben Gurion, keep the car in the event that we cannot catch a flight. We discover the U.S. is permitting El Al flights to enter New York City, but the matter of flights west out of JFK is uncertain. We finally take off uneventfully about 7 PM. We break through a low cloud and see below us the Mediterranean shimmering with the last light of the day as we head northwest direct to New York.

On the airplane we read the current *Post*.

> *Jerusalem Post*: (1) Peres: nixes Arafat meeting; makes Israel seem anti-peace, (2) America mobilizes: Bush to Arabs: Choose sides, (3) Palestinian police confiscates footage at Gaza rally, (4) Over 5,500 believed dead in US attacks, (5) 2 policemen hurt in grenade attack, (6) PA: Arafat fights terror 'by resisting the occupation', (7) Israeli air security might have foiled US attacks, (8) El Al resumes flights to US, (9) Bush mourns, visits 'ground zero', (10) Taliban threatens *jihad*

> *L.A. Times*: (1) Bush warns of long war, (2) Search for suspects (3) Broad new U.S. strategy emerging to fight terror, (4) Markets get ready to open, (5) Anti-U.S. displays worry Palestinians, (6) Poll: U.S. keen to avenge attacks, (7) "War is not the answer," pacifists tell their fellow mourners, (8) Amid caution and crowds, airports struggle to recover, (9) Israel strikes Palestinian security posts

Anxious now to get to U.S. soil, I look forward to settling down, catching up on sleep and reading news directly from American local newspapers. But meanwhile, we discuss the news as it appears in today's *Post*, now on the trip home, have time to reflect a little on the news situation and the Israeli media. There seems to be a recognition that what is happening in their country nowadays is on center stage. They know that many important events coming from neighboring countries are not appearing, as perhaps they should, in the media. It is in this way, they feel, the media is highly biased, if not controlled. They know that what the Israeli leaders say, how they say it, and particularly their military stance, is a focus of international attention with a range of possible consequences. They feel they are justified for their police and military actions in response to terrorist attacks. Most Israeli's, according to surveys and what we hear from the citizenry, want a stronger, more assertive confrontation with the system that supports the violence.

Whenever their Foreign Minister takes the stage there is a holding of one's breath hoping he doesn't give away any more security. Israelis are sensitive to compromising everyday security for the sake of what "the world" may think.

Israelis are aware of how taxing it is for their nation's leaders to deal with the distortions and myths so prevalent in the world media. The article on the Palestinian Authority in today's *Post* that tells of the taking away of footag of film on a Palestinian public response to the U.S. attack serves not only to reveal the variance of attitude towards the U.S. among the Palestinians, but also of the extent of control the Palestinian Authority exert control over what news might reflect favorably or unfavorably upon themselves. Their leaders follow the results of surveys as we do. As we stated earlier, we believe the leaders that organize and control the quantity and nature of the terrorist attacks in Israel measure its impact on survey results.

We think the leaders of the terrorist organizations, Fatah, Hamas, Hezbellah, Aksa Brigade and Islamic Jihad are now carefully following world accounts of the news. These people are probably hoping that whatever bias emerges into the world media stays within Arabic circles. They are watching the impact of their deeds on newspapers throughout the world, especially in Europe and Africa and North America. Many of them must be wondering now, after the New York and Washington attacks, that should further violent acts continue, how can their nation's leadership continue to draw support from the west.

The flight itself is uneventful. Yet, we have trouble resting during the flight and find we cannot sleep enough. There is a heightened state of security among the flight staff. Several times in a row when I left the seat to go to the restroom, the staff puts on the "seat buckle" sign and directs everyone back to their seats. Complicating the matter is that once I was able to get to the restroom, the door is locked. I drew the matter to the attention of the flight crew. They tensely came to the door, knocked, then not hearing anything, hesitated, looked through a peep hole. They stuck something into the hole, opened it up, inspected the area, adjusted the "occupied" sign. Without a gesture of emotion they gestured it was OK to go in. But then, the seat belt sign went on. Oh Well!

With all that is on our minds about the attacks on New York and the Pentagon. Our emotions do not give us much rest as we make our approach to New York, now five days after the hijacking and resultant suicide bombing attacks. It is dark and the lights below become murky as we approach Queens and Brooklyn from the northeast. My seat on the starboard side does not permit a view of Manhattan, but if so, the area could not be seen through the smoky and obscured sky night sky.

September 17, 1:00 AM: New York, John F. Kennedy Airport,

We arrive somewhat after midnight, New York time. Only two planes land at this time; the other one is from Africa. A long quiet wait is required going through customs and inspectors. Unlike what we have experienced in New York, people are speaking in hushed tones; they are polite. We find that airspace across the United States has opened, but flights are uncertain, and the prices quoted for LAX had inflated to equal the amount that we paid for the entire LAX-Ben Gurion round trip.

Two flights are found to LAX on two differing airlines. We do not know if they are direct to Los Angeles. We are told they are "expected" to leave in a "few hours" at a fare of $1,300 per person. Grateful that we had made it across the Atlantic; we are zonked from an almost sleepless flight and jet lag, and though the flight was uneventful, we do not want another sleep deprived trip, nor do we wish to wait for a flight.

3:30 AM: We will drive to California

We're in no mood to wait for an uncertain, expensive flight. We're not in the mood to wait for anything. What would we do if we found the flight over booked. We weigh options. We will rent a car. We call Hertz and arrange for a shuttle to pick us up outside. We walk out to a very heavily controlled and darkened street. It is strangely quiet. We see a car with an American flag on its antenna. We first assume there must be a diplomat inside. More cars appear with American flags. We wait, then call. We wait some more. Finally, the shuttle arrives. The driver explains that the communication signals have broken down. The antennae were on top of the towers that collapsed.

Driving home

By three o'clock in the morning, we are in a rented car removing shoes from our swollen feet, loosening our clothing; so glad to leave the macabre odors, eerie atmosphere of New York and potential traffic behind. We both give of a sigh as we pull out to find our way through Brooklyn to Manhattan heading for the Washington Bridge to New Jersey. We pass a check point. We explain our intent and with a slight understanding kind of smile, we are motioned to go ahead. All streets, freeways at this hour are quiet. Most of the vehicles in the area are either taxis, trucks or emergency vehicles. None have their red lights or sirens on.

The air is still. It is clammy, damp and smoggy. Visibility in Manhattan is reduced to about two miles. We can smell the debris. We enter New Jersey. We see opposite us that incoming traffic is being diverted away from lower Manhattan. We drive on southwesterly through foggy New Jersey and on through the entire beautiful but semi-foggy route through Pennsylvania, all the time listening to the sounds of American English on local radio.

We are inspired by the various displays of patriotism along the entire trip. Everywhere along the way, it is the same. American flags are draped everywhere, on cars, signs, fences, storefronts and homes. Never before have we seen so many American flags flying. The smallest of communities have flags waving in the breeze. Cars and trucks are adorned with flags. Flags were on the tops of cranes and silos. There are patriotic inscriptions posted all over along the freeway and byways. Talk shows and commentators are talking about their impressions of what happened and speculations on the "why and how" the perpetrators had done their deed.

We agree that the leaders and instigators of the hijacking and subsequent suicidal attacks on Washington and New York are having some second thoughts. We see on the front page of local newspapers of a pulling togther of American resources and hear the rhetoric of the might to fight terrorism. We hear from the President, of a plan for "Infinite Justice." to repel the "attackers of freedom." We recall the days following the seventh of December, 1941 Pearl Harbor attacks. We recall after the war reading about what Admiral Yamamoto's response of reporting on the success of the Japanese attack on Hawaii, as saying, "I fear we have woken up a sleeping giant."[15]

When the sun comes up we find we are in Pennsylvania. We stop at a truck stop for gas and refreshments. I purchase a road atlas and spread it out on a counter. A lady truck driver inquires where we are heading. To "L.A.!" There is interest as everyone is standing around. A couple of people offer best routes to take, and very supportive of not flying. A charity box lies next to the

---

[15]From east of the city of Lihouie, on the Island of Kauai, we saw from out hotel window looking upon the ridge paralleling the coast, a lengthy formation, a couple miles long, resembling a man sleeping on his back.

cash register, requesting funds to support the victims of September 11th. We are to observe the same request for funds all the way to California.

We find a sophisticated, well stocked supermarket in western Pennsylvania. We fill our ice chest with produce and drinks. We are able to purchase a number of items with symbols indicating they are kosher. We find a motel and fall asleep long before the sun goes down, The New Year of 5762, Rosh Hashanah is greeted in this way in Youngstown, Ohio.

A few days later we visit Hannah's brother Phil and sister-in-law, Elsie in their beautiful rural home in the outskirts of McAllester, Oklahoma. Two days later, we spend an afternoon with Hannah's friend Rosalie in Albuquerque. Talk centers on the significance of the attacks in the east. There is a sense of a common consciousness, despite where we were at the time, of the happenings and significance of the attack in New York.

Following a pleasant evening in the mountains near Flagstaff we arrive home in Los Angeles in time for Yom Kippur services with our Bel Air Chabad group.

Chapter 14
Jewish Presence in Palestine

Overview

That we have concluded that Jews have lived continuously in Eretz Yisrael for over 3,200 years to the present day, for some readers may not be as important as to how we approached the problem and went about reaching such a conclusion. The reader may refer to the Appendix, "Our Sources for Inferring Jewish Presence" for an outline of our sources of information and our methods.

Anyone having the interest in a fun week of travel in Israel, can determine for oneself the evidence and details of the continual Jewish presence. We are not the first, nor will we be the last to ponder the events and the role that Jews have had in this small corner of the world. Abba Eben, in *Land of Our Heritage* (1984) wrote,

> A thin but crucial line of continuity had been maintained by small communities and academies in Jerusalem, Safed, Jaffa and Hebron.... "Palestine never became the birthplace of any other nation. Every one of its conquerors had his original home elsewhere."

Some Key Points

1. Durant (1935) reviewed the history of civilizations in the Middle East, a landmark of study to that time. Though he described the ways of civilization throughout the eastern Mediterranean and eastward, including the Jewish presence, the classic textbook like others before and after, stop coverage in the Land of Israel beyond the time of Jesus and the Roman occupations.

2. A recent discovery of evidence of a population just before Jewish settlement in the area was that of the Philistines, a tribe allied to the Phoenicians who inhabited the southern coast of Palestine. They were spread over what is now Lebanon, Jordan, Crete and other Mediterranean islands. Very recent finds of

religious vessels near Tel Aviv by Israeli archaeologists (Kletter, 2002), date back to the 9th and 10th Century, BCE. Little is known about the Philistines because they left no written history. Records of neolithic times in Palestine are well exhibited in the Israel Museum in Jerusalem.

3. Several investigators, such as McEvedy, Jones and Burchardt (1978) have offered estimates of world population over the last few thousand years. These studies are important to understanding population changes and growth in relationship to resources throughout the world. For us, they offer a perspective of the general population throughout the world for the last two thousand years and serves as a basis of comparison to our population estimates in Eretz Yisrael.

A. The western world population in ancient days was remarkably smaller in number of people. Jews made up a higher proportion, especially during the first 2,500 years of Jewish history, especially in the Middle East and parts of Europe. At the start of the common era, Arabia contained but 2.0 million people. The entire Balkans, 4.5 million. Spain contained 4.5 million and France 5.0 million (Burchardt, 1992).

B. Population in much of the world had subsequently had grown disproportionately. By the 1500's Spain had grown to 6.5 million and Italy to 10 million. Yet, Arabia and the Balkans were still at 4.5 million. Five censuses were taken in Palestine between the year 1525-1573. The population had risen to about 0.3 million, mostly Moslems (Avi-Yonah, 2001). By 1700 Arabia remained at 4.5 million. The Balkan countries had grown to 6.25 million, Italy to 13 million, France up to 21 million and Spain way up to 80 million.

4. Biblical accounts shed light as to the presence of nations and societies in the Middle East and offers but clues to their number. The bible tells of where people settled and often for what length of time. The Old Testament offers much as where Jews resided, our historical roots, enterprises, style of life and leadership. Note should be taken that our interest in Jewish presence is limited to the time following the destruction of the Second Temple, 70 C.E., a period of time that takes place well after the epochs of the Old Testament where the details are reported in the first two books, Genesis and Exodus.

5. At the height of the First Temple, according to Burchardt (1992), there were about 2.0 million Jews throughout the world, mostly in *Eretz Yisrael*. At the time of the Babylonian exile, the number of Jews in *Eretz Yisrael* had been reduced to about 0.3 million. About 0.8 million lived in areas to the east of Eretz Yisrael. Many Jews lived throughout other parts of the Middle East, the Balkans, and in Western Europe. Multitudes followed the Roman occupation to all perimeters of the empire.

Table 9 Jewish Population Estimates Burchardt, 1992	
Year	Millions
B.C.E.	
1250	2.0
1000	1.3 - 0.8
538	0.31
500	0.5
100	2.45
C.E.	
70	1.5 - 2.0
800	1.3
1300	1.2
1450	1.0
1500	0.9
1600	1.1
1700	2.0
1800	4.0
1900	10.6
1920	14.0
1940	16.6
1945	11.0
1960	12.5
1980	12.8

6. At the end of the Second Temple era (Ben-Sasson (1976), the majority of Palestine's population remained Jewish. Most were concentrated in Judea, Galilee and the Peraea, the western part of what is now Jordan. Many lived in the coastal areas and outlying areas in communities still unknown. During the Byzantine era, it seems that most of the Jewish population resided in the northern parts of what is now Israel, still maintaining the majority.

7. Upon visiting archeological sites, it seems to us that much movement of Jews could be attributed to natural causes. There was little maintenance of the improvements following the Jewish and Roman occupations. Upon the departure of the Romans, there were extended periods of droughts and earthquakes. There were also religious and economic attractions which drew people from one part of *Eretz Yisrael* to another. Subsequent occupying powers were driven to take away whatever wealth existed and in so doing failed to maintain the existing infrastructure. We saw evidence climatic changes, droughts, earthquakes, fires, which had a significant impact on trade and living in Jeruslalem, Hebron, En Gedi, Katz'rin, Korazin, Tiberias and Safed. These shifts occurred during the time of the Second Temple days up through to modern times. In addition to these relatively large communities that were affected, there were a large number of smaller communities throughout *Eretz*

Yisrael that were more hospitable in terms of climate, fauna and flora. They thrived where water was ample and where there were agricultural possibilities.

8. Collections of letters were instrumental in revealing Jewish presence during the low periods in Palestine when people, including Jews were at their fewest. From the time somewhat before the Crusades on through the Turkish occupation, a reliable source on Jewish presence in Palestine were collections of letters and notes taken of travels throughout the area. We described these letters in chapters related to our site visits. These letters describe travels and adventures and visits with Jews residing in areas of Jerusalem, Haifa, Tiberias, Safed, Hebron and other centers active during the last 1,500 years. They enabled us to "fill in the gaps" that visits to archeological sites did not provide.

9. Perils awaited many who traveled. Travel to *Eretz Yisrael* from Europe was until recent years was hazardous. Venturing by sea was impeded by pirates. There were times however when transportation was relatively safe. One of these waves occurred in the 1500's when Jews came eastward to *Eretz Yisrael*. A wave of Spanish speaking Jews arrived in Safed and Tiberias in the 1500's, already with a formidable number of Jews and history of leadership in Jewish writings. As life grew perilous in the diaspora, particularly in the Iberian Peninsula, Jews came in larger numbers to established communities such as Hebron, Jerusalem, Naublus, Haifa, Acco, Jaffa, Safed and Jericho.

10. Like groups before them, the Turks let the earth go fallow. But they provided a measure of security not seen in earlier centuries. Life then improved over the years, but slowly. As areas became secure, Jews began to come to Palestine in increased numbers.

11. As the world population grew, people in general became more mobile. There seemed to have always been a pressure on the part of world Jewry to come to Palestine. It is mentioned in all major writings as something that Jews wish to see happening. It was quite natural for Jews to want to come to Palestine.

12. The acceleration of Jewish travel to Palestine began well before the First World War and the resultant Balfour Declaration of the British to re-establish a homeland for the Jews in Palestine, and well before the establishment of the

Table 10
Time Line For Selected Locales

Year	Hebron	Jerusalem	Tiberias	Safed	Haifa Acre
C.E					
	10,000				
100	Trace	500	100000	?	1000
200	Tarce	500	300000	?	3000
300	Trace	500	300000	?	500
400	Trace	100	300000	?	500
500	Trace	1000	100000	?	500
600	500	100	100000	?	500
700	500	100	75000	?	500
800	500	500	50000	?	500
900	Trace	50	50000	?	500
1000	Trace	500	500	Trace	1000
1100	Trace	100	500	Trace	1000
1200	Trace	1000	500	Trace	250
1300	200	25	500	500	0
1400	200	750	Trace	1000	50
1500	Trace	1500	1000	10000	Trace
1550	Trace	1900	1000	15000	0
1600	1000	1200	500	30000	0
1650	Trace	2000	500	1000	0
1700	200	6000	75	1000	0
1750	Trace	10,000	4000	1500	?
1800	1500	7000	4000	6000	?
1850	750	47000	Trace	2000	?
1900	1000	30000	7000	2000	?
2000	4000	750000	?		

Jewish Agency and the first meeting of the Zionist Congress in the late 1800s. For as the western world grew in numbers, and as transportation became faster and affordable and when pirates on the sea and vandals along the way became controlled, people came in big numbers to Palestine. We described Oliphant's observation during his travels throughout Palestine in the mid-late 1800s. He offered a rich description and many photographs of the area. He described a flourishing Jewish life through 1825-1885. He described land in the north, to the east of Haifa, that was exceedingly fertile and well cared. He wrote of the area as flourishing in agriculture with much exporting of goods and a good promise for the immediate future. Though Oliphant (1887) offered reports of vandals cruising the plains, mountains and rural areas, much of the area had become safe for travel. The infrastructure of modern Israel had already begun, by Jews and long before the Zionist movement started.

13.   History books focus on wars, battles, religious and political strife. This emphasis on battles exaggerates their influence on population growth and social changes.   Such emphasis leads to the production of enduring myths and distortions. Actually, for much of the time there was a great deal of tolerance from one culture to another. For when one group prospered, so did another. Evidence of this mutual prosperity was seen in the En Gedi and Jericho area in the first 700 years of the common era where trade flourished during the success of the Ptolemy empire in Egypt. We saw evidence of this cooperation in Haifa, Galilee, Golan and nearby areas where there were more peaceful times than war times. Most of the battles occurred in areas far away fro m one another. During the vast majority of time, when people of divergent culture shared common economical conditions they lived harmoniously.

PART II
THE ISRAELI - PALESTINIAN CONFLICT

PROLOGUE:

Being so close to the places to the sites of violence, hearing its sounds, listening to people's reaction, I became impelled to understand what could prompt the wide majority of Arabs in the area to claim support for such abhorrent acts. I wanted to know how it came to be that the majority of Palestinians, according to surveys, supported the violence and suicidal attacks, how such macabre acts were rationalized in the name of a religious cause and measured against the near and distant historical past.

This second part of the book was finished after returning home, and reflects my distress related to both the Israeli-Palestinian Conflict and the terrorist attack on New York. Because in part I was in Israel and later in New York being close to sites of terror, I wanted to know more about the why of it, specifically from the perspective of people that support the violence. The more I talked to people, both those that are supportive to Israel and those more supportive to the Palestinian cause (some people, of course, were supportive to both groups), the more I realized that their understanding of the events, as expressed, were based on specific matters that had recently took place -- a recent statement by a Palestinian or Israeli leader, a suicide attack, an expansion of a Jewish settlement, an Israeli attack in Palestinian territories or some other news making event. Regardless of position taken, there was little clue offered by anyone as to what could prompt a terror attack other than some sort of broad reference to misguided behavior. When the subject of suicide attacks did come up, I was often asked for my opinion on the matter, which at the time was of no help to anyone. I wanted more satisfaction than could be offered by opinions of those about me.

Pressing harder to find the answer to these question I began to regularly review the growing literature on Arab perspectives on the matter in periodicals and books as well as the Internet. I took a hard look at historical events forming interactions between Arab-Moslem and Palestinian views on history with that of mine in hopes of determining what might be the disparity in their precepts of the past and if found, what might be their significance. I soon found myself reading translations of current Arab media, reading translations of the *Qur'an*, guidebooks for conversion to Islam, translations of articles from Arab governmental newspapers and treatises on the matter from the perspective of the Arab-Moslem. Between Hannah and I we could at the time, understand but little Hebrew, none of Arabic, but could read enough French, Spanish, Italian and German to get the gist of an article. I read a number of articles embracing anti-Israel, anti-western rhetoric and anti-outsider views. I took special interest in articles that offered a linkage to the past, real, imagined or distorted. I collected these articles and began to sort them out by categories and periods of time. Included were opinion surveys of Arabs and Palestinians conducted from 1999 to 2003, historical texts, recent books and essays written by laymen, clerics and scholars, English translations of Arab-Moslem rhetoric appearing in various media, relevant sections of English translations of the *Qur'an* including a publication by the Saudi government, *Yearbook* recapitulations of 1947-1950, daily coverage of the conflict in the *Jerusalem Post* and *Los Angeles Times* and other U.S. and international newspapers including state controlled newspapers and governmental related sources such as the *Syrian News Agency* and the *Palestinian Chronicle* and other English versions of news organizations reflecting media coverage from the Middle East.

I sorted out the this Arab literature for the following periods going back in time to: (1) incidents and accords of the last twenty years, (2) the onset of Palestinian Nationalism in 1964 and the sudden pullout of the Jordanians from the West Banks and East Jerusalem following the 1967 war, (3) the Jewish and Arab refugee problems of 1945-1949, 1985 and 1967, (4) the Arab support for the Axis powers during and between World Wars I and II, (5) efforts on the part of the Arab League to control deliberations on the part of the United Nations in the matter of partition of Palestine, (6) back further in time to the 1300's and Moslem expulsion from Europe, and to the Crusades of 1000s to 1200s, and (7) even further back to where I eventually found the time and place of the terminus of this troublesome path, at its source, to events taking place in Medina, about the year 625 C.E., to the beginning of Islam.

I began to look at current precepts as an end of a linkage of a series of events connected to events believed to have taken place both in the near and distant past. These connections can be conceived as several layers of interwoven fibers woven together to form an assembly of connectors linking the present with the past. In this manner, I attempted to classify precepts inferred in the rhetoric of those supporting the cause of the Palestinian and of the Arab militants supporting the violence while we were in Israel.

Part II starts with a summary of the daily newspaper accounts of the violence throughout the country, our experiences and reactions of people around us. The subsequent chapters examine one or more of the common themes that are found in literature supporting the current forms of violent measures including terror and suicidal attacks. The final chapter in this second part of the book outlines and summarizes the several common precepts that I believe account for almost all motives of how it is that some support the violence.

Chapter 15
The Violence About us

We were ever mindful of the unrest and violence about us. We heard gun fire and explosions everyday as we traveled through the eastern and northern sections of this small country in the late summer of 2001. Occasionally walkways and roads were made clear of suspected placement of bombs. Though the populace treats these as inconveniences, they seem worrisome to us. The clear evenings skies were occasionally lit up with flashes of light. The deep noises and flashes, however, always seemed afar someplace, dull in sound without any shock or noticeable trembling of the earth. Occasionally I would hear the familiar and characteristic rat-a-tat-tat of machine gun fire, a reminder of trouble perhaps a few hundred yards away. The sound of sirens from nearby streets and the overhead drone and lights of helicopters in Jerusalem, the Galilee and Tel Aviv occasionally interfered with our sleep, signs of nearby trouble that we hoped to not read about later. The sounds of disturbances seemed to not be accelerating in our direction; rather, the action seemed to be drawing away. Some of the sounds, the next day, materialized into front page news of the *Jerusalem Post*. That there was a military presence and uniformed police officers nearby was reassuring. Despite the unrest, we curiously felt safe; it was not until the terror attacks in New York City and Washington that we felt impelled to leave to go home.

News Coverage

We found local and international newspapers available in many languages. We were able to keep abreast of events largely from reading the English version of the *Jerusalem Post*, often available at news counters in populated tourist centers, near large hotels and business districts. There were daily half hour morning and evening reports in English by CNN or British Skynews.

Following is a summary of the daily account of reported incidents that occurred while we traveled about Israel. Interestingly, these same incidents that we read with alarm in the *Jerusalem Post* in Israel were found published on the front pages of our *L.A. Times*. The *Post* articles contained more details of the names of victims, businesses affected, the perimeters of destructions as well as daily accounts of other terror incidents and related troubles.

Aug 26: A [Jewish] family from Ofarim were killed while driving in their car -- an Israeli was killed in a shooting attack near Kubbuz Magal – Palestinians infiltrated an IDF base, kill 3

Aug 27: Israeli killed, Zibri, PFLP terrorist leader

Aug 28: Mortar shell crashes into central Gilo

Aug 29: Israeli motorist killed in shooting attack near Nablus - a suicide bombing in Beersheba thwarted

Aug 30: Israeli murdered in restaurant near Green line -- Ashdod truck driver shot by terrorist

Aug 31: Modi'in man slain by gunman while driving -- a terror suspect caught on way to commit a terror attack -- high alert in north for Hezbullah attack

Sept 3: High alert in North Jerusalem -- back to school, amid security fears -- two soldiers & two civilians hurt in attacks -- attacks being planned from Lebanon

Sep 4: Suicide bomber wounds thirteen and blows himself up in Jerusalem -- Four bombings in 7 hours shake Jerusalem -- Hebron clashes leave 3 Israelis wounded, 2 Palestinians dead

Sep 5: IDF reinforces Jerusalem -- a pair of border police prevents a tragedy -- a terror cell planned multiple attacks

Sept 6: Man and woman shot -- Arab terror gang recruited by Fatah's Tanzim, uncovered in the North -- Neveh Tzuf man wounded as he drove home near Ramallah

Sep 7: IDF offficer killed, 2nd hurt in ambush -- Security cabinet to discuss seam plan,

Sep 9: Suicide bombing in Nahariya train station, Three killed and dozen wounded -- Two dead in attack on Jordan Valley teachers transport -- Cars, bus ablaze under Beit Lid bombing -- Cab driver spots bomb; police detonate

Sep 10: PA was repeatedly asked to arrest suicide bomber

Sep 11: Israeli embassies on alert -- Terrorists kill two border police officers -- NII must support Nahariya suicide bombers 2 widows, 10 orphans -- Passengers injured by stones thrown

Sep 12: Country mourns with Americans -- Woman slain in drive-by shooting near Alfei Menashe -- Israeli hotel industry harmed by grounded planes -- Palestinians celebrate as U.S. is attacked

Sep 14: First war of the 21st century -- No flights to US

Sep 16: Soldier killed in Ramallah -- One dead, one wounded in Jerusalem terrorist shooting -- Islamic Jihad leader lauds attack against US -- Palestinian police confiscate footage at Gaza rally

Political Groups Claim Responsibility

While we were in Israel, typically after an attack, one Arab-based political faction or another was quick to assume responsibility. Members of these several political parties make up the Palestinian Authority. They fill the seats of the Palestinian Council. As of this date, all parties support violence towards Israel. Such organizations include Fatah, with roots in Egypt during the days of the Egyptian leadership of the Arab world. They started in connection with the Muslim Brotherhood. Fatah is the major party. It underpins the current leadership of Yasser Arafat. Hezballah is in part a service organization in Lebanon, has become another source of support for armed resistance. Hamas, is another political party most active in promoting hostilities throughout Israel, often claiming responsibility for terrorist attacks. Relatively new and competing political groups, The Palestinian Jihad and the Al Aqsa Brigade are also bidding for political support, have also claimed responsibility for terrorist attacks throughout Israel (Lahoud, 2002).

Reactions to the Violence

From the Arab perspective, the conflict has become a battle for media support. Certainly, the news is hyped. Despite the intensity of the media coverage, the probably of injuries and fatalities to any civilian in Israel is quite small. The casualty rate in Israel is probably within the range of occurrences of serious injuries and killings as might take place in greater Los Angeles which hosts a similar number of people. Our riots, fires, earthquakes and incidents on highways as well as crime and accidents have also taken their toll on human life. Yet during most of this time, as we did in Los Angeles, we felt generally safe. As we pointed out, there was a sense of well being while in the Old City. Such thoughts became far away while appreciating the wonder amidst the beauty of agricultural Israel, and diffused by the feeling of being one among many in the huge population centers along the coast, and for the most part sensed a timelessness and serenity in the National Parks and historical sites. These factors seemed to offset the realization that trouble may be just around the corner.

In our travels we found ourselves unexpectedly close to active target sites. We conversed with Israelis, Arabs, Christians, Jews and Moslems about the violence about us. We presented some of their reactions in the preceding chapters. No one we spoke to supported the violence. Yet opinion surveys indicated considerable support among the Arab populace in Gaza and the West Banks for the perpetuation of the kinds of acts specified above.[16]

Precepts that Motivate the Perpetrators

In the remaining pages of this second part of the book I try to show how the present consciousness, precepts and behaviors of those that support the violence have been shaped, how it can happen that a few distortions and omissions of historical events can lead to recriminations, frustration, distrust and anger directed at western democracies. These events will be presented in chronological order from the past to the present in the hope that the reader may more readily anchor these events with standard textbook accounts of history.

---

[16]Opinion Survey: Pew Polls, Gallup Polls and surveys reported by the *Jerusalem Post* and the *Palestinian Chronicle,* 2001,2002.

Chapter 16
Arab/Moslem Precepts Derived from the *Qur'an*

Overview

Though much of the Qur'an is poetic and stirring, there are a number of *Sutras* that outline required conduct and personal tasks followed to this day. Notwithstanding the poetic and peaceful preponderance of the content, this chapter is limited to specific *Qur'anic* tenets embedded in the literature and rhetoric among those supporting the violence and terror

Upon reviewing the rhetoric supporting the violence that had occurred throughout Israel in 2001 I found several common themes related to *Qu'ranic* tenets. There are an abundance of references, often by innuendo, implicitly or explicitly referring to Sutras reciting the merits of *Dar al-Islam* (The lands and the world of Islam) and the other *Dar al-Harb*, (The Lands and World of War). There is also much reference in such themes to *Al-Firdaus*, (The After-Life), *Ad'n,* (Paradise), *Jihad*, (Holy War), which offer incentives for those who struggle with Kafir, (Enemies) at peril to their lives and as a result die, to become Martyrs. There is also the *Qur'anic* tenets of *Dhimma* (treatment of non-believers) of the prescribed attitude, social and civic procedures in the withstanding Christians and Jews.

The *Qur'an*

Followers of Islam learn the tenets and axioms of the *Qur'an* (recitation) as "revealed" to the "Messenger of Allah," Muhammad about 1,350 years ago. Muhammad told of his revelations and visions from 610 to 622 to the Companions who together compiled much of this material into the *Qur'an*. As part of submitting themselves to their faith and maintaining identification, Moslems are taught and are expected to implement teachings from the *Qur'an* into their daily lives. Much of the *Qur'an* is poetic and stirs imaginative thought and emotional response. But there is also much description of events, outlook on the land, and proscribing of thought and conduct without leap to allegory. Though monotheistic in its entirety, the nature of reality, truth, source of knowledge and eschatology is unique and differs critically from Judaism and Christianity. Variances include the role of the Patriarchs, the significance of Ishmael, the Exodus from Egypt, the identification with the establishment of the Jewish Temples, the repudiation of much of Jewish history and key Jewish and Christian tenets, a rejection of Palestine as being a homeland for the Jews and the entirety of Jewish post biblical writings occurring before the *Qur'an* was compiled. There is a revisionist view of Christianity with many references to Jesus and to the Children of the *Injeel* (Gospel), about 300 in total (See 3:48, 5:46,68, 7:157, 57:27).

The Timeliness of The Islam and The *Qur'an*

Moslems consider the *Qur'an* timeless in its applicability to everyday life. The *Qu'ran* and secondary writings form much of a common consciousness and cohesiveness seen in the Moslem approach to everyday matters. Throughout much of the Middle East, Islamic tenets continue to have a strong regulatory impact on the everyday as well as political life of its followers. The impact of the Islamic theology reaches far into everyday conduct, much more so than Judaism and Christianity. The axioms and tenets of the *Qur'an*, in much of the Arab triangle, have a direct impact on court proceedings, the criminal justice system, military activity, educational practices and a host of everyday practices. Arabs are keenly aware of their religious and cultural roots. Arab Muslims tend to see not a nation subdivided into religious groups as do Westerners, but that of religious groups subdivided into nations (Lewis, 2001).

The tenets of Islam provide a whole and integrative way of viewing the world. Noteworthy is the role of the clergy, the *Imams*, clerics, that continue to have discretional power to influence everyday conduct.

Lewis (2003, p 137) aptly points out that "Most Muslims are not fundamentalists, and most fundamentalists are not terrorists, but most present-day terrorists are Muslim and proudly identify themselves as such."[17] Extremist groups sanctify their action through pious references to Islamic texts, notably the

---

[17]For the fundamentalists, as for the natiohalists, the various territorial issues are important but in a different, more intractable form. For the fundamentalist, no peace or compromise with Israel is possible (or any other disputed territory), and any concession is only a step toward the true final solution – the dissolution of the State of Israel and to its true owners, the Muslim Palestinians, and the departure of the intruders (Lewis, 2003, p 150).

Qur'an. According to Lewis three different extremist groups, the subversive radicals of Al Qa'ida and the other groups that resemble it; the preemptive fundamentalism of the Saudi establishment; and the institutionalized revolution of the ruling Iranian hierarchy.

The "Afterlife", *Jihad* and the Martyr

Deeply interwoven among the basic thread is the important concept of life after death. According to Smith and Haddad (1981), so intense is the *Qu'ranic* concern for the "days to come" — when all will be held accountable for their actions -- that all ethical teachings contained in the Quran must be understood in light of this dual conception of reality. Though belief in some kind of life in the grave was ancient and common, it is nevertheless a critical concept for all Moslems. Life after death was part of Islamic understanding from its earliest times (2:216, 9:111).

A "sixth" pillar of Islam is the religious duty to apply the concept of *jihad* to war. The Kharjites raised *jihad* to the level of a pillar in the early days of Islam. When the situations warrants, men are required to go to war in order to spread Islam or defend it against infidels (2:216). Moslems are taught that individuals who offset the aggressor and/or occupier are entitled to rewards in the after life in *Ad'n*, paradise, where the souls of good people go after death (4:95, 8:73-74, 9:20-22, 61:12), a place that also awaits the martyr, those that die in the name of Allah (3:155-159, 169-172, 22:58, 59). Clair Tisdall (1973) and Shorrosh (1988) point out the importance of *jihad* throughout Islam, as does Al-Hilali and Khan (1998) in their comment on the *Qur'an*, published by the government of Saudi Arabia. The afterlife shall be as rich for those who try and succeed as those that die in the attempt, even if they fail in combating the *Kafir,* the infidel, aggressor and/or occupier. Even if one has conducted oneself in an undesirable manner, one can be redeemed if one makes an effort to stem off the aggressor or occupier at risk of their own life (4:74). These three threads form a very intrinsic part of the current group consciousness of all Arab Moslems. I believe it is fair to say that these concepts (the After-life, Holy War and Martyrdom) are so central to Islam that without incorporating them, them, one's identity as a Moslem might be questionable. Reference to one or all three of these precepts are prevalent throughout the current nationalistic government media from Syria, Iran, Saudi Arabia, Iran and the Palestinian Authority. It is indeed sad that tenets of a prominent religion with such strong overtones can so readily be illicited for state or political purposes.

Dhimma

Though there were massacres of Jews early on, they were soon considered "People of the Book," as like themselves, they were monotheists and subservient to the same God. As such, Jews were given an exemption from being forced to convert, be expelled or killed. They were given the option to accept the "protective" status of *dhimma*, which was extended to Christians as well, in exchange for their subordination to the Muslim populace. *Quranic* writings set forth the rationale for supporting discriminatory practices towards non-Moslems in Islamic societies. Because of their *dhimma* status, Jews and Christians could choose to remain in Moslem controlled territories. If Jews opted to reside in Moslem controlled areas, they were compelled to conform to many restrictions in business, given limited rights in courts of law, adhere to dress codes, restrictions on social relations with Moslems and refrain from open religious practices.

The tenet of *dhimma* is consistent with the objective of Islamic expansion of faith and influence. Islamic writings also focus on removing the threat of non-Moslems and non-believers, a process perceived as a cleansing of infidelity. For this reason we see much reference to synonyms in their current anti-West rhetoric today -- disloyalty, duplicity, faithlessness, treacherous, adultery, cheating, heresy, heathen, disbeliever, gentile, godless, occupier and *aggressor* -- depending on the context. These words are found throughout English translations of the *Qur'an*.

With the passage of over 1,300 years marked by practices of *dhimma,* a fourth thread had been generated, encased[18] with linguistic signals -- that non-believers should they be Christians or Jews -- are required to be treated under the law as second class citizens with limited human rights.

---

[18]The term, encasement, is a hypothetical construct that permits the transmission of linguistic signals to consciousness and unconsciousness (Margolis, 1991). See Glossary.

Islamic Colonization of Palestine

Embedded in the consciousness of all Arab Moslems is the significance of the difference between lands settled by Arab-Moslem communities and the lands that remain in the hands of non-believers. The global world is depicted by the *Qur'an* as divided into two portions. One portion of the world is that part ruled by Islam, *Dar al-Islam*, the Land of Islam. The other part of the world, is yet to submit to Islamic power, *Dar al-Harb*, the Land of Warfare (Warraq, 1995, Lewis, 1998, 2001).

Non Moslems, including the many Jews residing in areas in the 600s, in what is today Saudi Arabia, Iraq, and Iran, were dealt harshly with immediate massacres of Jews. In 630, Mecca surrendered to the Muslims, and afterwards numerous Meccans converted. This military-political-religious act established the pattern for *jihad*, holy fighting in the cause of Allah. This view continues to be promulgated today. According to Al-Hilali and Khan (1998) *Jihad* is one of the very fundamentals of Islam: the struggle against outsiders who are perceived as harmful to the Muslim community (See also Lee and Cherlin, 2002).

Palestine soon became subject to emigration from the east. Arab movement into Palestine accelerated.   Arabs cohabited the area with Jews under administration of various Arab occupying powers. All such administrations were quite colonial in nature. They varied in the extent they could draw out the wealth of the land and amounts of tribute from the indigenous populace for the crowns of Arab societies. Jews were taxed excessively as part of *dhimma*.

The hand of oppression varied with the rulers. The quality of life of all peoples in Palestine varied substantially with the occupying realm. We saw some of the Jewish communities as they stood in that period, En Gedi, Hebron, Katzr'in, Korazim, Capernaum, and Tiberias. None of these cities were found to be fortified during the early days of Islamic colonization. Though oppressed by Moslems, the population centers were degraded because of usurious taxation and neglect by the occupying Islamic based powers, but also by natural catastrophes and adverse climatic changes. As climates changed and with the natural disasters, floods, droughts and earthquakes, there seemed no inclination on the part of the occupying powers to maintain life and the land in Eretz Yisrael.

Jews had resided in Palestine for 2,000 continuous years before the Islamic conquests. By the 600s, wherever Jews resided, they continued to be active as evidenced by practices of immersion of utensils and one's body into water, *mikvot*, use of synagogues for study, prayer and community meetings, observance of Shabbot, Jewish holidays, evidence of dietary restrictions, study, preparing for *Bar Mitzvah* (training in preparation for adult religious participation), learning, interpreting and following *Halacha*, (Jewish Law). Those not living in Eretz Ysrael longed to "return" to the Jewish Homeland in Palestine as revealed by a number of letters which also indicated Jewish life throughout Eretz Yisrael was continuing. In addition to the above everyday richness of Judaism in Palestine during the Islamic expansion, there had been a finishing in the development in post biblical literature, the completion of the Talmud and other secondary writings on matters pertaining to further ramification of Jewish life and law. We saw evidence of Jewish life in this period in Hebron, Jerusalem, Tiberias, Katz'rin, En Gedi, and Safed.

Animosities reached a height with the Christian Crusades during the 1000s and 1100s as the Christian armies attempted to cleanse Palestine of Moslem and Jewish influence. The expulsion of Moslems and Jews from the Iberian Peninsula in the later 1400's laid further grounds for animosity that continue to this day. But this matter of their expulsion was largely between Christians and Moslems and Christians and Jews. Jews continued to be tolerated under the protection" of *dhimma*, but at the discretion of the local Imam

The next five hundred years would see the ending of the Crusader intervention in Palestine, the expansion of Islam to the east, throughout North Africa and much of Europe, some contraction starting with the expulsion of Moslems from the Iberian peninsula in the late 1400's to the period of growth in the late 1900s. But precepts of the existence and nature of the after-life, *Jihad*, martyrdom and *Dhimma* would remain deeply encased onto the consciousness of Arab-Moslems throughout the world to this day.

Chapter 17
Precepts Linked with Imperialism and Colonization

Overview

An apprehensive attitude and disdain towards colonization has long been embedded in the consciousness of anyone calling themselves an Arab. Since the demise of the Jewish state following the Jewish Roman Wars and the later failure of the Bar Kochba Revolt against Rome in 135-137, all areas of *Eretz Yisrael* and many areas in the Middle East had been occupied by powers whose home base was far away.[19]   How this common experience over centuries of time is manifested and reflected in the media, and the precepts that appear in the media supporting the kinds of terror in Israel, is the subject of this chapter.

Growth and Decline of the Ottoman Empire

The Ottoman Empire had grown out of the rule of the Seljuks, sultans of eastern Anatolia who had seen a constituent growth of Islamic civilization. The empire grew following battles in the east where they administered to Islamic and Arab speaking people. The armies of Suileman advanced across Hungary while in the east Ottoman fleets challenged the Portugese in the Indian Ocean. The empire, at its height in about 1670, extended through southeast Europe including the entirety of the Balkan states, northeast across the Danube, perhaps fifty miles from Vienna, eastward through the southern Ukraine, all of Anatolia, had infiltrated to the Caspian Sea, Iraq, Syria, Palestine, the entire southeast coast of the Arab triangle, Egypt, and almost the entire northern coast of Africa. The Ottomans had control of the Mediterranean until the naval battle of Lepanto in 1571. Turkish texts refer to the death of Suileman, the Magnificent, in 1566

---

[19]The reader may refer to Chapter 8, on Jerusalem, for a summary of the periods of occupying powers.

as the beginning of the breakdown in the Ottoman institution (Lewis, 1995).[20] A series of losses were beginning to occur to the north. Russian advances continued for three hundred years. With the advance towards Vienna, Islam offered a mortal threat to Christendom (Lewis, 1995). Beset with troubles in the east, largely in Persia, the Turkish thrust to the west to Vienna was finally repelled in 1683.

Turkish Colonization of Palestine

The Turkish administration, as was their Arab predecessors, colonial in structure. The main interest in Palestine was limited to pulling out of resources to support the Ottoman empire. The Turks were not interested in settling or improving the area, but fortunately, unlike the occupiers before them, the Persians, Umayad, Abbasid and Fatimid Caliphates, the Crusaders, Mongols, and Mamluks, they did provide a good measure of law and order. As a result, the populace of cities and towns became more secure from vandals. Life improved in a number of ways. Meanwhile the population of the western world was growing. Access to travel, though still limited, was available to more people.

The colonization of lands in North Africa and the Middle East by European powers from 1500 to 1946 contributed to an insidious Arab and Moslem disdain and contempt of western powers in general. Upon oil production, two world wars and diminishing of European colonialism, a pan-Arab nationalism evolved into its forms as seen today. As was the case with Turkey, Arab countries remain with greater ties to Islam than with either Judaism or Christianity. Other than Turkey and more recently, Egypt, Arab countries of today are characterized by monarchies and very strong ties with Islamic tenets.

Because Jews were considered believers of the same deity, but were not believers of Mohammad, they could be tolerated in Eretz Yisrael so long as they conformed to specific standards. The practice of *Dhimma* existed then, continues today, and in many ways had become so stringent that very few Jews

---

[20]

On the night of September 5, 1566, the Sultan died in his tent during the siege of Szigetvar in Hungary. The battle was still in progress, the issue uncertain, the heir to the throne far away. The grand vizier resolved to keep the Sultan's death secret. Once the new Sultan was installed in Istanbul, the secret was revealed (Lewis, 1995).

today can be found to reside in many of the Arab states. To remain in Islamic societies, as it was a thousand years ago, Jews always had to adhere to substandard positions in life. Jews were not permitted civil rights in courts of law when in conflict with Moslems. They continue to be denied positions of power, must adhere to differentiated dress codes, reside in specific areas, maintain social distance from Moslems. In many areas, as was the case throughout Palestine, Jews had to sustain extraordinary taxation merely on the basis of being Jewish.

Christians were also considered misguided. Though led by their "messenger" they have been described in the literature as a "a corrupted people" and are treated not much better than Jews (Lewis, 1995). Other ethnic and religious groups continue to be treated even more harshly -- convert, leave or in some cases, be imprisoned or killed.

We have seen historical manifestations of Arab and Moslem resistance to accommodating non-Moslems as we traveled throughout the country. This resistance to non-Moslem westerners became defined when we saw the extent of destruction and desecration of property. The destruction of Jewish facilities seems to have accelerated in the more recent years as occurred in Hebron and Safed in 1929, in Jerusalem during the Jordanian occupation of 1948-1967 and most recently in the West Bank with the desecration of the Tomb of Joseph last year near Nablus. But despite all this antagonism and desecration, we believe, the demise of most towns and cities in *Eretz Yisrael* following the colonization by Islamic forces were by natural causes or neglect, rather than desecration or direct hostile action, which at times did occur. As pointed out earlier, there was little maintenance or improvement of the Jewish and Roman infrastructure by subsequent occupying forces. The major interest on the part of all subsequent occupiers was taking whatever resources remained to fulfill the financial needs of the distant monarchial powers.

In the later years of the Turkish occupation, with the help of outside financial resources, much of the land was maintained. The infrastructure was improved. Christian, Moslem and Jews tended to get along quite well in *Eretz Yisrael*. In his first hand account, Oliphant (1976) described examples in detail where one minority helped another to prosper during the period 1825-1885. Unlike the stance of occupying powers before this time, monies began to come in and stay in Palestine to provide further growth. The Jews were long ready before the Zionist movement to set up an extensive infrastructure within the limits imposed by the Turks.

Encased on the consciousness of Arab Moslems today is much apprehension associated with foreign hegemony and occupation. The Ottoman Turkish empire was essentially Moslem. Perhaps with some mixed attitudes, their occupation and colonization was tolerated. That it was an occupation was not fully realized by the Arab populace until the defeat of the Central powers and the demise of Turkish control after the First World War and the subsequent British occupation in 1917. So long as the occupation force was Moslem in nature, there seemed little popular resistance on the part of Moslems to foreign control. This antagonism towards the west was to accelerate following the demise of Turkish rule and the resultant British mandate over Palestine in 1917. But in any event, by 1918, the matter of foreign encroachment became an integral paart of the collective Arab consciousness.

Chapter 18
Precepts Sanctioning Objectives of the Central and Axis Powers
And The Impact of the British Mandate of Palestine

Overview

Much is expressed in the Arab media of for the goals and aspirations held
by the European Central Powers of the First World War and the Axis Powers
of the Second World War. A positive sentiment for the Central and Axis
Powers had been born of fear and respect for western military strength,
economic power and perceived encroachment and colonization. There is strong
sentiment expressed when the subject arises. For centuries there has a been a
preoccupation and renunciation of western colonialism, a distrust of secular
democracy, a foreboding of western corruption, centuries of fear of Russian
intervention, Bolshevism and its later forms of Communism and more lately,
perhaps a contradiction, a distrust of big business in the hands of outsiders.
These matters all seemed to have come to a head with the defeat of the Central
Powers in 1918, the demise of Turkish control over the Middle East, the
establishment of the British Mandate of Palestine following the First World War
and the subsequent partition of the Mandate into a Jewish and Arab state
following the Second World War. These events provide the backdrop of history
that has energized the perceptual reality that European powers are responsible
for much of their troubles.

Early Sentiment for the Axis Powers

Much of the Arabic speaking world population had long been occupied by
Ottoman Turkish forces. The Turks had occupied *Eretz Yisrael* for from 1516
to 1917. The Turks had a positive sentiment towards Islam. This factor
contributed to the positive sentiment on the part of Arabs for the aspirations and
goals of the Axis powers in the First World War.
    Islamic Arabs are aware of the historical tendency for the strong to
overcome the weak, as they have seen done for centuries to themselves, each
other and outsiders. Arabs also know they treated Jews and Christians

differentially as second class citizens for centuries. The practice of *dhimma* continues today throughout all Moslem areas of the Middle East. As a result of their stance towards non-believers, they are likely to be very sensitive to any hint of religious persecution on the part of others. The history of Islamic growth and Arab ascendancy in the Middle East, North Africa, Europe and areas to the east has likely led to a heightened sensitivity, a reaction-formation, a perception that others may do onto them as they have done to themselves and to others over the centuries.

The Demise of Turkish Control

The First World War brought the end of the Ottoman Empire as a great power. At the end of October, 1914, Turkish warships, accompanied by two German cruisers, bombarded the Russian Black Sea ports of Odessa, Sevastopol and Theodosia. The sultan-caliph proclaimed a Jihad against all who bore arms against him and his allies – Britain, France and Russia, the three principal Allied powers, ruled over vast Muslim populations in Central Asia, North Africa and India. The Turks and their German allies hoped that these Muslim subjects would respond to the call to *jihad* and rise in revolt. That was not to happen. The Ottomans confronted Russia and Britain on their eastern and southern borders (Lewis, 1995).

With the demise of Turkish control, a number of stressor situations developed related to the dramatic changes that occurred in governing power and administration. With control by the Allied powers, a period of a new kind of freedom set in. Not an anarchy or monarchy, but of a unstable democracy. In this vacuum a number of Arab groups soon sought power and influence over one another. Though there were elements of a common geography and contemporary culture, the overall cohesive element that held Arabs together was the fabric and threads of their common ties to the past including the adherence to Islamic tenets (afterlife, martyrdom, *Jihad* and *dhimma*) and fear of local and foreign hegemony.

Prior to World War I much of the world Arab populace were occupied by Turkish forces. The First World War saw support for the Turks and other Axis powers, but as pointed out by Lewis (1995), Arabs did not significantly join the militarily ranks. As the First World War was coming to an end, attempts were made by France and England to accommodate both Allied and Axis interests in the areas previously held by Turkey. Russia, because of the losses in Europe in

1914 and the revolution in 1917, had little influence on the matter. After the Hussein-McHahon talks and the May 1916 signing of the Sykes-Picot agreement, the stage was set for dividing the area administered by the Turks between Britain and France.

The Defeat of the Central Powers

The outcome of the war, the defeat of the Central powers, Germany Austria and Turkey, and the French and British occupation was a very hard blow for the Arabs to accept. Islamic leaders could not accept that a war, believed as religious and whose participatory action would result in a rich afterlife, could end in an ultimate defeat. Though perhaps not apparent to the west at the time, the allied victory was denied in much of this part of the world, as it came to pass in Central Europe. The allied victories and failure of the Turks and the resultant French and British occupation of the Middle East were to have a marked effect on events to occur.

Arab revolts began to occur throughout Africa and the Middle East. The defeat of the Germany-Turkish Axis, served as a encasement of both a brusque reminder re-affirming the significance of being left behind by both a scientific and technological advance of the west and perceived as a failure to gather in the defense of Islam. [21]

The British Mandate

Following the collapse of the Turkish army in 1917, The British set up a mandate over much of the Middle East, including what is now Israel and Jordan. The Balfour Declaration, an outcome of the war, outlined the British plan for the development of a Jewish homeland (not given a name) in the area of *Eretz Yisrael*, the biblical description of the Land of Israel, Palestine and

---

[21]This form of denial continues to the date of this writing. At the time of the fall of Baghdad, in many capitols throughout the Arab Middle East, Arabs expressed anger at Hussein for not fighting to defend his capital. Much of the anger is related to the feeling of betrayal, of being taken in to believe Hussein that the Battle for Baghdad would be decisive. A common sentiment expressed is that the Iraqi government has merely gone underground and preparing for the real war (David Lamb and Kim Murphy, L.A. Times, Apr 11, 2003).

adjacent areas including southern parts of Lebanon and Syria and much of what is today Jordan. Following the the war, Pan Arabist leaders soon urged the British to curtail emigration of Jews to Palestine. In 1922, the British minister for colonies, Churchill, due to Arab pressure, published the White Paper excluding the area east of the Jordan river from the Balfour declaration and called for organizing Jewish immigration according to economic capacity of Palestine.

The Mandate had set up a workable governmental body. Palestine was administered by a British High Commissioner, who was assisted by various officials–British, Jewish and Arab. The country had been divided into six districts, each under a district commissioner. Considerable autonomy was given to the Moslem, Jewish, and Christian communities. The religious affairs of the Moslems were controlled by the Moslem Supreme Council, and questions involving their personal status, were under the jurisdiction of the *Sharia* courts. The Jewish community was organized under an elected assembly and a general council, *Va'ad Leumi*. The Jewish community operated its own schools, courts with jurisdiction over matters of personal status. Much of the same situation existed for the several Christian communities. There was also the Jewish Agency, a quasi-governmental body, which concerned itself with the establishment of the Jewish National Home. The police force was composed of British, Arabs and Jewish elements. The official languages were English, Arabic and Hebrew. A British census in 1931 reported 1,035,154 people in Palestine, 73% Muslim Arabs, 16.9% Jewish and 8.6% Christian. Of the area that is now within the green line of Israel, Jews formed the largest group.

For the most part, Jew, Christian and Arab got along quite well during the British Mandate and despite strong religious differences, as one individual prospered, so did another. German Jews had come in during the 1800s and developed commercial enterprises which drew employment from local residents. They cooperated well on economic and political levels. Jews and Arabs moved into the area working together in agriculture and commerce.

Clashes and riots accelerated between Arab Palestinians and the British and between Arabs and Jews. As Jewish interest in Palestine developed into further immigration, Arab and Moslem organizations resorted to insurgency and terror to stem the British policy of permitting Jews to migrate to Palestine. Arab clashes occurred in the Old City of Jerusalem. Jews were attacked in riots in Hebron and Safed in 1929. Following the riots and as Jewish immigration increased, Irgun, a Jewish militant group, split off from Haganah as a response to Arab terrorism. The League of Nations investigated the situation.

In 1936, Haj Amin Husseini, overseer of Jerusalem, headed the Arab Higher Committee. In protest to the British, Husseini called for a stop to tax payments. These clashes accelerated with the implementation of anti-Semitic policies throughout Europe, which he supported.

Arabs Remodel Support for the Axis Cause

Germany and Italy offered an attractive alternative to the French and English administrations –– which were not doing well anyway -- and a return to the sentiments of the Axis powers, which among other things included a bitterness for the powers of Western Europe seen as imperialistic. In this environment the Arab position easily became aligned with the aggressively pursued Nazi position of anti-Semitism. In 1933 the British-appointed Mufti of Jerusalem, Haj Amin al-Husayni made contact with the German Consul to declare support and offer his help. Along his way to Berlin in 1941 he stopped in Baghdad in April 1941 and assisted Syria to set up a pro-Axis regime. The group from Syria that supported the Axis take-over became the Ba'ath party, that eventually came to power to govern both Iraq and Syria. Among the many that supported or sympathized with the Axis during the war years included Nasser and Sadat. Rashid Ali has been resuscitated as a hero in Saddam Hussein's, Iraq (Lewis, 1995). According to Lewis (1995) the Axis powers launched massive programs of propaganda which penetrated the Arab world. By preaching hatred of the Jews, the Germans and Arab leaders were able to exploit *dhimma*, a problem that existed in the area for centuries, to become a common cause.

Revolts occurred as Arab volunteers entered Lebanon to help fight the British occupation. In 1937 the Peel committee report recommended partitioning Palestine into a Jewish state and a Palestinian Arab state with British protectorates including Jerusalem. The Arab Higher Committee rejected the plan. The Germans recruited Arabs, some of the volunteer forces in the so-called Orient Legions. The Allies supported a Transjordan Brigade and a Jewish Brigade from Palestine.

The Arab position was consistent with the developing Nazi programs at the time. It is known that Adolf Eichmann met with Feival Polkes, a spokesman for the Haganah in November, 1938 in Cairo. On the agenda, according to Schleunes (1990) was a discussion regarding possible emigration of Jews to

Palestine. But the meeting was held to gather intelligence regarding the growing Jewish center, a common fear shared between leading Nazis and Arabs. The Nazi's feared the centralization of the Jews anywhere; the Arab leaders feared the centralization of Jews in Palestine. During the days preceding the war as well as during the war, the Arabs and Germans concurred on halting immigration to Palestine.

Arab-Nazi Consortium

Both the Nuremberg and Eichmann trials revealed the conspiracy between the Arabs and the Germans. Adolf Eichmann met with the British-appointed Mufti in Palestine in 1937. On April 25, 1941, the Nazis sent the Mufti to German occupied Bosnia, where he assumed the Title "Protector of Islam."

Later in 1941, the Jerusalem Mufti, Haj Amin al-Husseii, the Arab spokesman at the time, went to Germany and met with Adolf Hitler, Heinrich Himmler, Joachim Von Ribbontrop and other Nazi leaders. In a recorded meeting on November 28, as printed in the *Israel-Arab Reader*, edited by Lacquer (2001), he attempted to persuade them to extend the Nazi anti-Jewish program to the Arab world (*Response*, 1991). The Mufti sent Hitler 15 drafts of declarations he wanted Germany and Italy to implement concerning the Middle East. They called upon the two nations to declare the illegality of the Jewish home in Palestine. Upon meeting with Hitler in November 1941, he told him the Jews were his foremost enemy. He pleaded: "the Arabs were Germany's natural friends because they had the same enemies as had Germany...the Jews." Hitler is recorded as responding favorably:

Germany stood for uncompromising war against the Jews. That naturally included active opposition to the Jewish national home in Palestine....Germany would furnish positive and practical aid to the Arabs involved in the same struggle....Germany's objective...solely the destruction of the Jewish element residing in the Arab sphere.

Documents on German Foreign Policy, 1918-1945, Series D, Vol XIII, London, 1964, p.88ff in Walter Lacquer and Barry Rubin, *The Israel-Arab Reader*, 1984, pp 79-84

By 1942, soon after their meeting, the stage had become ready for the cleaning out of six million Jews from Europe. A group estimated by Morse to of approximately 100,000 volunteers in 1943 formed the Nazi SS-Division, Hanzar, with the Mufti serving as chief administrator (Morse, 2003). The Mufti implemented the Nazi "Pejani Plan" resulting in the killings of approximately 200,000 Christian Serbs, 40,000 Gypsies and 22,000 Jews.

Germany at the time was engaged in its decisive offensive towards Stalingrad and Rostov. According to the agreed upon plan, once the tank divisions and air squadrons were to make their appearance south of the Caucusus, the public appeal as requested by the Grand Mufti for a mobilization would get out to the Arab world. Germany anticipated a large number of eager volunteers to join the Arab Legion to join efforts for the common cause against England. The Grand Mufti advised the Germans to bomb Tel Aviv and pointed out their mutual interests including the demise of English and Jewish power (Lewis, 1995).

The mufti went on record as clarifying his position regarding the scheme. He claimed on behalf of Islam that this German offensive was "indeed a just war." Therefore, "Islam not only supports the war," but further argued that "the Germans are to be assured of victory because Islam can never support an unjust war" (Lacquer and Rubin, 1984). Though the German advance to the Caucuses was eventually halted by the Soviet Army, the mufti and those supporting his position could never accept the allied victory and could not concede the defeat of the Axis powers nor disavow their political objectives (Morse (2003). In 1943, Hitler appointed the Mufti as head of a Nazi-Moslem government. From his headquarters in Berlin, he laid out plans for a concentration camp for Jews near Nablus in Palestine modeled after the concentration camp, Auschwich. That year the Mufti was installed as head of the Nazi-created Islamische Zentralinstitut in Dreseen where he set out to begin the process of educating future Islamic leaders in Nazi idealogy.

Arab Denial of the Holocaust

The reason Arabs today deny the Holocaust took place is that they disavow their guilt for supporting German anti-Jew policies. In 1945, Yugoslavia sought to indict the Mufti as a war criminal for his role in recruiting 20,000 Muslim volunteers for the SS, who participated in the killing of Jews in Croatia and Hungary (Bard, 2001). He escaped from French detention in 1946, however, and continued his fight against the Jews from Cairo and later in Beirut.

Most of the Arab states sat on the fence for six years since the beginning of the war waiting in vain for signs of nearby Axis victories. Meanwhile, Iraq, established in 1932, was taken over by pro-Nazis in 1941 to join the Axis powers. England moved quickly and forced the new government out of power. Even as the war continued to its inevitable end, the Arabs were most reluctant to enter the war against Nazi Germany. Only Transjordan went along with the British in 1939. Later, in 1945, seeing that all hope was lost for an Axis seizure of the Middle East and as the Axis powers collapsed, Egypt declared war against Germany on February 25; Syria on February 27; Lebanon on February 28; and Saudi Arabia, on March 2, in order to join the newly formed United Nations. By contrast, some 30,000 Palestinian Jews fought against Germany.[22]

Even as the war in Europe was coming to its end, Haj Amin el Husseini, continued his Anti-Jewish propaganda broadcasts as he had been doing for the Axis powers during the war. For him and for many Arab leaders, the war seemed to continue on. He landed in Cairo in June 1945. A photograph is offered in the 1947 *Universal Yearbook* (Funk and Wagnall, 1948) of a large group of Arabs listening to a speech in British-controlled Palestine. The Arab League (composed of Egypt, Iraq, Lebanon, Saudi Arabia, Syria, Transjordan and Yemen) warned the United Nations that the partition of Palestine would be considered a hostile act by 400,000,000 Moslems. In Saudi Arabia, on December 12, King Ibn Saud said he hoped the U.N. would "correct" its "mistake" on Palestine's partition.

Colonialism was in its final years; Arab nationalism was on the rebound. The axis powers lost the war, but the new Arab states did not yield in their supporting the axis cause, and were reluctant to yield to democratic directions following the war. It was in this climate that new Arab states were being formed. After the war, with increasing pressure from Jews for a homeland and from Arabs to keep them out of the area, the British were at a standstill. World Jewry and many of the allied powers supported the new Jewish state. Many European Jews that survived the war were among the large number of "displaced

---

[22]On September 3, 1939, the Zionist Executive in Jerusalem published a call to all young people to enroll in Jewish units to fight Hitler. In a few weeks 130,000 men and women registered. According to Ben-Gurion (1974), the British at first refused to accept Jewish volunteers unless an equal number of Arabs came forward. Few Arabs volunteered; most of the leaders in Palestine and the neighboring countries supported Hitler and prayed for his victory. It was not until 1944, as a result of Churchill's personal intervention, that a Jewish Brigade was formed, which fought in Italy and took part in the decisive battles.

persons" looking forward to emigrate to Palestine. The Arabs rejected any move that might lead to the development of a new state in Palestine declaring the partition as illegal.

The positive sentiments with that of the Axis powers of World War I and II are now encased on top of the already strong and well developed linkage to the past. This newer thread, given the quality of the older ones, and enlivened by the years of promise held by the Axis Powers, has not only intensified the potency of the inner core of linkage to the past, but had added this newer thread encased with a rebuff of western democracy, secular government, big business, with British and French hegemony.   Beyond that of a fear of non-Arabic religious beliefs, there is also a more recent fear that Islam may succumb to the secularism that they perceive has taken hold over Judaism and Christianity.

This attitude is so prevalent and had been going on for so many years that it has led to the development of another thread that connects the current consciousness of Arab Moslems with that of the past -- a very positive, yet disavowed sentiment for much of the objectives of the Axis Powers of both world wars. That there was a common interest with Germany in the days preceding and during the Second World War in eliminating the Jewish problem was a further bonus that bonded Arab leaders associated with Ba'ath with that of the German National Socialist Party, the Nazis.

Chapter 19

Arab Precepts of the "Illegitimacy of Israel"

Overview

A dominant theme running through the fabric of the rhetoric of those that support the violence and terror in Israel is the precept that Israel is an illegal country. The Arab League had its pact signed in March 22, 1945. The one issue to which they could agree upon was not resolving issues involved with the ending of the British Mandate of Palestine. The Arab League would not accept the U.N. partition of Palestine into the two areas, "Jewish" and "Arab" as recommended and stipulated by the United Nations. Upon passage, the argument offered by the Arab committee at the time was that proceedings were illegal. The Arab media at the time protested, and referred to Israel as illigitamate. The threads linking such a notion to the past at that time were even more active then at this juncture of time. This chapter reveals how it happened that the league failed in preventing the establishment of Israel, but was indeed successful in preventing a new Palestinian state from being formed.

The Plan for Partition of Palestine: (1947-1948)

It seems that it is easier for Arabs to agree on what together they are against, then as to agree on how to go about doing something constructive. According to Woolbert (1948, p381-382), whose summary of Palestine appeared in the *Universal Yearbook*, the Arab League agreed to "prevent Palestine, or any part of it, from being made into a Jewish state." Woolbert went on to state, " the countries represented used whatever instruments of policy that were at their disposal." Sometimes they acted singly, as in the case of Iraq's embargo on Jewish goods from Palestine, or collectively as a cohesive block in the U.N. The League, not being a state or federation, was not eligible for membership in the U.N. However, it often brought pressure to bear on that body through the concerted action of its members.

The British studied the matter of partitioning Palestine into Jewish and Arab sections. They listened to proponents of various solutions and offered variants to the Jews and Arabs in the area. Much rhetoric and threats were offered by spokes people of the developing Arab League.

The Arab League rejected the British plan for partition. The British passed the matter on to the United Nations with the recommendation for an immediate formation of a Jewish and a Palestinian state (Khalidi, 2002). The center of the Jewish state was to be in Tel Aviv. The center for the new Arab state was to be in Jaffa. It seemed at the time that two more nations would soon be born in addition to the new Arab states in the Middle East, one a national homeland for Jews and another, next door, a home for the new Arab state, mostly Moslems, residing in Palestine.

The Arab states, some of them very new at the time, did not want a newer one with the fabric of the Palestinian Arabs. They already had their hands full building their own infrastructure. Within a few days the Arab League, influenced by Syria, Lebanon, Jordan, Saudi Arabia, Iraq and Egypt declared the partition illegal and supplied the Arab Committee, influenced by Husseini, with weapons and volunteers.

Meanwhile, the pan-Arabists, now at their height of influence, were urging the British to continue placing limitations on Jewish emigration to Palestine even though the war had ended though the Arabs had not participated in the war as allies. The Pan-Arabist movement, sympathetic to the Axis cause, continued on in ways as if the war was still going on. They denied the holocaust had taken place in Europe. They resisted settlement of the Jews. They scorned western style democracies and secular governments. They perceived the U.S. and England as wanting to control the Middle East and the world's energy. They asserted Jews controlled the world's money supply and business supply. They maintained anti western attitudes and supported the "New Order" of the Axis cause.

As the post year months passed, the Arab leadership became further tied to Islam, which also served as a cohesive political force binding them together. They continued their anti-Jewish policies. With strong fervor, but with clear error to their polemics, they denounced the legitimacy of permitting Jews to come to Palestine. They were successful in impeding Jewish emigration to Palestine until May of 1948 when Israel declared its independence. We recall that the leaders of the Arab states seemed unable to recognize the reality of the situation. They seemed to hang on to notions of past glories.

In his autobiography, Abba Eban (1977) covers the immediate period leading to the establishment of Israel. In 1947, during what he considered "a moment of climax" in this part of his political career, he been engaging in discussion with political leaders involved in the partition plans, including Abdul Rahman Azzam Pasha, Secretary-General of the Arab League. At the time the Arab League had a central position in Arab diplomacy and could be regarded as the central power in Arab nationalism which was approaching its height. Others present were David Horowitz, then a senior Zionist official in charge of political work in Jerusalem, John Kimche, correspondent of the London *Observer*, the *Economist* and the *Tribune*. David Horowitz was selected by the Zionist leadership for representation to the 1947 Assembly. At that time Horowitz and Eban stressed a single theme: would it not be better for Arabs to work out a plan, instead of clinging to vain resistance, so that we might live in cooperation and compromise? Azzam's reply was "courteous, but firm."

> The Arab world is not in a compromising temper...Get one thing into your heads You will not get anything by compromise or by peaceful means. You may perhaps get something, if at all, by force of arms....

Eban pointed out, "Even if there is a war, we would not disappear. We would have to meet afterward to negotiate.... Since negotiation would have to take place after the war, why not have negotiation before and instead of war."
Azzam replied,

> You are too rational. The Arab world regards the Jews as invaders. It is going to fight you. War is absolutely inevitable. If you win the war, you will get your state. If you get your state by winning a war, you have a chance that the Arabs will one day have to accept it, although that is not certain. But do not consider for a single moment that you will ever have a chance of our accepting you in advance. This is a question of historical pride. There is no shame in being compelled by force to accept an unjust and undesirable situation. It is shameful to accept such a fact without attempting to prevent it. This conflict has its roots deep in history. There will have to be decision; and the decision will have to be by force.

Eban, Abba (1977), p 86

Events in Palestine in 1947

In January, the British made a desperate attempt to find a way out of the impasses. The Palestine High Commissioner, Sir Alan Cunningham left for London on January 1st. In his absence the question arose as to who should represent the Arab state. The Arab Higher Committee were able to chose the Arab delegation. The Grand Mufti was excluded by the U.N. because of his pro-Axis activities during the war. The result was that the representatives were closely allied to the Mufti. The outcome seemed predictable. Their stance would be as if the Germans had not been defeated at Stalingrad and a road from Rostov to Iraq had been secured by the Werhmacht and that there had been no defeat of the Axis Powers.

The British developed a plan. The plan provided for 100,000 Jewish immigrants to be admitted to Palestine during the following two years; the Jewish Agency and the League Mandate were both to be abolished; in their place would be a U.N. trusteeship under a British High Commissioner to be set up for five years – during which time Palestine would be divided into two zones, one with a Jewish majority and the other with an Arab majority. If the Jews and Arabs agreed, Palestine would become independent; if they did not agree, the issue would go to the U.N. There was to be no agreement.

There was supposed to be a truce during the period of the London conference, but it was poorly kept. Insurgent attacks by Jewish groups ensued upon British personnel and installations increased. On January 12 the police station in Haifa was shattered by a bomb blast that killed 5 policemen and wounded 142 persons in all. Appalled by this outrage, the Va'ad Leumi and the moderate Jewish organizations talked of using force to repress the insurgents. For their part the British imposed taxes to pay for the damages. In addition to all this anti-governmental action was the arrival of ships loaded, often badly overloaded with Jewish refugees from Europe and North Africa, seeking admission to the Promised Land. Most were intercepted and taken to refugee camps on Cypress, not to be released until Israel declared its independence in May, 1948.

Between April 28 and May 15 the General Assembly held 15 plenary meetings, while the Political and Security Committee met 12 times. On May 1st, with the U.S. leading the anti-Arab forces, the Assembly voted 25 to 15 not to accept the Arab proposal to establish Palestine's independence.

On August 31, the UN Special Committee on Palestine, that had its first meeting on May 27, came up just before its deadline with a number of recommendations. Items agreed upon included: speed of action to terminate the mandate, a transition period to be as short as possible, responsibility to the UN, sacred places to be preserved with access ensured, alleviation of distressed European Jews, the political structure to be democratic with a constitution to safeguard rights of minorities, an economic unity of Palestine and an end to violence. The two states were to be independent after a two year transition period starting September 1, 1947, during which 150,000 settlers were to be admitted to the Jewish area.

The Zionists were pleased, though not satisfied with the boundaries of the suggested Jewish state. The Arabs were enraged. They repeated their threats to fight against the partition "to the last drop of blood." One of the foes of the mufti, a labor leader named Sami Taha, was assassinated in Haifa on September 12.

Syria saw the area to their south as an extension of Syria. They wanted Palestine for themselves and did not recognize any form of Palestinian nationalism.[23] In 1937, a local Arab leader, Auni Bey Abdul-Hadi, told the Peel Commission, which ultimately suggested the partition of Palestine: "There is no such country....Palestine is a term the Zionists invented!....There is no Palestine in the Bible....Our country was for centuries part of Syria." (Yaniv, 1974, p39 in Bard, 2001). As late as 1947 the spokesman for the position of Syria said "Palestine is a Province of Syria," and that "politically, the Arabs of Palestine were not independent in the sense of forming a separate political entity." Later, Ahmed Shuqeiri, the chairman of the PLO, told the security Council: "It is common knowledge that Palestine is nothing but southern Syria." (Palestine Royal Commission Report, 1937, p 51, in Bard, 2001).

The Arab population of Palestine accepted the British plan for their new Arab state (Woolbert, 1948, p376). The "shadow government" of the Mufti even agreed to pay the taxes that would be imposed. But on September 29, Jamel El-Husseini, representing the Arab Higher Committee, the group became further aligned with the Mufti. They informed the UN Committee that an Arab

---

[23] Palestinian Arab nationalism is a post World War II phenomenon that did not become a significant political movement in Israel until after the 1967 six Day War and Jordan's release of the West Bank

state for all of Palestine was the only solution his people would accept; otherwise the country would be drowned in blood.

From October 7 to 9 the Council of the Arab League met in Lebanon. They asked the Arab states to send troops to the border of Palestine, ready "for any emergency." The much awaited news on U.S. policy was spoken on October 11, the verdict: a favoring of partition. Two days later the Soviet delegation concurred, calling the need for setting up a Jewish state "urgent." On October 16, the Committee was told that Great Britain was determined to withdraw from Palestine. November 3 found the Soviet delegation asserting the mandate should end by January 1, 1948, with the British leaving by April 1. On November 17, the British informed the Committee they would leave by August 1, and thus not be available for enforcement of the partition. A London Times correspondent in Jerusalem on November 17 sent a dispatch declaring the British withdrawal was already under way. On November 17, the subcommittee agreed on a timetable for partition: the mandate was to end on August 1, 1948, and the two new states were to be created within two months after British evacuation, or supposedly by October 1. The issue was passed on to the General Assembly. After several delays a vote was taken on November 29 and partition by October 1, 1948 carried by 33 to 13 with 10 abstentions including Great Britain and China, while among those voting affirmatively were the US, USSR and France.

After the vote was taken the representatives of Iraq, Saudi Arabia, Syria and Yemen declared their governments would not be bound by the decision and, accompanied by the Lebanese and Egyptian delegates, walked out of the meeting. The U.N. came out with its first unequivocal decision made possible by active American and Soviet support in the face of opposing opinions and votes of the Middle Eastern states, most of whom supported the Axis powers prior to, and during the Second World War. This obstruction to the U.N. plan seems but another manifestation of Arab denial of the Axis defeat and of the allied victory.

Events of 1948

Throughout the year there was an abundance of bellicose rhetoric on our radio, newspapers and on motion picture, notably on *Movietown News* denouncing the U.N. and the Zionist movement. Outspoken Zionist and new Jewish leaders presented their views in support of the Jewish state to be. Arab states declared their intent in destroying the budding nation using similar rhetoric seen among the pro-Nazis. Leaders of the attacking Arab countries declared the U.N. partition proceedings invalid. The Arab leaders denied the Holocaust; it was "an invention, a Zionist ploy, to rationalize their evil plans of controlling and corrupting the world."

On the approach of the armies of Lebanon, Syria, Jordan, Saudi Arabia, and Egypt, the word was passed around to Arabs of the coming defeat of the new Zionist entity. They would advance their armies, come in and liberate the area. They attacked on several fronts. In the meantime the populace were given the instruction to flee areas under contention. They were led to believe they would return soon after the military units secured the area. Their propaganda was effective. Yet, we recall, there were no promises of promoting the development of the new "Arab state"as outlined by the United Nations partition. Emphasis was not on creating a new state, but on occupying the area and planting their national flags. Their propaganda: We'll get rid of the Zionist entity, then come back and live under our administration. I assume that part of their plans were to convert non-believers to Islam. If the Jews resisted they would be removed by force, or perhaps consistent with *dhimma,* they could stay as a second class of persecuted foreigners in the new extended borders.

Some of the Arab countries immediately succeeded in occupying some of the land. Some of these were quite strategic. Within their occupied perimeters they could readily defend their hold while at the same time set themselves at overlooks above lower areas designated to be part of Israel. areas. They quickly set up martial law. Though a truce occurred, none of the attacking nations relinquished their hold on areas designated to be part of the new Arab state. Once the area was occupied, they set up martial law under the flag and auspices of the invading nation. The Arab residents that were to inherit a state of their own following the U.N. partition became subject to whatever power occupied the land. Lebanon claimed northern sections along the northwest borders of Palestine. Syria held on to the Golan heights down to the east banks of the Sea of Galilee. Egypt, already extended into the Gulf of Sinai, encroached northeast along the Mediterranean coast, occupied Gaza and annexed a finger of land along the coast known as the Gaza Strip. Jordan occupied Samaria and Judea, extensive highland sections between the coastal plain and the Jordan River, and eastern portions of Jerusalem including the entire Old City. Arabs that resided in Lebanon remained under Lebanese administration. Those living in the Golan area remained under the supervision of Syria. Gaza became subject to Egyptian administration. Arabs remaining in Israel found themselves living under Israeli administration.

The UN debates reflected the developing crises in Palestine. Both Jews and Arabs mobilized. December clashes of 1947 mushroomed into fighting and bombing. Evacuation of British troops had started in March and was accompanied by the suspension of mail, money orders and all ensured services. By April the fighting was full fledged. Significant among the battles were those for the Old City of Jerusalem and the Jerusalem-Tel Aviv Road. Fighting in Jaffa occurred in April, but by May 13, became an open city policed by the Haganah. On May 15 the British High Commissioner left, thereby ending the British Mandate, two Egyptian columns advanced from the south, and the State of Israel was declared. Israel was immediately recognized by the U.S.

The Arab powers were successful in denying a new Arab state. In this aspect, the Arab combatants, forces from the more distant countries, Iraq and Saudi Arabia, claimed this as a victory. But on the matter of removing the newly formed state of Israel, the combined striking forces of Egypt, Jordan, Syria, Lebanon, Saudi Arabia and Iraq had failed.

The Arab League accomplished half of what they were against. Iraq and Saudi Arabia had no succession of real estate, but took credit for participating in the successful effort to avoid the set up of the new Arab state. And, interestingly, urged the war to continue so as to drive out the Jews from the "Zionist" entity. The fact that there was now to be no new Arab state evaporated amidst the Arab rhetoric of their "victory." They wanted all of Palestine, Arab and Jewish, for themselves. There was to be no new Arab state. The U.N. did nothing about the Arab attack nor anything about the Syrian, Jordanian and Egyptian occupation of Palestine, nor was there any military reaction to the darkness that set in. The Arab states were quick to go on record as not accepting the new state of Israel and vowed to continue the fight even after the armistice went into effect!

The identification with the Axis Powers seem to explain much of the Arab stance today towards Israel today as well as during its formation. What is uncanny here, is that much of the sentiment and activity on the part of Arabs during the period of time of the emerging of the Axis Powers (1912-1945) is altogether avoided in both the Arab and Western texts and media. This avoidance may be understandable when one considers that much of the early obstruction to both the development of Israel and the Palestinian state on the part of Arab powers is disregarded or down-played even today by western writers. There seems to be very little or no recognition in English texts of the role of the Arab leaders and of the strong favorable sentiments of many Arabs with that of the Axis Powers and the heavy hand of Arab leaders to obstruct both the development of the new state of Israel and the new Arab Palestinian state.

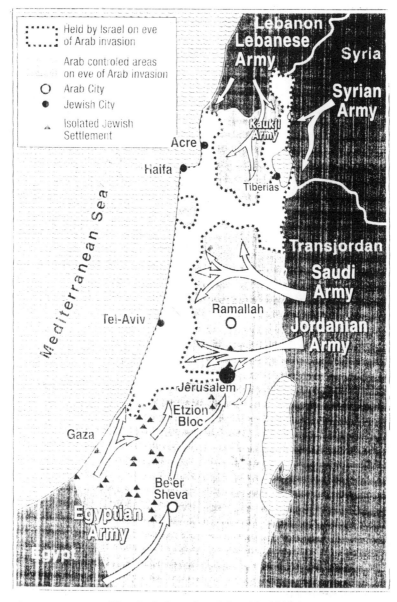

The Arab Invasion: May 15, 1948

The combined military offensive operations by Lebanon, Syria, Saudi Arabia,
Jordan and Egypt to occupy and prevent the development of the new Arab state.
From Bard and Hertz (2001), p64

Chapter 20
Arab and Palestinian Precepts of Entitlement to the Land:
The Refugees

Overview

Current surveys conducted in Israel reveal a widespread sentiment on the part of Arab Palestinians for a claim to all of Palestine (PEW survey, 2002, JMCC Poll #46, 2002). The nationalistic rhetoric supporting the violence always contains reference to themes or precepts of unprovoked victimhood. In such a theme, in one way or another, there is a precept that they are the "hapless target of a Zionist grand design to dispossess them their land, a historical wrong for which they are entitled to redress"(Karsh, 2002, p 120). What is clear is the anti-Israeli, anti-British and more recently, a general anti-western animosity including the United States in such rhetoric, often with comments about western and U.S. hegemony in Arab lands. This negative form of rhetoric consistently appears in current media supporting the Palestinian cause. At times the claim appears limited to the West Bank areas of Samaria to the north and Judea to the south, East Jerusalem and the Gaza strip, all currently under the semi-control of the PA. This claim of entitlement to *Eretz Yisrael*, when presented in Arabic in the Arab media, is understood by readers to eliminate Israel. This chapter examines the issue of Jewish and Arab refugees, Arab and Palestinian precepts to entitlement to the land, and the rationale and roots of such precepts.

Arab Colonization of *Eretz Ysrael*

For centuries following the 135-137 Jewish Revolt, with the exception of early Christian developments in the Galilee and during the Crusade period, whatever interest there was on the part of occupiers in the land was limited to sapping the area of resources to provide revenue for distant governments and crown families in some foreign land. The indigenous people, be they Jews or Christians, and Moslems after 625, were without representation by governing power for 1,800 years. The British brought reforms and a modicum of self-government in 1917. But it was not until the establishment of Israel that Eretz Yisrael became free of occupying powers.

Whoever lived in the area during this long period spent much of their efforts in agriculture, probably local, in trade, as merchants, artisans, or engaged in some religious activity. Other than Jews, all other religious and ethnic groups had their original home elsewhere. All records indicate that every occupier and conqueror had households and a family history elsewhere in some foreign land.

The Arab/Moslem claim to entitlement to this land is an extension from that built upon the older religious/political belief, the carte blanche license by tenets of the *Qur'an,* to claim this part of the world as Islamic. The fundamental expansionist themes found in the *Qur'anic* tenets of *Dar al-Harb* and *Dar Al Islam,* the World of Islam and the World of War.

The latter part of the Turkish occupation was characterized by some order and improvements in the land with a slowly developing Jewish infrastructure developing in some areas. This trend continued during the times of the British Mandate. By 1947 there were workable local Arab and Jewish governments operating well under an umbrella of a higher level of British control.

At the price of a great deal of denial and distortions in recanting the recent and distant past, there seems to continue to be a carte blanche claim to the land. The estrangement from Jordanian, Israeli, Syrian and Egyptian life have now become part of the consciousness of Arab Palestinians. Arousal of these matters cause a great deal of anguish among Palestinians who search for answers in a past embellished by illusions of political and religious glories.

In 1948, Syria, Lebanon, Jordan, Iraq, Saudi Arabia, Yemen and Egypt conspired together to invade the eastern side of Palestine, west of the Jordan River. Their objective: (1) obstruct the development of Israel, (2) prevent the new Arab Palestinian state from being started and (3) to facilitate the occupation of western Palestine by Lebanon, Syria, Jordan and Egypt.

Many Arabs fled contested areas in Palestine in 1948 in the anticipation of the approaching military units. There continues to be a claim in support of the Arabs that fled the area in 1948 for a right of return to properties that they once held, or to be so compensated for the loss that had occurred. This obstruction by the Arab countries were occurring as hundreds of thousands of Jews throughout Arab lands in the Middle East were becoming uprooted from their homes. Of all those uprooted, there were probably more Jews than Arabs.[24] Almost all the Jews were resettled, many in Israel. There is a movement among Jews that were forced to leave a number of Arab countries to demand as part of a peace settlement, reparations for the uprooting of Jews during this period, an equal number of Jews.[25] Rachel Pomerance (2002), in an article entitled, "Compensation sought for Jewish refugees," argues that upcoming peace negotiations in the Middle East include reparations from Arab states for causing the fleeing of Jews from their respective countries, and that these funds contribute to Arabs who claim a loss of property in Israel. Over 135 million refugees were created during the Twentieth Century. In 1947 Britain was withdrawing from India, leading to the birth of independent Pakistani and Indian states. The Indians and Pakistanis agreed to transfer millions of their people across the border to defuse ethnic and religious tensions. India sent Muslims to Pakistan, which in turn sent Hindus to India. Both states had granted citizenship to these refugees (Lewis, 1995). Such sanctioned transfer was not promoted by the United Nations; the participants in the struggle were able to work out such difficulties.

At the price of a great deal of denial and distortions in recanting the recent and distant past, there seems to continue to be a carte blanche claim to the land. The estrangement from Jordanian, Israeli, Syrian and Egyptian life have now become part of the consciousness of Arab Palestinians. Arousal of these matters cause a great deal of anguish among Palestinians who search for answers in a past embellished by illusions of political and religious glories.

---

[24]A group, "Justice for Jews From Arab Countries" is seeking redress from Arab countries on behalf of 865,000 who fled or were expelled. What form it will take should be determined in Israeli-Palestinian peace talks. (Rachel Pomerance, 2002.) In 1945 there were nearly 900,000 Jews in communities throughout the Arab world. Today there are fewer than 8,000 (Lerman, 1989).

[25]Following the War for Independence it is estimated that 820,000 Jewish refugees fled from Arab lands of which 586,000 were resettled in Israel at great expense and hardship to the new state. According to Bard (2001) Between 1948 and 1972, there were 602,000 Jewish refugees from Arab countries. Though treated with the "protection" of *dhimma*, the lives of Jews became suddenly in greater peril immediately following the U.N. partition and again after the War of 1967. Jews and Moslems were both aware that attitudes towards Jews varied with individuals, but all were aware that persecution of Jews was consistent with Islamic writings. They had to leave their ancestral homes, property and assets, travel a great distance to another culture, take up a language and customs foreign to them and take on new economic and social roles. Very few Jews now remain in Arab countries.

Palestinian Refugees

Soon after hostilities broke out in May of 1948, almost all Palestinian Arabs chose not to fight the Israelis nor join the foreign Arab units, but to leave for other Arab areas not in the path of military action. They left the fighting of the Jews to the hands of the existing armies of Lebanon, Syria, Jordan, Iraq, Saudi Arabia, Yemen, and Egypt. At the time these "armies" seemed quite ominous. There was a great deal of hope that one or more of such Arab units would soon enter in their area and beat off the Jewish defenders.

On May 14, 1948 crowds of Arabs stood by the roads leading to the frontiers of Palestine, enthusiastically welcoming the advancing armies. Days and weeks passed, sufficient to accomplish the sacred mission, but the Arab armies did not save the country

Middle East Journal, October, 1949

Karsh (2002) describes the exodus of Arabs as largely because of the tendency of Arab leaders to leave the country. As the leaders left, there was an acceleration over the months for Arabs to leave. The intellectuals, according to Karsh, claimed their battle was "an intellectual one," leaving the fighting to outsiders. Though we know of areas of Israel where Arabs were under duress to leave, such as in Safed, it was under military action during a fight for the city that led to their fleeing and not as a result of a policy or overall sentiment of the people. Karsh describes much animosity between the Palestinians and the Arab armies that came to save them. The Palestinians felt they were derelict for having issued wild promises of military support for which they never made good, whereas the Arab League regarded the Palestinians as a cowardly lot who had shamefully deserted their homeland while expecting others to fight for them.

In those areas the Arab legions occupied, they planted their respective national flags. As the fighting spread into areas that had previously remained quiet, the Palestinian Arabs began to see the possibility of the failure of the Arab Legion to finish off the "Zionist entity." As the possibility turned into reality, the flight of the Arabs increased. More than 300,000 departed after May 15, leaving 160,000 Arabs in the State of Israel (Prittie, 1972). Although most of the Arabs had left by November 1948, there were still those who chose to leave even after hostilities ceased, as was the case with the evacuation of 3,000 Arabs from Faluja, a village between Tel Aviv and Beersheva. An ordinance was passed creating custodial care of abandoned property, "to prevent unlawful occupation of empty houses and business premises. to administer ownerless property, and to secure deserted fields (Schechtman, 1963).

The word had long been put out by the Arab media of the invading countries that the "occupiers" were not them, but the Jews, the new "aggressors" in the Middle East, the" Zionists." There was little attention at the time to the fact that the armies of Jordan, Egypt and Syria were occupying non-Jewish areas and little coverage in the papers of the persecutions and massacres of these Arab peoples throughout neighboring Jordan, Syria and Lebanon and other countries. These Arab countries put out an integrated propaganda campaign focused on arguing the illegitimacy to the State of Israel, at that time being made out to be a common enemy. At the time the propaganda served to work well to turn the anger of the Palestinians away from their Arab occupiers onto the Israelis. In retrospect, it seems that this stance was a ploy to politicize the plight of the refugees at the expense of their internal difficulties as well as an attempt to position themselves favorably within the power struggle among the Arab bloc of nations. This direction of psychological warfare capitalized on latent sentiments for the Axis Powers and was consistent with the anti-Jewish common interest on the part of members of the Arab League, thus accounting for much of the source of the precept of entitlement itself.

The General Assembly of the UN voted on November 19, 1948, to establish aid to the refugees with a budget of $50,000,000. By the mid 1950s it became evident neither the refugees nor the Arab states were prepared to cooperate on the large-scale development projects originally foreseen by the Agency as a means of alleviating the Palestinians's situation. Early in 1949, the Palestine Conciliation Commission (PCC) had opened negotiations. The Arabs insisted Israel yield the territory won in the 1948 fighting and agree to repatriation. The Israelis told the commission the solution of the refugee problem depended on the conclusion of a peace. Later, on April 1, 1950, the Arab League adopted a resolution forbidding its members from negotiating with Israel. The PCC made another effort to bring the parties together in 1951, but finally gave up reporting "...the Arab Governments have evinced no readiness to arrive at such a peace settlement with the Government of Israel (Palestine Conciliation Commission Report, 1948-1952; in Bard, 2001).

The camps are now in the hands of the Palestinian Authority. Though much was attempted, little was accomplished to improve the lot of the Palestinians living in them. Journalist Netty Gross visited Gaza and asked an official why the camps there hadn't been dismantled. She was told the PA had made a "political decision" not to do anything for the more than 400,000 Palestinians living in the camps until the final-status talks with Israel took place (Jeruslaem Report, 1999).

By the middle of 2000, the number of Palestinian refugees on UNRWA rolls had risen to 3.7 million, five or six times the number that left Palestine in 1948. One-third of the registered Palestinian refugees, about 1.1 million, live in 59 recognized refugee camps in Jordan, Syria, the West Bank and Gaza Strip. The other two-thirds of the registered refugees live in and around the cities and towns of the host countries, often in the environs of official camps. As of June 2000 the total of Palestinian Refugees Registered by UNRWA was:

Location	Registered Refugees	Camps	Registered Refugees in Camps
Jordan	1,570,192	10	280,191
Lebanon	376,472	12	210,715
Syria	383,199	10	111,712
West Bank	583,009	19	157,676
Gaza Strip	824,622	8	451,186
Total	3,737,494	59	1,211,480

It was the intent of the U.N. to dismantle the camps and put into place a costly social-economic program. Not only was there no support from the Arabs involved, but resistance offered by neighboring Arab states. As of today there seems to be insufficient infrastructure, even with aid, to solve the social and economic problems of the Palestinian refugees. The Palestinian assertions of the right of return for themselves and their descendants is at the expense of a general Arab denial of reality which is now apparent in their distortion of critical historical events.

Their appeal for the right of return is linked with the support of many Arab Palestinians to revert the borders back to the lines of the British Mandate of 1917 and have the area controlled by a Palestinian state. Not only would this be an affront to Israel, also to Jordan. Though the Arab states wish to get rid of Israel, and some are willing to take risks to enjoy Islamic control throughout the Middle East, no Arab country seems to be able to tolerate a new Arab state in the Palestine area. The Arab states continue to appear to not want a Palestinian state in any current conceptual form.

The Palestinian Claim

The Palestinian precept of entitlement seems fairly clear, as does the sources for the distortions of facts. From an Islamic viewpoint there seems little doubt that the operations of the *mujahidin*, warriors for the cause of Islam, against the Jews in Israel are legitimate. The usual basis of the precept goes back to the Islamic view as Palestine being a *Dar al-harb*, a territory of war. In a review by Lisa Palmieri-Billig in the Jerusalem Post, issue, June 9, Magdi Allam, the Italian columnist of Egyptian origin who writes regularly about the Arab and Muslim world for the national daily *La Republica* (2003), the new Imam of the Grand Mosque of Rome, the largest in Europe, Abdel-Samie Mahmoud Ibrahim Moussa, called for the "victory of Islamic fighters in Palestine, Chechnya and others in the world." He was further quoted as having told Magdi Allam that suicide attacks in Israel are religiously legitimate, whereas they are not in Saudi Arabia, Morocco or Italy. Such a precept seemed sufficient to offer a rationale for the violence and terror tactics amidst us when we were in Israel in 2002. The argument goes that these are missions of martyrdom and those who commit them are martyrs of Islam because all Palestine is a *Dar al-harb*. Magdi Allam, author of several books on Islam in Italy, considered the position as not an isolated phenomenon of the preaching of hate. The lack of outcry by the Italian community is worrisome as there are one million Mjuslims in Italy, by far outnumbering the numerically small but historically important 35,000 Jews in Italy.

The feeling of wanting a land, even coveting a land in of itself is understandable. But such a feeling or attitude cannot in any way change the reality of the situation, only the way that it may be perceived or described. The Palestinians cannot make a real case of entitlement to the land because the evidence of such is not supported. That they may believe they had founded the land is but a wish. Who was it that claimed it? What were it's borders and its capital and major cities? What may have constituted its economy and the nature of its administration and who provided security for its people? What was its coinage, language and religion? Yet, this innermost thread appears throughout the Palestinian controlled media and has become a part of anti-war slogans, and quite likely forms a parcel of the consciousness of almost all Palestinian Arabs.

When the links in previous chapters are connected together with this false precept of entitlement, and when all are believed as true, incorporated into a perceptual reality with working defense mechanisms, such individuals can be considered dangerous to others and self.

Contributing to the problem are the many distortions and half-truths, appearing throughout the contemporary Arab media. For example, the *Syria Times*, May 28, 2003 in an editorial entitled "Who are the Palestinian Refugees?" argues that (a) No settlement can be just and complete if recognition is not accorded to the right of the Arab refugee to return to the home from which he has been dislodged in 1948 so Israel could establish a State for Jews in Palestine and (b) those Arabs that fled Israel during the 1967 War when Israel launched a war against Jordan. Both premises are blatantly false. The Arabs left in 1948 because of the invasion of Palestine by military units from Lebanon, Syria, Jordan and Egypt who occupied the area preventing a new Arab state from forming. In 1967, Jordan attacked Israel without pretense other than that of an impending and expected victory by Egyptian forces. The Jordanians had forsaken the Arab population in the West Bank.

Chapter 21
Palestinian Nationalism

Overview

Nationalism and patriotism have similar meanings. According to Webster's abridged Dictionary, nationalism refers to loyalty and devotion to a nation, a sense of national consciousness exalting the culture and interests as opposed to those of other nations. Patriotism stems from the word, patriot, anything derived from one's father, but generally refers to someone that demonstrates love for one's country and zealously supports its authority and interests. This chapter explores the roots of Palestinian nationalism and patriotism and the rhetoric espoused supporting its cause.

Much of the arguments, position statements and objectives seen in today's rhetoric supportive of the Palestinian cause are little different than that addressed by spokespeople for the Arab cause during the U.N. partition of 1948. Later, in 1974, when Arafat addressed the United Nations, about ninety-five percent of this lengthy address contained a historical critique of Israel, the United Nations and the West very similar to the Arab rhetoric continuing since the Second World War. About two percent of this address iis focused on the merits of the Palestinian Liberation Organization. The balance, about one percent, refers to positive objectives such as "eternal presence...a cultural heritage...a self-determination...being uprooted from the land...freedom. But even these matters are filled with references to the Zionist entity, the occupiers...aggressors, the struggle with the era of colonialism....Jews are the instruments of aggression....of Zionist theology... Israel as imperialistic, colonialist, racist, reactionary and discriminatory and blocking the "right of return" (Arafat, 1977).

The Jordanian Withdrawal from the West Bank

Despite Israel's effort to avoid incursions into West Bank areas occupied by Jordan since 1948, Jordan attacked Israel in 1967 from the east. The attack began early in Six Day War when Jordan supposedly anticipated a successful

Egyptian attack in the south. Within three days, Jordan relinquished their hold over Jerusalem, Samara and Judea. East Jerusalem and the Old City also suddenly came under Israeli rule. The advance of the Syrian army to the north as well as that of Egypt to the south, were stopped. A truce was established that permitted Israel to hold on to the Golan, the Sinai Peninsula and the Old City of Jerusalem. Israel suddenly found itself reluctantly in control of the entire West Bank areas to the Jordan River.

Arabs residing under the Jordanian occupation had already begun to identify themselves as "Palestinians." The Palestinian Liberation Organization had been recognized in hopes of developing an infrastructure that many hoped that would lead to economic growth, greater security and welfare for residents in the West Bank areas.

Meanwhile Jews throughout the Arab world continued to be persecuted, but with increased intensity. Jews residing in Saudi Arabia, Iran, Iraq, Syria, Jordan, Egypt and other Arab countries, though perceived as Mid Easterners, were considered likely to be supportive of Israel. By Islamic tradition, they were outcasts and subject to further restrictions than had existed on and before 1948. More Jews from Arab lands were displaced in this way than Arabs that left the Israeli controlled areas in Palestine.

Palestinian Nationalism

The Palestine Liberation Organization (PLO) and its parent, Fatah, grew out of the Fedayeen, an anti-Jewish organization that had begun perpetrating terrorist tactics against Jews in the British Mandate since the 1930s. The Fedayeen were active til the Suez War of 1956 when Fatah, influenced by the Muslim Brotherhood, took over their role (Ben-Sasson, 1999, Ben-Gurion, 1974). A draft resolution issued at an Arab summit in Cairo in 1963 established the PLO which became operational in the West Bank in 1964.

Since 1964, Arabs residing in Jordanian controlled areas called themselves "Palestinians." Arabs residing in other countries who claim a residence in Palestine after 1946, according to the PLO, may also refer to themselves as Palestinian. Prior to 1964, people living in Palestine, whether in the West Bank, The Golan, Gaza or throughout Israel who were not Jewish were called, Arabs. Though some Arabs could speak Hebrew, French or English, their language was Arabic and the predominate religion was Islam. Though most were Moslem, some Arabs were of Jewish, Samaritan, Christian or Bahai backgrounds.

Under Jordanian occupation, there had been little effort extended on the part of the Palestinians to create an infrastructure leading to a responsible administration.   When the Jordanians moved out, there was no Palestinian infrastructure to maintain the area.   The vacuum was filled by the Israeli government.   The situation in many areas were improved, especially East Jerusalem where water and power were connected and developed.

The Palestinian Liberation Organization, from its beginning shared the sentiment denying the defeat of the War of 1967.   The Arabs residing in the area became quite vulnerable to anti-Israel sentiment.   Much of the energy seems focused on accusing Israel and her allies of intensifying economic pressure on the Palestinians to achieve political goals.   As reported by the *Jerusalem Post* (2002), Peter Hansen, commissioner-general of the United Nations Relief and Works Agency, stated "few places have ever undergone as steep and rapid a decline in income and living standards and as rapid an increase in mass deprivation; more than 60% of Palestinians in the West Bank and Gaza Strip are now living in poverty.   According to Palestinian Authority Labor Minister Ghassan Khatip, the PA needs $15 million a month to solve the problem of unemployment.   Arab countries are not giving the PA financial aid to help reduce the rate of unemployment, Khatip said.   They are helping to pay the salaries of the PA civil servants.

Much of the rhetoric of Palestinian leaders today remains the same as did in 1948 as stated by their predecessors, the Fedayeen prior to, and during the Second World War, and later by Fatah, and its outgrowth, the PLO and the Palestinian Authority.   Fatah has become the dominate political party of the Palestinian Council, the party of its current Leader, Arafat, a party just ahead of PFLP (Palestinians for the Liberation of Palestine), Hamas and Islamic Jihad.

Despite the passage of fifty years, there has not been any significant single positive change in the relationship between Israel and the Palestinian Arabs. The rhetoric remains largely the same.   But time has passed.   Both areas are more populated.   Israel has become more affluent and stands among other countries in the world in terms of import-exports, technology and tourism.   The Palestinian Authority, for the most part, remains basically unchanged in its structure and society and as a result of the conflict, more isolated.   The Arabs in the area seem more impoverished, more restricted in travel, and to this date continue to show little readiness to become a viable nation.

Chapter 22
Justification Offered for Terror Attacks

Overview

This chapter examines current themes throughout the media supporting the violence, terrorism and suicide bombing attacks while in Israel in 2001. Underlying precepts were selected on the basis of their commonality of appearance in public address, governmental news releases, position summaries of the Arab League, periodicals, secondary reviews of Syrian textbooks and Arabic literature, opinions expressed in American and English language newspapers, especially the *L.A. Times* and *Jerusalem Post* and identifiable material available through the Internet. Much of the material gained from the Internet included English versions of the *Palestinian Chronicle*, translations and versions of the Iranian, Egyptian media and English and French translations of the *Syrian News Agency*.

Current Precepts and Motives

Entitlement to the land: The basis of Arab claims of entitlement to disputed land (lands once claimed to be occupied by Islamic powers or by Islamic control), including *Eretz Yisrael*, stem from the *Qur'an*. As pointed out in Chapter 17, according to *Qur'anic Suras*, there are two "worlds" or kinds of lands or populations of people. One is *Dar al-Islam*, the world of Islam, consisting of people who had submitted themselves to Islam. The other land is *Dar al-Harb*, the land of war, disputed lands inhabited by non-believers. The people of these lands are deemed destined to submit themselves to Islam, if not willingly, by force. There are several parts of the today's world that are at stake in this theological/political conflict, now apparent in Afghanistan, Iran, Pakistan, Lebanon and Jordan. Such matters of entitlement are occurring throughout much of the southwestern Pacific, most notably in Indonesia and the Philippine Islands. Palestine, by nature of its strategic position, its close proximity to Europe, Asia and Africa and being in the Middle East, and for centuries a home for Jews, Christians and Moslems, to Mid- Easterners,

Europeans and Africans, and being in the crossroads of world trade, has the attention of the world. For these reasons, and many more, *Eretz Yisrael*, the lands of Palestine and Israel has been, and is now, the focal point of Arab/Moslem conflict with the world of the west, the land of many non-believers. The rhetoric goes that Palestine, as that of much of the *Dar al-Harb*, has been corrupted by the sins of Judaism and mediocrity of Christianity and its western ways. As such, the entitlement lies in the hands of believers of Muhammad. The non-believers are to submit themselves to the authority of the Almighty as described in the *Qur'an* or be driven out The nature of the claim seems more religious and political than economic or cultural. The precepts of entitlement are more emotional and theological than they are factual, unless one considers the *Qur'anic Suras* as epistemological truths, as Moslems are so taught. The preceding chapters details how and when this claim for the land started and how it became deeply encased onto the Arab-Moslem consciousness. The claim to the land seems to have formed an adhesive core bounding together other linkages to the past. It is this linkage to the past, tenuous as the claim appears, is what underlies much of Arab trepidation and the disquiet stance towards Israel.

This primary link of entitlement stems back to the days of the early Islamic expansion, and as such is based on legendary and perhaps the right of divine revelation, if not sheer attempts at colonization. But if the entitlement is believed as written in the Suras, and if taught and believed as told by many clerics, such admonitions can lead to torment.

The idea of a Jewish presence in Palestine since the days of the Roman occupation is absent in the Arab media. The denial of the Jewish presence in *Eretz Yisrael* for the 1,300 years subsequent to the writings of the *Qur'an* is also quite noteworthy. The Arab/Moslem belief that Jews had no presence in the area is widely shared by many Christians, and unfortunately by some Jews as well. The anti-Jewish or anti-Israeli basis of such a denial is apparent in of itself.

After fifty four years of Israeli statehood and development of its Department of Antiquities, anyone, Christian, Moslem or Jewish, can travel through Israel today and see for themselves, as we did, the evidence of 3,200 years of Jewish presence, a confirmation for a Jewish entitlement to the land.

The dualistic concept of "afterlife": including *jihad* and martyrdom are such important concepts throughout Islamic literature that it is central to understanding the essence of Islam. Much of the rhetoric pertaining to such spiritual aspects is now connected to nationalistic and political aims. The fundamental concepts have become distorted, yet remain quite strong as reflected by the growth of institutional support. Acceleration of recent funding from Saudi Arabia, Syria, the Palestinian Authority, and until recently, Iraq keynotes the matter. In some cases, the welfare system in Israel also supports families of "martyrs" who had ventured out to defeat or destroy the non-believer, the occupier and aggressor -- in the very tradition that was taught and supported a thousand years ago. The use of terror as it was occurring when we were in Israel, we think would not be as endemic if there were no encouragement nor financial incentives offered to the people connected with their acts. Not only does the Israeli government provide welfare assistance to family survivors of the "martyr" but that stipends are offered to the family by the Palestinian Authority as well as from internal and external organizations supporting attacks on Israel. During Israel's Operation Defensive Shield in Ramallah, 2002, documents were found that linked Iraqi President Saddam Hussein with transactions reaching $15 million that were transferred to families of suicide bombers and wounded Palestinians in the territories. Such transfers of funds were conducted with full knowledge of Yasser Arafat and other PA officials. According to the October, 9, 2002 *Jerusalem Post*, Plans had been made since 2000 to transfer $15,000 to families of suicide bombers. Seriously wounded Palestinians received $1,000 and lightly wounded Palestinians received $500. Financial support to the Palestinian Authority comes from areas of the world, some of them continuing to look for ways to eliminate Israel.

Children are being taught to connect dying for the Islamic cause and being granted a choice spot in the after life. Dudkevitch (2002) reported two Arabic publications that encourage children to view suicide bombers as role models. One is an Iranian newspaper for children printed in Kuwait, also distributed to the Moslem world via the Internet, while the other is a children's newspaper printed by Hamas.

Jihad: When the situations warrants, men are required to go to war in order to spread Islam or defend it against infidels (Sutra 2:216). Moslems are taught that individuals who offset the aggressor and/or occupier are entitled to rewards in the after life, in paradise where the souls of good people go after death. (*Qu'ran, Sutra* 4:95, 8:73-74, 9:20-22, 61:12). The afterlife shall be just as rich for those who try, but die in the attempt even if they fail in combating the infidel, aggressor and/or occupier. Even if one has conducted oneself in an undesirable manner, one can be redeemed if one makes an effort to stem off the aggressor or occupier at risk of their own life (4:74). The individual who martyrs oneself in the attempt to ward off the non-believer is entitled to an entrance to the afterlife whereupon thy will be "well-pleased." (22:58,59).

Dhimma* and the timeliness of the *Qu'ran: What had applied in terms of practices thirteen hundred years ago, applies to believers as if time stood still. The concept of *dhimma*, and the Islamic attitude towards the Christian and Jewish unbelievers does not seem to have changed. So long as Jews are in the *Dar al-Islam*, Land of Islam, they are to be treated differentially under the law, with limited rights, restrictions in career choice, business practices, social functioning, and special taxation. As much as many Arabs complain about life in Israel, hundreds of thousands prefer being there than to be in other Arab countries. Yet, this enduring *Dhimmic* outlook towards Christians and Jews seems to have broken away out of the confines of the *Qur'an* and is contributing to the current unrest throughout much of the Arab triangle.

Fear of Western hegemony and colonization: is deeply rooted onto the consciousness of all Arab-Moslems. Chapter 17 discusses current precepts relate to the early expansion of Islam, the Christian Crusades and Turkish occupation of Arab lands from 1516 to 1917. Much of the current themes in Arab media consists of the apprehension connected with foreign hegemony and occupation. Much of this anti western concern comes out of the denial of hegemony of one Arab state over the other, akin to a reaction-formation and projection of blame onto the west, with all the guilt and denial involved upon recognizing their troubles.

Sentimentality for the Axis cause. The sentiment for goals of the Axis Powers does not seem to have been diminished with time. The sentiments continue for the elimination of English and Russian power, overthrowing democratic institutions, and democratic states, setting up a world order free of European colonialism, and a society based on strong central control of trade, business, social and human rights. Sympathies were clearly with the German war plan, under control of the Nazis, to destroy the Jewish element wherever found including those residing in the Arab sphere. Encased on this thread is the extension: since Islamic leaders decreed the struggle as a just war, there can be no public recognition of such a defeat. With this theologically based rationalization, a defeat can be denied and the cause can continue, a theme that perpetuates the sentiment.

Obstructing the development of Israel and the Palestinian state: is connected to the belief that Israel is "illegal", an "aggressor", and an "occupier" that is "encroaching" onto the land. These ideas, as distorted as they seem to be from a western outlook, come about logically as extensions to of the above precepts of entitlement, *jihad, dhimma* and linkages to the aspirations of the Axis powers -- so long as the information encased in the links to the past is believed as true. For so long as Israel is seen as the aggressor, and so long as they believe the War of 1948 and 1967 were to provide Jews with Arab land, there may be little heed to the historical facts that it was indeed, Lebanon, Syria, Jordan and Egypt, with the support of Yemen, Saudi Arabia and Iraq, that aggressively moved in with their military units and occupied what was supposed to become a Palestinian state fifty years ago. What prevented a Palestinian state was not Israel, but the countries that occupied the Arab sections in 1948, Lebanon, Syria, Jordan and Egypt. But for a Palestinian to express such a thought in public, in writing or in any way to be identified with questioning the reality of this link to the past is very damaging, not only to one's self concept but quite dangerous to express publically.

The Palestinians seem to have either forgotten that it was the armies of Jordan, Egypt and Syria that had taken over land intended for the new Arab state, or, they had never learned of the invasion.. The propaganda deflected anger and blame from the Arab states by portraying the Israelis as the new "aggressors" in the Middle East.

American social psychologists, active with the Office of Strategic Services in early 1940s, discovered that if you change the behavior of a group, attitudes tend to favor and support the conduct. Such seems to be the case now in the attitudes of many Palestinians as they see amongst themselves anti-Israeli, anti Jewish and anti-western behaviors, promoting their conflict with Israel.

Recent Developing Aspects

The new-style terrorists that engage themselves in the slaughter of innocent and uninvolved civilians is not "collateral damage." The attacks upon civilians and private property is the prime objective, and almost always involved with media and television coverage. As pointed out in Chapters 3, 9, 12 and 19, attitude surveys can be used to measure the impact of local and world response. The purpose is to inspire fear – a psychological victory, serving to deny a defeat, armistice or treaty -- a situation occurring when some of the losers cannot accept a defeat and hope to turn it around in hopes of an eventual victory. This kind of turn around follows the logic pursued in the past: if a war is justified as being just, it is required through faith to be won, for a just war cannot be lost. The logic of denial was applied by the founders and followers of the Ba'ath Party in Syria and Iraq after the French surrender to Germany in 1940 (See Lewis, 2003), by the Grand Mufti in reference to the Second World War battle for Stalingrad (Eban, 1984), following the failure of the invading Arab armies to drive out the Jews following the U.N. partition of Palestine in 1948 (Universal Yearbook, 1949), by the Muslim Brothers in the early 1950's in Egypt (See Lewis, 2003) and subsequently after every Arab military and political setback in the Middle East.

Suicide missions were pioneered by military /religious organization like Hamas and Hezbellah who from 1982 onward carried out a number of such missions in Lebanon and Israel. The word, *fedayeen*, comes from the Arabic *fider'i*–one who is ready to sacrifice his life for the cause, an identification with the assassins who carried out violent acts following the will of God in 656, first against Moslem rulers, portrayed as impious usurpers (Lewis, 2003).

The recent fundamentalist trend throughout Islam – the turning towards the fundamental values of Islam in response to failures in dealing with western and eastern hegemony -- is not a movement whereupon all fundamentalists support such forms of terrorism. As pointed out above, most Muslims are not fundamentalists, and most Moslems who are fundamentalists are not terrorists nor support such terror tactics. It is significant that Ehud Olmert, the past Mayor of Jerusalem told us while we were in Jerusalem in late August of 2001, that of the 200,000 Arabs residing in Jerusalem, none were known as supporting the terror and violence throughout Israel and even preferred Israeli rule over that of the Palestinian Authority, which they saw as corrupt and unable to provide a satisfactory infrastructure for everyday life.

EPILOGUE

This final segment provides a summary of the findings reported in Part One, our visits to sites of continuous Jewish presence, and of Part Two, the identification of Arab precepts that support the current forms of terrorist action. This final segment ties together the matter of entitlement to Palestine and Israel and the rationale of those individuals that supported terror attacks while we were in Israel in 2001.

SITE VISITS 2000 AND 2001

Our trip was to be a combination vacation and a fun self-tour throughout Israel, to visit sites and experience Jewish life in Israel. These goals were met in 2000. Following our visits to Masada, En Gedi, Hebron and Katzr'in in 2000 we began to experience and learn of history first hand that seemed at a variance with what we had anticipated. At Masada we heard of alternative explanation as to what happened on top of the mountain following the Roman siege. At En Gedi we happened onto a recent excavation of a Jewish city active before, during and after the siege of Masada. While traveling through the West Bank to Hebron we experienced Arab hostility in our approach and visit to the Tomb of the Patriarchs -- in the heart of a city where Jews have lived for long periods of time -- a city now that we believe has become a flashpoint of the Israeli-Palestinian Conflict. There, we witnessed the onset of a confrontation between two misguided Arab youths and an Israeli soldier. A few days later at the ancient city of Katzr'in we were impressed with the advanced state of Jewish life as contrasted to the picture we got at the British Museum in London on life during this time in Europe and England. These four experiences formed the germ of my decision to pursue the matter of Jewish presence throughout Israel.

At home, I searched the literature for additional sites to visit that were likely to provide the evidence I was looking for. These sites included the sites happened upon in 2000, Masada, En Gedi, Gamla, Hebron, Jerusalem, Katzr'in,.Tiberias and Safed Put on the list were specific sites in the above areas as well as an additional visit to Ashkelon, Peki'in, Merin, and the Haifa area. Though there were so many places where Jews had lived in the near and distant pass in *Eretz Yisrael*, that I concluded we could limit our search to these places where we might readily find evidence for the Jewish continuous presence.

Because of the terrorist attack upon New York and Washngton D.C., we were in too much distress to visit Peki'in nor to stop at Haifa. We did agree though that we had already visited enough sites and had gained the supportive data to conclude: Jews have continuously lived in *Eretz Yisrael* since days of the construction of the First Temple continuously to current times, a period of 3,000 years within the perimeters of what is now central and northern Israel.

On Entitlement to the Land

That Jews had lived continuously in what is now Israel for three thousand years is indeed a viable claim to the land. That such a presence is not generally recognized in texts is more than simply noteworthy. It is critical. Many facts not well integrated into history of the Middle East. Facts such as this one, if it were known and accepted might go far to alleviate many of today's problems.

There are a number of myths and distortion among Jews, Christians and Moslems that need to be undone. Some Israelis and Jews still hold on to the view that before the Zionist Congress and Jewish Agency became active in the late 1800s there was little or no Jewish organization in Palestine. There is the newly outdated Catholic position that Judaism was in a degenerate state and thus disappeared after the coming of Jesus -- as a punishment for their various sins (Isaac, 1964). Western college textbook accounts of Middle Eastern History typically omitted the presence of peoples in the Land of Israel after the rise of Christianity, e.g Durant (1935). Though Moslems do recognize the Children of Israel as God's people at the time of the Exodus (Lewis, 2003), there is an absence of recognition of the continuity of Judaism and presence of Jews from those days to the present day throughout the area. Hannah and I saw the implications of such denial and resultant anger on the part of Arabs during our attempt to visit the Tomb of the Patriarchs in Hebron upon witnessing the hate of a two Arab teenagers, and discovering because we were Jewish we were not permitted to enter the site.

The connection between the Jews of Davidic times to the establishment of the modern state of Israel has indeed been continuous, and as such may not need as much support as it did in the past for a connection based on literacy, *Haggadic* literature (the order of readings for Passover), general prayers and poetic sentiment to fuse present Jewish entitlement to *Eretz Yisrael* and Israel. The continual presence of Jews, even if small in numbers, is sufficient in of itself for a claim to entitlement to the land.

There seems to be a tendency for some Jews to overlook the ongoing presence of Jews in *Eretz Ysrael*. Such a recognition may be perceived by some as downplaying the importance and the impact of the Zionist Congress in Europe. Also, in so viewing the Jewish presence as continuous, may be contrary to the lore of giving credit to the European movement and the *habonim* (the pioneer workers) and veneration of the kibbutzim (communal living groups), especially in agricultural development of the twentieth century, a nationalistic claim of the mid 1900s.

There is no question that the Jews have an entitlement to what we now call Israel and parts of greater Palestine. We do not question that other ethnic/religious groups may also have claim to the land. That Palestinians may feel a need and wish to have a land and be free of outside intervention in affairs is quite understandable. But wishing and wanting is not the making of an entitlement. The Arab or Moslem entitlement that I reviewed seemed to be largely rhetoric with little evidence that suggests an entitlement to a land. For a claim to entitlement for such a land, I would think what needs to be known are the boundaries, the language, the nature of the government, coinage, the culture, the artifacts, architecture, tools, and the religion. Thus far, I am unaware of any such claims other than references to plots and properties once owned -- claims that can be resolved through local court.

Some Not Well Known Historical Facts

The Jewish presence in the Diaspora started well prior to the coming of the common era. The Diaspora was not the making of the destruction of the Second Temple, of Christianity, nor was it an Islamic enterprise ,but took place well before the Jewish Roman War, the times of Jesus and the onset of the Byzantine occupation. Jews had traveled east to Babylon and Persia and to within all perimeters of the growing Roman Empire before all these epochs began. Later, the perils of travel increased and was feared by all who traveled.

Following the time of the Jewish Temples, the population decreased significantly for Jews and gentiles as well. As we have seen during our brief travel throughout Israel, there was evidence of a large number of ongoing communities throughout *Eretz Yisrael*. Following the Roman occupation many areas continued to be resided by various cultural groups, including Jews -- so long as natural resources permitted, people chose to stay. The impact of battles, wars, politics and religious strife, though important, are highly exaggerated. The written accounts also tend to promote nationalistic and exigent political cause deemed important at the time. Such drama also makes the reading of history more enticing to the reader as comparted to the everyday existential problems of people adjusting to difficult times. Such emphasis on violence has led to the production of many enduring myths and distortions. What seems to be more the case, and what happened time and time again in *Eretz Yisrael*, when one group prospered, so did others.

From about the time of 1000 B.C.E. the only occupying power that was home-based was that of Jews. Palestine never became the birthplace of any other nation, as Eban so eloquently stated (1984), everyone of its conquerors had his original home elsewhere.

As pointed out in earlier chapters, foreign occupiers had let the earth go fallow and let improvements deteriorate. With the exception of the Christian Crusaders, a common interest on the part of all occupiers was to colonize the area so as to provide resources and revenue for their home base, far away. Even the Christians did not significantly maintain nor improve the land. As a result all the occupiers other than Jews let the earth go fallow.

As the world population grew and life became more mobile and safe, it was quite natural for peoples to come to Palestine for visits and immigration. The acceleration of travel to Palestine began well before the Balfour Declaration, before the Jewish Agency and the first meeting of the Zionist Congress in Europe. Once travel became relatively safe, Jews were among the first of ethnic groups in that period to come to *Eretz Yisrael*.

On the Support for Terror Attacks

The Violence in Israel, when it occurs is terrible, but the occurrences are highly exaggerated by nature of the large presence of reporters in the area. The war is largely a psychological war, as it was from the early view of the Palestinian elitist Arabs in 1948. The rhetoric coming from articles, speeches and interview that do support the violence were summarized in the previous chapter. Along with their underpinnings, six common precepts were found in the media supporting the violent nature of the conflict:

(1) A broad kind of entitlement to the land seems to come from *Qur'anic Suras*. Present day Muslims for the most part do not recognize the modern state of Israel as the legitimate heir of the ancient Children of Israel. (2) There is much reference to the After-Life including *Ad'n* (Paradise), a place where defenders of the faith and martyrs are redeemed. (3) *Jihad*, as used in the context of struggle with enemies, when so decreed and when executed, is believed to lead to an afterlife in *Ad'n*. (4) Because for centuries, Jews and Christians were treated differentially and tolerated only as second class citizens, Arabs would naturally be apprehensive and over sensitive to possible designs on the part of Christians or Jews to turn the table about. (5) There continues to be a strong propensity towards the goals and aspirations of the Central and Axis Powers in both world wars. (6) There is much in the media indicating that Arabs, as a whole, tend to view the establishment of Israel and the development of a Palestinian state, as illegal and (7) the wars of 1948 and 1967 were fought so that Jews can take over Arab lands.

The history of personal attacks and violence of the kind seen in terror attacks today seem to have roots in identification with the *assassins* who carried out the will of God, 656 CE, first against Moslem rulers, portrayed as impious usurpers. They called themselves *fidayeen*, from the Arabic *fida'i* – one who is ready to sacrifice his life for the cause. The term re-appeared in Iran in the so-called *fida'i Islam*, the *fida'is* of Islam, a political-religious group in Tehran. Between 1943 when it began its activities and 1955, when it was suppressed, the group carried out a number of political assassinations. The term was revived again by the militant wing of the Palestine Liberation Organization from the 1960's onward.

These Arab groups might have looked back at what was happening in the 1900s when there was a renewal of anti-western action in the Middle East, though of a different type and for different purposes. Terrorism had gone through several phases. During the last years of the British Empire, imperial Britain faced terrorist movements in its Middle Eastern dependencies that represented three different cultures: Greeks in Cypress, Jews in Palestine, and Arabs in Adeb. All three groups, according to Lewis (2003) acted from nationalist, rather than religious motives. Their purpose was to persuade the imperial power that staying in the region or pursuing a policy was not worth the cost in blood. Their method was to attack military and, to as lesser extent, administrative personnel and installations. All three operated only within their own territory and generally avoided collateral damage. All three succeeded in their endeavors. (Lewis, 2003).

Regular warfare for the Arabs had again failed in 1967 and subsequent wars. Out of the defeats came the new-style terrorists, the slaughter of innocent and uninvolved civilians. Such injury and damage to property is not "collateral damage" as was the case earlier when civilian property and non-combatants were killed or injured during attacks and battles. In the new-style terrorism, such is the prime objective and is measured by media coverage, especially television. The purpose is to inspire fear. As the killings and destruction was carried on television and carried on the front pages of newspapers, it was noted by photographers that the populace often celebrated. More importantly, perhaps to the leaders, was the impact of the attacks on international opinion surveys. If the results were anticipated to be satisfactory, the attack was also likely to be regarded as a psychological victory, and quite likely if they were not effective, the nature and location of the next series of attacks would be modified.

Hijacking of aircraft, murder of Israel athletes at the Munich Olympics, seizure of the Saudi Embassy in Kartoum, murder of two Americans and Belgian diplomat; the takeover of the Italian cruise ship Achille Lauro, in 1985, and subsequent suicide missions were pioneered by religious/political/social organizations like Hamas and Hizbullah, who from 1982 onward carried out a number of such missions in Lebanon and in Israel.

One may visit the same sites as we did and come to their own conclusion. I believe they would reach the same conclusion as we did: Jews lived continuously in the land for over 3,000 years. What is important here, is that such a view of Jewish continuous presence is inconsistent and incompatible with much of the precepts of Christian, Moslems and some Jewish groups. Each group has their unique reasons for perpetrating the myth. Christians, to recent times, have views that support the contention that the strength of their faith replaced the Jewish population following the days of the destruction of the Second Temple. Moslems, though believing the authenticity of the account of the Children of Israel, do so only up through to the beginnings of the common era, but the connection from that early period to that of the present is either denied or minimized.

The drama of the persecutions in Europe in the late 1800s and throughout much of the 1900s seems to have overshadowed the importance of the role of Jews already in the Middle East as well as Jews residing in Palestine who had set up an infrastructure long before the Zionist dream and subsequent activities of the Jewish Agency in Europe.

Throughout Part II of the book, the Israeli-Palestinian Conflict, several points were offered that seemed to reflect the Arab stance in regards to the Israeli-Palestinian Conflict. If there is a single key point, what seems to impel the movement towards violence is the impetus of the *Qur'anic* tenets that claim the area as part of *Dar Al-Islam*, the world of Islam. It should be no surprise to realize that much of the Arab claim is energized by reverting to the fundamentals of Islam. Though the wars in Israel, Afghanistan and more recently in Iraq are seen in the perspective of most western countries as a war against terror and a prevention of further dangers. The general struggle between east and west in the perception among Arabs supporting the violence in Israel, Afghanistan and Iraq has taken on, for many is a religious Islamic struggle. All Arab Moslems, and perhaps Moslems in general can readily relate to this matter, though with various degrees of commitment.

The key protagonists, the U.S., Britain, Spain, Australia, India, and others choose to see the struggle without reference to religious views, and as a result are at a disadvantage in not being able to utilize ways to implement resistance to this form of Islamic cause without recourse to miliary options. For largely these reasons, the Palestinian-Israeli Conflict seems to be the flashpoint between the two claims to entitlement for the land. Our travels had taken us to sites that reveal the ongoing presence of Jews in the land thus offering one important premise for a Jewish and Israeli claim to the land.

APPENDIX A

Common Consciousness as Reflected by Language Usage

The uniqueness of words and phrases in a language reveals the distinctive qualities of the common consciousness of a group of people with a common language. These matters become apparent upon translating important subtleties from one language to another. There are several key words currently seen in the rhetoric of those supporting the violence in the Israeli-Palestinian Conflict that belie the commonality of precepts among the Arabic speaking groups.

The word, "occupier" is bantered around "loaded" with attributes of meaning different from western usage. We would like to point out several of these words and how they serve to distort facts and confound people. We think, to the Arabist, the word, "occupier" has a different connotation than to westerners. It is first unclear to our western mind as to what the Palestinians are trying to denote. We do know when we now hear these terms, we become upset, then angry. So do others. Here is why. To westerners, an occupier is an outside or foreign power administering territory following a display of force. In this book we use the term to identify the rulers and foreign power during much of the 3,200 years of Jewish presence in Palestine.

To an Arab-Moslem, the word "occupier" appears in context with an occupation force, administration or an overseer consisting of non-Moslems, "non-believers" or "infidels." The Arab literature and Arab media takes little heed when a governing power is tyrannical so long as there is a close association with Islamic control. Arabs write about the "occupation." It is Israel, they claim that now occupies the land in which their fathers and mothers, grandparents or uncles once claimed as theirs. Though there seems yet no foundation for such a claim, there is an implicit plea of entitlement to the land. I am not talking about personal or business property, which when disputed is handled in civil courts, but the land within boundaries or borders, *Eretz Yisrael*, the land of Israel. There is an attitude that they had lost something they want back. The rhetoric is false, only serving to prevent them from dealing with the angst that it was never theirs to begin with. Such denial, angst and disavowed feelings seem to have gotten into the unconscious of the youth. Now they are hampered by defense mechanisms doing battle with their angst.

Another word often heard in close context is "aggression" or "aggressors."

These are terms generally applied to the country of Israel or to Israelis. To the Arab mind these terms "occupier" and "aggressor" are used interchangeably but with somewhat differing connotations. There is a *Qu'ranic* foundation for the use of these words. As pointed out earlier, the idea behind the word implies an individual is an "occupier" and "aggressor" when deemed to threaten the existence of the Islamic ideal. Imams have a great deal of discretion in applying such rhetoric. At their will, they can dis-inhibit the propensity to strike out at anyone or anything said to threaten Islamic society. The same rules are applied under condition of *dhimma*. The *Qu'ran* is quite clear on this matter. It is the obligation of all Moslems to stem off such a threat, be it by a person or entity that symbolizes infidelity to their religious cause. We believe it is largely for this reason that Palestinians and Moslems do not feel obligated as do westerners to respect historical and religious sites of other religious groups. In fact, as we discussed earlier in our chapter on our visit to Hebron that doing so is not only discouraged but leads to a tolerance that unfortunately is unacceptable among Moslems in the area.

There are several meanings to word, "return." One use is the reference to the right of claim on the part of Palestinian refugees for property that they had once owned prior to fleeing Palestine following the establishment of the Israel. The concept is also linked with precepts related to return to the days of *Dar al-Islam*, the Land of Islam. According to this more common view, Palestine was a part of the world destined to become *Islamic*. Another meaning of the term refers to the reversion of the borders of Israel to become a Palestinian state and/or Islamic controlled area.

The term, "martyr" is generally perceived by English speaking persons as someone that sacrifices something very important, sometimes even their lives for a cause. Moslems relate the term to those individuals, who, because of their action to offset the aggressor and occupier, are entitled to rewards in the after life as well as welfare payments to the family should they be killed in the process. Even if one has conducted oneself in an undesirable manner, should they be victorious or killed in the process of combating the infidel, aggressor and/or occupier, they become benefactors to their survivors and have a special "place" for themselves in the afterlife.

People clinging to these precepts summarized above can readily get into trouble. The acting out of precepts can take on bizarre forms. In an 11-13-02 article in the L.A. Times, Dick Laars, reported that Shahid Nickels, a 21 year old convert to Islam sai d in a Hamburg court that a group of young Arabs including three were among the hijackers in the September 11 attack. They were described as constantly searching for ways to join a Muslim holy war. The group was described as "almost obsessed with *jihad*, cheerfully singing songs about martyrdom and talking of little else." The hijackers themselves were thought to be among the most radical of the fundamentalists in Hamburg. In another *Times* article of the same day, an excerpt from tape played appeared in *Al Jazeera*, reported by AP, 11-13-02. The transcript refers to the hijackers as "zealous sons of Islam in defense of their religion and in response to the order of their God....The prophet, Bush, the Pharaoh of this age...is killing our sons in Iraq...and Israel [is] bombing houses that shelter old people, women and children with U.S. made aircraft in Palestine." Much of the rhetoric leaps into fantasy and jumps from reality, but syllogistically follows from the above precepts: Islamic colonization, the richness of afterlife and jihad, the satisfactions coming from dis-inhibition of *dhimma*, the denial of the defeat of the Axis powers of the two world wars and strive to undermine the legality of the United Nations when it does not serve their purposes.

Appendix B
Our Sources for Inferring Jewish Presence in Palestine

Our attempt in providing evidence of Jewish populations and estimates of numbers was borne out of a personal interest developed as we toured the area. The following is a compilation of our sources and of relevance of the category.

1. **Archaeological sites** revealed the extent of Jewish presence throughout the area. The National Park Service is making an extraordinary effort in developing and reconstructing historical sites throughout Israel. Information developed by the Israel Department of Antiquities were often posted, including dates of activity in the area. The park service typically offers booklets depicting features of the communities. Such booklets that were cited appear in the Reference Section.

2. **Water sources**, remnants of existing viaducts, cisterns were taken of indications of habitation over the years. Where and when there was water, so must there have been people. The greater the quantity of collected water, and the more accommodating the nearby land appeared, the greater we thought would be the likelihood of a larger population.

3. **Personal observations** were offered from people familiar with the sites that we had visited. We also came across a number of people who were associated with families that had resided in the area for many generations.

4. **Post-Second Temple Jewish writings**, particularly Gaonic and communiques to and from Eretz Yisrael from authorities in the diaspora regarding interpretations of laws and observances. Dates of many of these communiques were recorded.

5. **Contemporary well known writers** of various periods, for example, Josephus, Maimonides, Nahmonides, Benjamin from Tudela and many travelers through time to Oliphant's account of the mid 1800s.

6. **Personal letters from ordinary people** over the centuries (see Kobler, 1952). A number of communiques are showing up over the years as people communicated with friends and business connections, in and out of Eretz Yisrael over the years.

7. **Reports of military actions** by occupying powers over the years. These include Josephus on through to British observers from 1917 to 1948.

8. **Caches of coins.** They were often dated, thus offer clues as to activities of that particular period of time.

9. **Writings on Christian life**, artifacts and activities. Though the focus is typically on Christian history, much can be deduced as to reported activities of the populace, including Jews.

10. **Translations of Arab and/or Islamic writings.** Such records were found to be particularly helpful during the European middle ages. Interest in such literature is typically on matters pertaining to Islamic issues, but matters of Jewry come up from time to time, including the special taxes that were collected from Jews.

11. **Records of tax and tribute by occupying powers.** Jews were tolerated if taxed. Tax records were kept on the basis of family units, thus offering an estimate of Jewish population in an area.
The Turks conducted population surveys and kept records of community payments.

12. **Communiques stored in the Cairo Genizah.** Discovered in the old synagogue of Fustat, in ancient Cairo. A host of communiques were saved because they had inscribed on them, references to the Almighty; if the name was enscribed it would not be destroyed. They were catalogued. They reveal much of the commercial and travel experiences of Jews, especially during the twelfth and thirteenth centuries (see Baron, 1958).

13. **Studies of world population.** Works by McEvedy and other specialists in world population offer a general picture of population changes throughout sectors of the world including the Middle East (McEvedy and Jones, 1978).

14. **Visits to sites ancient synagogues.** We visited a number of historical and archeological sites which offer visual evidence of Jewish religious and social activity.

15. **Burial sites** are common throughout the land. We saw them from a distance as we tended to avoid them. People have found the details as to dates difficult to interpret.

16. **Historical literature.** Much has been written in books and periodicals pertaining to the Middle East. There is a wide selection of literature available in English on Middle East history. Much of this work was obtained from the Library at the University of Judaism in Los Angeles, California.

17. **Travelogues and guidebooks.** Contemporary guidebooks and travelogues were found to be helpful, especially recent ones (For example, Israelowitz, 2000).

18. **Museums.** Exhibits at The British Museum in London, the Israeli Museum in Jerusalem and Museum of History at Katz'rin had displays of artifacts, tools and of the arts of the kind found in the areas we visited. We were quite impressed with the state of progress of the tools found in *Eretz Yisrael* in comparison to the tools found during the same period in Europe.

19. **Presumptions on our part.** We try to give the source of facts and conclusions. We did not hesitate to offer our own opinions and deductions on many matters; upon doing so, we hope we have made it clear that responsibility is ours and valid to the extent you find it reasonable.

GLOSSARY

HEBREW WORDS AND PHRASES

Avino Shalom Aleichem	A song. Lit. Our father, peace throughout the world
Bar Mitzvah	The coming of age and duty of a boy to participate in services, manhood, to be counted in a *min'yon,*
Be'it hamikdash	Lit. The holy house: The temple.
Chev'ron	Lit. Friend, loved one. Ancient and current name for the city of Hebron
Cohanim	Jewish Priests active with the First and Second Temples. A descendent of Aaron (brother of Moses) and (in the male line of descendents from the Temple priests).
Dovening	Reading or chanting classical prayers
Eretz Yisrael	The land of Israel (an ancient and modern term)
Hakotel	Lit. The wall. The western retaining wall of the First Temple.
Halacha	Jewish Law
Me'orat ha'machpela	Tomb of the Patriarchs, Family/ancestral burial site.
Kaleb	Dog, doggy
Kashrut	The supervision of food content, production, distribution, cooking and serving of food. The labeling of food as Kashrut. Keeping Kosher.
Kibbutz	A work-oriented-social commune characteristic of Israel.
Kiryat Arba	District of Four (the patriarchs); ancient name for Hebron and a current city in the area.
Manishma	How are you doing?
mikveh/mikvot	immersion pool/s
Min'yon	A group of ten qualifying Jews that enable a Torah service
Mitzpah	Outlook, viewpoint, overlook
Shabbaton	A gathering for shabbot-oriented, catered experience.

Shabbot	Jewish sabbath. Dusk Friday through dusk Saturday
Shul	A synagogue, typically orthodox.
Yiddishkeit	Lit. Yiddishness; The culture of the Yiddish speaking
Yom Kinneret	The Sea of Galilee

ARABIC WORDS AND PHRASES

Dar al-Harb	The world (lands) of unbelievers, war
Dar al-Islam	The world (lands) of Islam
Dhimma	From the Qur'an. "Protection" given by law to follows of the Almighty who are not Moslems. The protection of dhimma can be lifted by decree of the Imam..
Imam	An Islamic cleric with much influence over everyday conduct
Injeel	Gospel, New Testament
Jihad	An internal struggle to be a better person in the sight of Allah, a struggle to establish Islamic life, holy war.
Kafir	The infidel; a general term for the enemy, the aggressor, the occupier
Mujadeen	Warriors for the cause of Islam
Qur'an	Recitation. The Koran, the classical book of Islamic writing. Believed by Moslems to consist of visions and revelations of Mohammad.
Sharia	Courts. During the Mandate, British shared authority with Arabs to settle disputes among themselves.
Sutra	Section of the Qur'an, consisting of a sequence of verses identified by number.

STRUCTURES / SITES

| The Cardo | A Roman boulevard. Revealed through digging in the Old City of Jerusalem |
| First Temple | Temple built in Jerusalem by King Soloman, ca 1000-587 BCE. |

Knesset	The building of the Parliament in Jerusalem. The leading party selects a prime minister, who selects a cabinet.
Tomb of the Patriarchs	The site where the patriarchs are believed to be Interred, below the massive structure built by the Romans and modified by the Ottoman Turks (once a synagogue, a church and a mosque) in Hebron.
Second Temple	Rebuilt on the site of the First Temple ca. 445 B.C.E. destroyed by Romans in 70 C.E..

ORGANIZATIONS, JEWISH/ISRAELI

Chabad	A chassidic orthodox group with roots from Lubavitch, in Eastern Europe.
Chassidic	A movement with characteristic spiritual, musical style, and expressed concern with philosophical matters, stems from writings of the *B'al shem Tov* (the good name), in eastern Europe about 1790.
Genizah	Lit. a collection. A collection of Jewish writings. Usually refers to the collection of notes, letters and communiques in Cairo.
Haganah	The Jewish military organization that merged with the Israeli Defense Forces following the War for Independence.
Irgun	A Jewish militant organization active following the Second World War, disbanded and joined forces with the Haganah during the War for Independence.
IDF	Israeli Defense Force. Combined army, naval and air force
Knesset	Israel national governmental center in Jerusalem (See Structures)
MEMRI	Middle East Media Research Institute; a recent Israeli non-profit group that translates Arabic media into Hebrew and English.
Pew Research Center	An international research center specializing in international opinion surveys

Va'ad Leumi	Elected assembly and general council during the British Mandate
Yishuv	Jews of the local area communities. Also means a Jewish community.
Yeshiva	A classical Jewish school. The yeshiva method is of small groups often discussing current matters and issues in terms of accumulated knowledge.
Zionism/Zionist	The movement starting in Europe in the late 1800s supporting the establishment of a homeland for the Jews. One who supports a Jewish Homeland.

ORGANIZATIONS, ARAB AND PALESTINIAN

Al Aksa Brigade	Lit. the brigade of the Temple on the Mount, a more recent political party, terrorist in nature..
Arab Higher Committee	An advisory committee made up of appointees by Arab Organizations in 1947 to offer recommendations to the United Nations regarding the intended partition of Palestine.
Arab League	An organization of Arab interests started following the Second World War.
Fatah	One of several political parties of the Palestinian Authority. An outcome of the pro-Axis Powers, Ba'ath party, Muslem Brotherhood, Fedayeen, the party of the current leader of the PA, Yasser Arafat.
Fedayeen	An anti-Jewish organization active during the days of the British Mandate
Hamas	One of several political parties forming the Council of the Palestinian Authority. Maintains the highest profile among claimants for violent attacks in Israel.
Hezbellah	A social and military activist group stemming from Syria and Lebanon, also a political party among others that form the Council of the Palestinian
Islamic Jihad	Another political party making up the current Palestinian Authority. Among claimants of violent attacks in Israel.

PFLP	Palesinians for the Liberation of Palestine. A political party comprising the Council of the Palestinian Authority.
PLO	Paletinian Liberation Organization, grew out of the Fedayeen
Sharia	The court system for Arabs under the British Mandate

MISCELLANEOUS

Arab/Misrachi Jews	Jews stemming from eastern areas, with Arabic or Farsi culture.
Ashkenazic Jews	Jews stemming from Central and Eastern Europe with Yiddish culture.
Casting	A psychobiological term. An electro-chemical process enabling a sensory volley to be transmitted upward and capable of transmitting linguistic signals and made compatible with processing at higher nervous centers. This is a hypothetical construct developed by the author (Margolis, 1991).
Chaparral	Type of flora found in dry areas of North America
Diaspora	The Jewish life away from Jerusalem and Eretz Yisrael -has always coincided and communicated with the Jewish presence in Eretz Yisrael. Also refers to migration to the east following the destruction of the First Temple to the east. And later to the days of the Second Temple to migration to areas occupied by the Roman Empire, even within Eretz Yisrael..
Encasement	A psychobiological term posited by the author to be a physical result of encoding and casting of afferent sensory signals. Once a signal is encased, it can become part of, and influence memory and consciousness.
Intifada	A quasi-military movement among Arabs in Palestine who support an uprising against Israel.

Moslem Fundamentalist	Those who feel that the troubles of the Muslim world are the result of excessive western modernization resulting in a betrayal of authentic Islamic values (Lewis, 2003, p 134)
Partition, the	A U.N. plan of 1948 to partition Palestine into a Jewish and Arab state.
Seam/Green Line	A boundary between Israeli and Arab interests. May be merely historical or an actual barricade, fence or wall constructed by Israelis.
Sephardic Jews	Jews of Spanish speaking descent. Many were expelled during and following the Spanish Inquisition.

REFERENCES

Abu,Tomeh, Khaled, "Hamas to PA: No Alternative to Suicide Bombings," *Jerusalem Post* Internet Edition, November 5, 2002.

Al-A, Aref, "Who are the Palestinian Refugees?" An editorial from the *Syria Times,* May 28, 2003.

Al-Hilali, Muhammad Taqi-ud-Din and Khan, Muhammad Muhshin. *The Noble Qur'an.* King Fahd Complex for the Printing of the Holy Qur'an: Madinah, K.S.A. 1998

Allam, Magdi, "Reports by Magdi Allam," in La Republica, (Italy) June, 2003 reported by Lisa Palmieri-Billig, *Internet Jerusalem Post*, June 9, 2003

Arafat, Yasser, "Yasser Arafat' Address to the UN," November, 1974, in *Extreme Islam: Anti-American Propaganda of Muslim Fundamentalism*, Adam Parfrey, Ed., Los Angeles: Feral House, 2002.

Ari-Yonah, Michael. *A History of Israel and the Holy Land.* Continuum Publishing Group, Inc: New York, 2001.

Azad, Mohamed and Amina, Bibi. *Islam Will Conquer All Other Religions and American Power Will Dimish: Read How Allah's (God's) Prediction Will Soon Come to Pass.* Bell Six Publishing: New York, 2001.

Bard, Mitchell C. *Myths and Facts: Guide to the Arab-Israeli Conflict.* American-Israeli Cooperative Enterprise, 2001.

Bar-Illan, "Israel's New Pollyannas," in *The Mideast Peace Process*, Neal Kozodoy, Ed. Encounter Books: San Francisco, 2002.

Baron, Salo Wittmayer. "High Middle Ages, 500-1200", Volume III, *A Social and Religious History of the Jews.* Second Edition, Columbia University Press: New York, 1957

Baroud, Ramzy, "Condemned by Terrorism," *Palestinian Chronicle*, http://palestinianchronicle.com, November 5, 2002.

Ben-Gurion, David, Ed. *The Jews in their Land*. Doubleday and Company, Garden City, New York, 1966, Revised, 1974.

Ben-Zvi, Itzhak. *The Exiled and the Redeemed*. Jewish Publication Society: Jerusalem, 1976.

Bier, Aharon. *Eretz Israel, Old and New: A Jewish Pilgrim's Companion*. World Zionist Organization: Jerusalem, 1976.

Camiel, Deborah, Roman, Yadin and Shkolnik, Ya'akov. *Golan Pocket Guide*, English Edition,
Golan Tourist Association: Eretz Ha-Tzvi Inc. 1998.

Candor, Frank, *The Root of the Problem*, f_candor@hotmail.com and Answering-Islam.org/t_root.html, 2001.

Cohen, Ammon. *Jewish Life Under Islam: Jerusalem in the sixteenth Century*. Harvard University Press: Cambridge, 1984.

Cohen, Richard, "Where Bigotry Gets a Hearing," *Washington Post*, www.washingtonpost.com/wp-dyn/articles/A9032-2001, October 29.2001.

D, Jonathan, "Understanding the breakdown of Israeli-Palestinian negotiations," *Jerusalem Letter/Viewpoints*, Jerusalem Center for Public Affairs, Dec 29, 2002.

Davis, Leonard J, "Myths and Facts: A concise record of the Arab-Israel Cobnflict," A Near East Report, *Washington Weekly on American Policy in the Middle East*, Near East Research, Inc: Washington D.C. 1989.

Dothan, Moshe. *Hammath Tiberias: Early Synagogues*. Israel Exploration Society, Ben-Zvi Printing Enterprises Ltd: Jerusalem, 1983.

Dudevitch, Margot, "Peace with Israel is not to be found in PA schoolbooks," *Jerusalem Post*, November 23, 2001.

Dudevitch, Margot, "Peace with Israel is not to be found in PA schoolbooks," *Jerusalem Post*, November 23, 2001.

Dudkevitch, Margot, "Arabic paper, book encour age kids to emulate suicide bombers," *Jerusalem Post,* Dec 23, 2002.

Durant, Will. *The Story of Civilization: Part I: Our Oriental Heritage.* Simon and Schustrer: New York, 1935.

Eban, Abba. *Abba Eban: An Autobiography.* Random House: New York, 1977

Eban, Abba. Heritage: *Civilization and the Jews.* Summit Books: New York, 1984

Ellis, Raff. "Arabs Beware; the Trojen Horse is in Your Midst," *Palestine Chronicle*, January 31, 2003

Encyclopedia Judaica, Keter Publishing House, Jerusalem, Ltd, Jerusalem: 1972

Franck, Dorothea S, "Palestine," *The New International Year Book for 1948*, Henry E. Vizetelly, Ed. Funk & Wagnalls Company: New York, 1 949, 413-415.

Franck, Dorothea S, "Palestine," *The New International Year Book for 1949*, Henry E. Vizetelly, Ed. Funk & Wagnalls Company: New York, 1949, 414.

Galilee Touring Map, 1:118,000 Corazin publishing: Rosh Pina, Israel, 1998.

Gortein, Schlomo Dov, "What would Jewish and general history benefit by a systematic publication of the Documentary Geniza papers?" *Proceeding, of the American Academy for Jewish Research*, v 21, 1954, 29-39.

Golan: Pocket Guide. Golan Tourist Association, English Edition, tour@golan.org.il PO Box 175, 12900 Katzrin, Israel, Eretz Ha-Tzvi, Inc, Israel, 1998.

Golan Tourist Map, Golan Tourist Association. Qatzrin, Israel. Ca. 2001

Grayzel, Soloman. *A History of the Jews: From the Babylon Exile to the Present.* Jewish Publication Society of America: Philadelphia, 1968

Gross, Netty,[on Palestinian refugees, find title] Jerusalem Reports, 1999

HaCohen, Ran, "Ethnic Cleansing: Past, Present and Future," *Palestine Chronicle*, 31 Dec 2002

Ha'aretz, Article on PA corruption, Feb 11, 2001

Haetzni, Nadav, "In Arafat's Kingdom,"in *The Mideast Pece Process: An Autopsy,* Neal Kozodoy, Ed., Encounter Books: San Francisco, 2002, 57-68.

Halevi, Yossie Klein, "Dar El-Harb," *Olam*, Olam Publications, Los Angeles, Winter, 2001

Hameiri House (Brochure) Beit Hameiri, Safed, Israel, undated.

Hamat Tiberias National Park. (Brochure) Israel Nature and National Parks Protection Authority, Ramat Gan, Israel. No date.

Heidbreder, Edna. *Seven Psychologies.* Appleton-Century-Crofts, Inc., New York, 1933.

Hellander, Paul, Andrew Humphreys and Neil Tilbury. *Israel and the Palestinian Territories. Guidebook*, Lonely Planet Publications: Oakland, 1999.

Hill, John "Objectives, Roots and Arguments on the Part of the Palestinians," by, Yahya Abdul Rahman, *Palestinian Chronicle*, Dec 27, 2002.

Isaac, Jules. The Teaching of Contempt. Holt, Rinehart and Winston: New York, 1964

Horesley, Richard A. *Galilee: History, Politics, People.* Trinity Press International: Valley Forge, PA, 1995.

Hourani, Albert. *A History of the Arab Peoples.* Belknap Press of Harvard University:
Cambridge, 1991.

Israel Tourist Map 1:400,000. Issued through Traffic Rent a Car; Target Maps and City Guides, Ltd.: Tel Aviv, 2001.

Israel Tourist Map 1:400,000. Survey of Israel, 1994.

Israel Tourist Map 1:500,00. Atir Publishing & Publications Co. Ltd: Rehovot, Israel.

Israelowitz, Oscar. *Israel Travel Guide.* Israelowitz Publishing, Brooklyn, New ork, 1996.

Jerusalem: The Old City; Map (based on aerial photography) and Guide. Jewish Quarter Tourism Administration (M.T.R.) 1983.

Jerusalem: Israel Pocket Library. Ketter Books, Jerusalem: 1973.

Jerusalem Post www.jpost.comJeff Barak, Editor-in-Chief, The Jerusalem Post Building, PO Box 81, Romema, Jerusalem 91000, Israel 02-531-5666.

Jerusalem Post, An article on monies transferred to families of suicide bombers, October 9, 2002

Jerusalem Post, "Report 1.2 million Israelis living below poverty line, 5 percent increase," www://jpost.com, November 4, 2002.

Josephus Flavius. *The Jewish Wars.* [publisher, city, date]

Karam, Zeina, "Syria Schools Portray an Evil Israel," Middle East Media Research Institute, Associated Press, April 27, 2000.

Karsh, Efraim, "On the Right of Return,"in *The Mideast Pece Process: An Autopsy,* Neal Kozodoy, Ed., Encounter Books: San Francisco, 2002, 119-130,

Kertzer, David I. The Popes Against The Jews. Alfred A. Knopf: New York, 2001.

Khalidi, Walid, "Palestine-Net: Chronology of Palestinian History," *Palestinian Chronicle*, 10-29-2002.

Kobler, Franz. *Letters of Jews Through the Ages.* vl, Horowitz Publishing Co.: New York, 1952.

Korazim National Park (Brochure) Israel National Parks Authority, Ramat Gan, Israel, August, 1999.

Kursi National Park, (Brochure) Israel Nature and National Parks Protection Authority, Ramat Gan, Israel, 2001.

Laars, Dick, in a feature article describes transactions in a court in Hamburg, Germany. *L.A. Times,* November 13, 2002.

Lacquer, Walter and Rubin, Barry, "The Israel-Arab Reader," *Documents on German Foreign Policy, 1918-1945*, Series D, Vol XIII, London, 1964, p88f.

Lahoud, 2002, Jeruslam Media & Communications Center, [comp0lete reference]

Lamb, David and Murphy, Kim, "Iraqi Collapse Is a Dagger in the Arab Heart," *Los Angeles Times, p A17*, Friday, April 11, 2003.

Lee, Risha Kim and Cherlin, Amelie. [Guidebook] *Let's Go: Israel and the Palestinian Territories.* St. Martins Press: New York, 2002.

Lerman. *The Jewish Communities of the World.* Facts on File: New York, 1989.

Levy, Thyomas E, *The Archaelogy of Society in the Holy Land.* Facts on File.: New York, 1995.

Lewis, Bernard. The Middle East:A Brief History of the Last 2,000 Years.Simon and Schuster: New York, 1995.

Lewis, Bernard. What Went Wrong: The Clash Between Islam and Modernity in the Middle East. Harper Collin Publisher: New York, 2002.

Lewis, Bernard, "The Revolt of Islam: When did the conflict with the West begin, and how could it end,*" New Yorker,* November, 2001

Lewis, Bernard. *The Crisis of Islam: Holy War and Unholy Terror.* Modern Library: New ork, 2003

Los Angeles Times, an excerpt from a tape played by Al Jazeera, reported by AP November 13, 2002.

Macoz, Zvi Uri, "Ancient Synogogues of the Golan," *Biblical Archaelogist,* June, 1988.

Macoz, Zvi Uri, and Killebrew, Ann, "Ancient Qasrin: Synagogue and Village," *Biblical Archaeologist,* March, 1988.

Margolis, Hannah, "Implications of the Teachings of Roman Catholic Church on the Holocaust: Focus on Relationships with the Jews," Silogram Corporation, Unpublished, 2002.

Margolis, Harold J. *Inhibitory Control Theory: A Psychobiological Theory on the Fusion of "Mind"and Body.* Silogram Corporation: Beverly Hills, Calif. 1991.

Masada National Park [brochure] Israel Nature and National Protection Authority: Israel, . 2000.

McEvedy Colin and Jones, Richard. *Atlas of World Population History.* Penguin Books: 1978d

McGeown, Kate and Asser, Martin, "Right of Return: A Palestinian Dream?" *BBC News*, http://news.bbc.co.uk, November 16, 2002

Meyers, Eric M. *Galilee Through the Centuries: Confluence of Cultures.* Eisenbrauns: Winona Lake, Indiana, 1999.

Marx, "Importance of The Geniza for Jewish history," *Proceedings of the American Academy for Jewish Research*, 1947, 194-201.

Megiddo National Park (Brochure) Israel National Parks Authority, Ramat Gan, Israel, undated.

Morse, Chuck, "Nazi Origins of Arab Terror," *Arutz Sheva*, Israel National News.com, March 5, 2003

Nellhaus, Arllynn. *Into the Heart of Jerusalem: A Travelers Guide to Visits, Celbrations, and sojourns.* John Muir Publicatiions: Santa Fe, N.M, 1999.

Netenyahu, Benjamin, "Choosing survival," *Olam*, Winter 2001/5701.

Nirenstein, Fiamma, "The Journalists and the Palestinians," in *The Mideast Pece Process: An Autopsy,* Neal Kozodoy, Ed., Encounter Books: San Francisco, 2002, 111-117.

Northern Region: Haifa, Acre, Nazareth, Safed and Tiberias, Millennium Issue. Ministry of Tourism: Israel, 2001.

Oesterreicher, John M. *Jerusalem.* The John Day Company: New York, 1974.

Oliphant, Laurence. *Haifa: Life in the Holy Land 1882-1885.* Canaan Publishing House: Jerusalem, 1976.

Palestinian Conciliation Commission Report, 1948-1952 [p191 Myths]

Palestinian Media Center, "Israel army kills more Palistinians, prepares for Hebron Judaization," *Palestinian Chronicle*, December 4, 2002.

Palestine Royal Commission Report, 1937 [see Bard, p51]

PASSIA diary, "Palestinian history beyond 1949," *Palestinian Chronicle,*
2000

Patai, Raphael. *The Arab Mind.* Charles Scribner's Sons: New York: 1983.

Podhoretz, Norman, "Intifada II: Death of an Illsion,? in *The Mideast Peace*
Process: An Autopsy, Neal Kozodoy, Ed., Encounter Books, San Francisco,
2002, 87-109.

Pomerance, Rachel, "Compensation sought for Jewish refugees," *Jewish*
News of Greater Phoenix, October 4, 2002.

Prager, Dennis, "Rewinding 9/11," *Olam,* Winter 2001/2002. and
www.dennisprager.com.

Pipes, Daniel, "Israel's Moment of Truth," in *The Mideast Peace Process:*
An Autopsy, Neal Kozodoy, Ed., Encounter Books, San Francisco, 2002, 75-
86.

Pearlman, Moshe and Yannai, Yaacov. *Historical Sites in Israel.* Chartwell
Books: Secaucus, NJ, 1977.

Prittie, 1972 [On Palestinian refugeees, find reference]

Rabinowitz, Allan, "Acre: History on display," p11 *Jerusalem Post,*
September 6, 2001.

Response, "Grand Mufti plotted to do away with all Jews in Mideast," Fall,
1991

Rossoff, Dovid, *Land of Our Heritage.* Targum Press: Spring Valey, New
York.

Rossoff, Dovid, *Safed: The Mystical City.* Sha'ar Books: Jerusalem, 1991.

Roth, Cecil. *Dona Gracia: Of the House of Nasi*. Jewish Publication Society: Philadelphia, 1977

Roth, Cecil. *The Duke of Naxos: Of the House of Nasi*. The Jewish Publication Society of America: Philadelphia, 1948.

Rahman, Yahya Abdul, "Indigenous activist expresses solidarity with the Palestinian people," Palestine Chronicle, December, 27, 2002.

Sa'ar, Eran, "Ever Yours, Peki'in," *Eretz Magazine*, August, 1997, 36-45

Smith, Jane Idleman and Haddad, Yvonne Yazbeck. *The Islamic Understanding of Death and Resurrection*. State University of New York Press: Albany, 1981.

Tsuk, Tsvika, Ed. Korazim National Park. The Israel Nature and National Parks Protection Authority Publishing: Israel, August, 1999.

Safed Tourist Map 1:7,500 Benjamin Blustein Publications, Israel, 2000.

Schechtman, 1963 [on Palestinian refugees]

Schleunes, Karl A. *The Twisted Road to Auschwitz: Nazi Policy Toward German Jews, 1933 - 1939*. University of Illinois Press: Chicago, 1990.

Shalem, Yisrael and Shalem, Phyllis. *Safed: Six Self-Guided Tours In and Around the Mystical City*. Safed Regional College, Bar Ilan University: Israel, 1997.

Shorrosh, Anis A. *Islam Revealed: A Christian Arab's View of Islam*. Thomas Nelson Publishers: Nashville, 1988.

Survey Report, "How the world thinks in 2002," http://people-press.org, December 4, 2002.

Syman, Fiona, "The Hostility of Hebron," *BBC News*, http://news.bbc.co.uk, November 16, 2002.

Temmo, Barry M ," Speech by Syria's Foreign Minister, Farouk Al-Shara, "Proceedings of the annual Conference of the Arab Writers Union," as reported in the *Syrian Arab News Agency* , January 30, 2002.

Tiberias (Map and Travel Guide) Michal Productions: Achat, Israel, 2000

Universal Jewish Encyclopedia, Patrons Edition, Isaac Landman, Editor, Universal Jewish Encyclopedia, Inc: 1943

Universal Yearbook, Events of 1947, Henry F. Vizetelly, Ed.. Funk and Wagnall,, 1948

UNRWA, 2000 [on Palestinian refugees]

USA Today http:/remembering.usatoday.com, 10000 Wilson Blvd., Arlington, VA.

Warraq, Ibn. *Why I am not a Muslim*. Prometheus Books: New York, 1995.

Woolbert, Robert G., "Palestine," *The New International Year Book for 1947*, Henry E. Vizetelly, Ed. Funk & Wagnalls Company: New York, 1948, 372-378.

Woolf, Richard, *Guide to the Sea of Galilee Area*, Caprice, Michal Productions: Israel, 2000.

Wurmsevr, Meyrav, "Schools of Ba'athism: A study of Syrian Schoolbooks," A MEMRI Monograph, Middle East Media Research Institute, [memri.org/booksummary.htm], 12/31/2001

Yaniv, 1974 [on "Palestinian Arab nationalism," in Bard, Mitchell C. *Myths and Facts: Guide to the Arab-Israeli Conflict*. American-Israeli Cooperative Enterprise, 2001. p39.

Yehoshua, B. *Municipality of Safad*, no date.

244

INDEX

PLACES

EVENTS